Behavior Analysis for School Psychologists

Perfect for students preparing for a career in school psychology and for current practitioners, teachers, and consultants, this book translates behavior analysis theory into practice. In concise chapters illustrated with school-based examples, *Behavior Analysis for School Psychologists* guides readers through the basics of behavior analysis, including observation and measurement, experimental analysis, and intervention design and implementation, while providing academic, behavioral, and mental health interventions from research-based principles of learning and behavior.

Michael I. Axelrod, Ph.D., is Director of the Human Development Center and Professor in the Department of Psychology at the University of Wisconsin-Eau Claire, USA. His primary clinical and research interests include helping parents and schools solve problems involving academic, behavioral, and social/emotional functioning.

Behavior Analysis for School Psychologists

MICHAEL I. AXELROD

 Routledge
Taylor & Francis Group

NEW YORK AND LONDON

First published 2017
by Routledge
605 Third Avenue, New York, NY 10017

and by Routledge
2 Park Square, Milton Park, Abingdon, Oxon, OX14 4RN

Routledge is an imprint of the Taylor & Francis Group, an informa business

Library of Congress Cataloging-in-Publication Data
Names: Axelrod, Michael I., author.
Title: Behavior analysis for school psychologists / Michael I. Axelrod, Ph.D.
Description: New York, NY : Routledge, 2017. | Includes bibliographical references.
Identifiers: LCCN 2016056925 (print) | LCCN 2017021979 (ebook) |
ISBN 9781315650913 (ebook) | ISBN 9781138121492 (hbk) |
ISBN 9781138121485 (pbk) | ISBN 9781315650913 (ebk)
Subjects: LCSH: School psychology. | Behavioral assessment of children. | Behavior disorders in children. | Behavior modification. | Behaviorism (Psychology)
Classification: LCC LB1027.55 (ebook) | LCC LB1027.55. A98 2017 (print) | DDC 370.15—dc23
LC record available at https://lccn.loc.gov/2016056925

ISBN: 978-1-138-12149-2 (hbk)
ISBN: 978-1-138-12148-5 (pbk)

Typeset in Dante
by Keystroke, Neville Lodge, Tettenhall, Wolverhampton

Dedication

For Henry, my creative inspiration
For George, my intellectual inspiration

Contents

List of Figures

List of Tables

Preface

My journey as an educator began when I accepted a position as an elementary school counselor in northern New Hampshire. Equipped with a new Master's Degree, I set out to change the world. Regularly being referred students with challenging behavior, emotional, or social problems, my formula for change consisted of therapy directed at underlying causes. I worked with students in my office, on the third floor of an old and beautiful school building, far away from the locations of their problems. I talked, they talked (some much more than others), and this exchange went on for about 30 minutes. These students were improving—following instructions, interacting appropriately, and saying what I wanted to hear. Following each session, I sent them back to the classroom where the referral problems reemerged. My referral sources, primarily teachers, seemed satisfied with the results but I knew they were looking for something more. I knew these students were not making the improvements we were hoping for.

While I worked hard and helped many, I found my training and, more specifically, my approach was not enough. I decided to leave the friendly confines of my third floor office and observe these referred students in the places the problems existed— classrooms and hallways, the playground and cafeteria, and the bus. The more I observed, the more familiar I became with the settings in which these students' problems were occurring. I considered that, perhaps, these problems were somehow related to these settings, that they were caused by some feature of the environment rather than an underlying pathology, disability, or characterological flaw. I thought that maybe we could solve these problems by doing something to the environment. Thus, my journey with behavior analysis began.

Behavior analysis is a science of behavior that offers rigorous methods of analysis and empirically-derived principles. And from these methods and principles have come methods of assessment, intervention, and instruction, all grounded in empiricism. These features of behavior analysis appeal to me as a school psychologist. I tell people that I prefer behavior analysis over other orientations because, as a science, it satisfies my spirit and, as a tool, it helps me to solve problems. My commitment to behavior analysis comes from my interest in helping others in meaningful and socially important ways.

As far back as 25 years ago, scholars predicted a shift in how students would be served by school psychologists. This innovative service delivery model highlighted a major role change. School psychologists would conduct fewer standardized assessments and engage in less paperwork, while consulting more with teachers. No longer would the field be exclusively partnered with special education. Rather, school psychologists would address problems presented in both general and special education. School psychology would emphasize data-based decision making and evidence-based practices. This vision of school psychology is what drew me to the field. Although the paradigm has never fully shifted, I remain encouraged by the roles school psychologists are now playing in schools. For example, school psychologists in my home state of Wisconsin are taking on leadership positions in both general and special education, furthering their scope of influence. However, more responsibility and influence means more accountability.

I wrote this book to help school psychologists solve school-based problems. Solving problems to enhance student success necessitates an evidence-based perspective. School psychologists have recognized this for some time, which is probably why the field has become so closely aligned with behavior analysis. However, I did not want to simply present assessment or intervention protocols to be followed blindly (that is what the internet is for). Rather, I wanted to facilitate school psychologists' understanding of the fundamental principles of behavior analysis that underlie methods and procedures often employed via assessment and intervention. There are undoubtedly times when experimental control is required to establish instructional effectiveness, understanding behavior is necessary to change behavior, or an intervention supported in the literature fails to work with a particular student and a new solution is required. I hope this book serves as a resource for when the unexpected (and expected) occurs and all eyes turn to the school psychologist for answers. This book is also for other school-based professionals (e.g., teachers, school counselors, administrators) who are committed to supporting students using scientific approaches for understanding learning and behavior. Behavior analysis is not just for the school psychologist.

Several years after my revelation in that small New Hampshire town and four years after starting graduate school in school psychology, I came across a quote by Father Edward J. Flanagan, the founder of Girls and Boys Town in Omaha, NE, writing about society's failure to help marginalized youth in the 1930s. Paraphrasing, he said, "there is no such thing as a bad kid, just bad environments." I hope you find this quote as encouraging as I do. Arranging environments to facilitate student success offers tangible solutions that are within everyone's reach.

Acknowledgments

I would like to thank my many mentors and colleagues from St. Lawrence University in Canton, NY, School Administrative Unit #58 in Northumberland, NH, Indiana University Bloomington, Father Flanagan's Girls and Boys Town in Omaha, NE, the Eastern Maine Medical Center in Bangor, ME, and the University of Wisconsin-Eau Claire. Special appreciation is extended to Scott Bellini, Ph.D., Melissa Coolong-Chaffin, Ph.D., Patrick Friman, Ph.D., Thomas Huberty, Ph.D., and Mary Beth Tusing, Ph.D.

Recognition goes to my research assistants, Hannah Effertz and Adrienne Reyerson, for the countless hours they committed to supporting this work. I would also like to thank my current and former students and supervisees who have helped refine my ideas about, and become fluent with, this book's content.

At Routledge, gratitude is extended to Rebecca Novak for providing advice, insight, and positive reinforcement while I was developing the concept for this book and drafting the proposal, and Daniel Schwartz, for offering guidance as I prepared and submitted manuscript drafts.

I offer special gratitude to Angela Fontanini-Axelrod, Ph.D., my school psychology colleague and loving wife, for her support and wisdom.

Last, a special thank you goes out to all the children, families, and schools that I have had the honor of working with over my many years of practice.

Behavior Analysis and School Psychology

1

Experimental Analysis of Behavior (EAB) was founded as a science of behavior. Its approach, including a rigorous experimental methodology, was designed to determine functional, or causal, relationships between an organism's behavior and specific environmental variables (e.g., reinforcement, punishment, extinction). Early research efforts, mostly with animal models, established important empirically-derived principles of behavior that have since been applied to work with children and adults. Research in the early 1960s by early pioneers like Azrin, Baer, and Bijou utilized both EAB's methods and principles to apply a science of behavior to socially important problems that informed child development, psychology, and education. When the first issue of the *Journal of Applied Behavior Analysis* (*JABA*) was published in 1968, the field of Applied Behavior Analysis (ABA) was already well established.

ABA has close ties to education. The first article of the first issue of *JABA* investigated the effects of contingent teacher attention on the behavior of two elementary school students (Hall, Lund, & Jackson, 1968). The study was conducted in a general education public school classroom in Kansas City. Using a reversal design, a methodology common in EAB, Hall and colleagues found that both students' on-task behavior increased over baseline when the teacher provided positive attention contingent on on-task behavior. Since then, applications of empirically-derived principles of behavior analysis have informed educational practices (Bordieri, Kellum, & Wilson, 2012) and, as Polsgrove (2003) noted, years and years of accumulated science in the field of ABA has offered educators answers to difficult questions. And although early research efforts focused on improving behavior of individuals with low incidence disabilities (e.g., autism, intellectual disability), ABA has more recently informed educational practice across a variety of populations and problems. In doing so, ABA has contributed significantly to curricular planning, instructional design, assessment and measurement, and prevention and intervention programming (Cooper, 1982; Heward, 2005).

Despite ABA's track record, it has not been as widely adopted in education. In 1991, Saul Axelrod suggested ABA research demonstrating effective educational methods was regularly overlooked by those in education, noting that ABA was hardly mentioned in several timely and influential publications within the field of education. More recently, Doabler and colleagues (2014) and Burns and Ysseldyke (2009) reported empirical data indicating teachers rarely use evidence-based instructional strategies derived from principles of behavior analysis. Heward (2005) offered an exhaustive list of reasons why educators might view ABA as irrelevant. Included were the incompatibility of ABA's basic assumptions about education with current educators' perspectives, educators' perceptions that ABA lacks creativity and is overly simplistic, and ABA's insistence on the use of data to inform practice. Yet, reports published by educational policy groups, (e.g., the National Reading Panel and the President's Commission on Excellence in Special Education) have recommended greater educator accountability, direct and explicit instruction, research-supported practices, regular assessment of progress, and problem-solving approaches that use data to inform decisions (Reschly, 2008). Recently, these recommendations have made their way into federal legislation. The Elementary and Secondary Education Act and Individuals with Disabilities Education Act each emphasize using data-based decision-making models and evidence-based practices for improving student learning outcomes. Accordingly, current reform efforts are calling on educators to be more scientifically minded in their practices.

The School Psychologist and ABA

Reform efforts and legislative changes have led to major shifts in the delivery of educational and related programming. For example, school districts have reported implementing multilevel systems of supports for students (e.g., Response to Intervention or RtI) that provide ongoing measurement of student progress and match instructional need with intensity of support (Spectrum K-12, 2011). Moving from traditional education models to RtI, for example, has created controversy and posed challenges (Castillo & Curtis, 2014). However, the shift has opened opportunities for school psychologists and other educational professionals (e.g., special education teachers, speech-language pathologists) to expand their roles. For example, school psychologists are no longer just special education gatekeepers. Rather, they are being asked to play a more pivotal role in supporting the entire educational system. Fagan (2014) noted that school psychologists have taken on responsibilities other than the assessment of individual students. Specifically, he indicated that school psychologists regularly design and implement interventions, consult with stakeholders (e.g., teachers, parents), and engage in systems-level activities including designing and evaluating school- or district-wide programming (e.g., curriculum, prevention efforts).

School psychology's expanding role requires a different framework for practice and an expanded skill set. School psychologists can no longer just play the part of psychometrician. An expanded role that is consistent with educational reform efforts necessitates a broader awareness of the process of education (e.g., curriculum, resource allocation) but also a deeper understanding of learning and behavior. As Reschly (2008) noted, the paradigm shift in education and school psychology is calling for a problem-solving model that uses data to drive programming, emphasizes research-supported practices, regularly measures student performance, and adjusts instruction and intervention based on ongoing progress monitoring.

Not surprisingly, a longstanding relationship exists between school psychology and ABA. Over the years, ABA has made several significant contributions to the field of school psychology, both directly and indirectly. ABA has introduced more objective and less inferential ways of assessing school-based phenomena (e.g., academic functioning, behavior), provided a behavioral context for school-based consultation, addressed gaps in the school-based intervention and prevention literatures, and offered a more experimentally-oriented methodology to evaluate outcomes and use data to inform decision making (Kratochwill & Martens, 1994; Wilczynski, Thompson, Beatty, & Sterling-Turner, 2002). From a practice standpoint, ABA is highly regarded within the field of school psychology as evidenced by the increasing emphasis graduate training programs give ABA within their training scope and sequence. Regarding research, publications that cater to school psychologists, such as the *Journal of Applied School Psychology* and the *School Psychology Review*, feature methods (e.g., single case experimental design) and techniques (e.g., positive reinforcement, extinction) consistent with ABA.

To summarize, a more scientifically-oriented approach to education is being called for at the federal level and schools are increasingly in need of effective problem-solvers who can directly measure student outcomes, offer evidence-based practices directly or via consultation, and make decisions about students based on valid data. Moreover, accountability remains a buzzword in education. Teachers and other educational professionals need strategies now, more than ever, that work. Taken together, school psychologists adopting an ABA framework are well positioned to support students and shepherd education toward a more prosperous future.

Assumptions

Before introducing concepts, procedures, or principles associated with ABA, it is important to first recognize several fundamental assumptions. The remainder of this chapter reviews assumptions of ABA beginning with Skinner's statement about the science of behavior to more practical matters such as ABA's position that all students can learn. While this list does not pretend to be exhaustive, it does represent features of ABA that are relevant to education and school psychology practice.

ABA is a Science

Skinner (1953) proposed a science of behavior, noting specifically that science was a way of thinking more than a set of procedures to carry out an experiment. This way of thinking is characterized by a balance between skepticism and open-mindedness. The scientist is cautious about unsupported assertions, open to new information, and adamant about needing evidence when making or supporting claims. The enterprise of education has been plagued by fads and pseudoscientific conceptualizations and practices, and school psychologists have not been immune to this problem. Surveys of school psychologists have found that to be the case as they endorse engaging in activities not supported by research (e.g., administration of projective assessments; Lilienfeld, Ammirati, & David, 2012). Orienting to a model that emphasizes a scientific way of thinking might prevent questionable practices and improve outcomes for students. In addition, thinking scientifically means having high standards for evidence. School psychologists and other educational professionals cannot rely on unreliable sources to inform practice. Evidence from personal testimony, anecdotes, case studies, and even supposed authority figures is not likely to meet the high standards required for effective practice. Thinking scientifically implies considering data derived from experimental methods (e.g., peer-reviewed scientific literature, experimental analysis of practice-related procedures).

Other features of science worth noting include description, prediction, and control (Cooper, Heron, & Heward, 2007). For the school psychologist, this means describing behavior using clear and precise language, predicting future behavior based on repeated observations of previous behavior, and establishing control over behavior by identifying causal relationships. Regarding this last point, scientists look to establish laws that explain the natural world using repeated experimentation. Behavior analysts attempt to do the same. As a result, laws or principles have been established in behavior analysis that help explain the relationship between behavior and environmental variables (e.g., reinforcement, punishment).

Behavior is the Unit of Analysis

Skinner (1953) wrote that in a science of behavior the behavior, itself, is the unit of analysis. That is, behavior is the variable under investigation. However, Skinner cautioned against thinking of the study of behavior as easy or simple. Instead, he noted that behavior is complex, constantly changing, and never "held still for observation" (p. 15). Yet, he and others that followed conceptualized behavior as observable events that could be reliably measured. This view of behavior has several implications in educational settings. First, educators must emphasize observable events not unobservable constructs (e.g., cognition) or internal states (e.g., anger). In doing so, an objective definition of the target emerges that, in many ways, simplifies the task. Rather than attempting to address some difficult to understand construct, like cognitive processing, the school psychologist targets an observable, measurable behavior like oral reading fluency. Second, school psychologists and other educators can count or measure the phenomenon under investigation when using an objective definition. Objective definitions also eliminate inferences and establish reliability among observers, thus reducing error and improving the validity of conclusions drawn from data. Finally, repeated measurements are conducted to reliably detect changes in the phenomenon over time. This should all sound appealing to school psychologists and other educational professionals who are interested in assessing students' academic, behavioral, and social progress, and intervening when problems develop or persist.

The Analysis of Behavior

Both as a scientific enterprise and an applied discipline, ABA is analytic. It features a systematic method for observing, measuring, and analyzing behavior. Observation and measurement are discussed above. The analysis utilizes experimental methods to show a change in the environment resulted in a change in some behavior (Cooper, 1982). Establishing a causal relationship between behavior and the environment using experimental methods is the primary aim of behavior analysis. To paraphrase Baer, Wolf, and Risley (1968), behavior analysts want to demonstrate that a behavior can be 'turned on or off' by manipulating something specific in the environment. Of course, experimental methods (e.g., reversal technique, multiple-baseline design) are required to determine causal relationships and replication to establish some level of predictability is necessary. Yet fundamentally, behavior change lies in the manipulation of the environment.

Identifying environmental causes of behavior that can be manipulated should hold great appeal to school psychologists. Getting one's hands on the knobs and dials of behavior is what allows practitioners to change behavior or teach skills. Consider other commonly cited causes of behavior, such as genetic or psychological factors, that are impossible or near impossible to manipulate directly. Not being able to manipulate a variable directly reduces the possibility of successfully influencing that variable. How do we intervene when the cause of aggressive behavior is genetics or the cause of poor peer relations is a disordered personality? Changing behavior or teaching skills by changing the environment is empowering and suggests to a change agent (e.g., teacher, parent) that he or she can have control over student behavior and learning.

The Environment Can Be Arranged to Promote Positive Outcomes

ABA attributes causes of behavior to the environment (Fisher, Groff, & Roane, 2011). For example, praising a student for saying 'thank you' can influence the probability of that student saying 'thank you' in the future. Similarly, educators can systematically arrange the environment to elicit specific behavior. For example, modeling an academic behavior, such as multiplying six and eight, can serve as a cue for students' accurate responding. We can also match the learning material to a student's current skill level, provide visual prompts to increase the likelihood a student transitions appropriately from one activity to another, or increase the amount of reinforcement available to a student who is socially withdrawn. ABA provides educators with a science that enables them to effectively arrange environments to promote successful outcomes.

All Students Can Be Taught

Principles of behavior have been successfully used to teach students who were previously thought to be unteachable (Heward, 2005). Research has demonstrated ABA's effects across students (e.g., with and without disabilities), settings (e.g., general and special education, residential treatment), and instructors (e.g., teachers, paraprofessionals, parents). Furthermore, the published literature has reduced the scope of problems that have not been successfully managed by ABA to a small number. Problems that were once considered unresponsive to intervention, such as self-injury, have responded positively to treatments employing behavior analytic principles (Betz & Fisher, 2011). ABA's success addressing challenging, as well as everyday, problems offers an optimistic outlook but it also suggests that school psychologists and other educational professionals might be best served conceptualizing student learning and behavior change as an attainable goal rather than an impossible task. Equipped with the technology of ABA, school psychologists and other educational professionals can have a profound impact on student learning and behavior.

Conclusion

ABA offers school psychologists more than just a set of procedures to implement when students' fail. It provides them with a way of thinking, an objective unit for change, a method for establishing causation, and a location to intervene. Specifically, ABA presents to school psychologists a scientific orientation to problem-solving that focuses on behavior (including academic behavior) and the role the environment plays in both eliciting and changing behavior. ABA also delivers hope to school psychologists and other educational professionals looking for solutions to challenging problems. Explanations for problems are not rooted in internal causes. Rather, causes for problems are attributed to environmental variables that can be manipulated directly by teachers, parents, or even students themselves to promote positive outcomes.

References

Axelrod, S. (1991). The problem: American education, the solution: Use behavior analytic technology. *Journal of Behavioral Education, 1*, 275–282.

Baer, D. M., Wolf, M. M., & Risley, T. R. (1968). Some current dimensions of applied behavior analysis. *Journal of Applied Behavior Analysis, 1*, 91–97.

Betz, A. M., & Fisher, W. W. (2011). Functional analysis. In W. W. Fisher, C. C. Piazza, & H. S. Roane (Eds.), *Handbook of applied behavior analysis* (pp. 206–225). New York: Guilford.

Bordieri, M. J., Kellum, K. K., & Wilson, K. G. (2012). Editorials: Special issue on behavior analysis and education. *The Behavior Analyst Today, 13*, 1–2.

Burns, M. K., & Ysseldyke, J. E. (2009) Reported prevalence of evidence-based instructional practices in special education. *The Journal of Special Education, 43*, 3–11.

Castillo, J. M., & Curtis, M. J. (2014). Best practices in system-level change. In P. L. Harrison & A. Thomas (Eds.), *Best practices in school psychology: System level services* (pp. 11–28). Bethesda, MD: National Association of School Psychologists.

Cooper, J. O. (1982). Applied behavior analysis in education. *Theory into Practice, 21,* 114–118.

Cooper, J., Heron, T., & Heward, W. (2007). *Applied behavior analysis* (2nd ed.). Upper Saddle River, NJ: Merrill/Pearson Education.

Doabler, C. T., Nelson, N., Kosty, D., Fien, H., Baker, S. K., Smolkowski, K., & Clarke, B. (2014). Examining teachers' use of evidence-based practices during core mathematics instruction. *Assessment for Effective Intervention, 39,* 99–111.

Fagan, T. K. (2014). Trends in the history of school psychology in the United States. In P. L. Harrison & A. Thomas (Eds.), *Best practices in school psychology: Foundations* (pp. 383–399). Bethesda, MD: National Association of School Psychologists.

Fisher, W. W., Groff, R. A., & Roane, H. S. (2011). Applied behavior analysis: History, philosophy, principles, and basic methods. In W. W. Fisher, C. C. Piazza, & H. S. Roane (Eds.), *Handbook of applied behavior analysis* (pp. 3–13). New York: Guilford.

Hall, R. V., Lund, D., & Jackson, D. (1968). Effect of teacher attention on study behavior. *Journal of Applied Behavior Analysis, 1,* 1–12.

Heward, W. L. (2005). Reasons applied behavior analysis is good for education. In W. L. Heward, T. E. Heron, N. A. Neef, S. M. Peterson, D. M. Sainato, G. Y. Cartledge, . . ., J. C. Dardig (Eds.), *Focus on behavior analysis in education: Achievements, challenges, and opportunities* (pp. 318–448). Upper Saddle River, NJ: Prentice Hall.

Kratochwill, T. R., & Martens, B. K. (1994). Applied behavior analysis and school psychology. *Journal of Applied Behavior Analysis, 27,* 3–5.

Lilienfeld, S. O., Ammirati, R., & David, M. (2012). Distinguishing science from pseudoscience in school psychology: Science and scientific thinking as safeguards against human error. *Journal of School Psychology, 50,* 7–36.

Polsgrove, L. (2003). Reflection on the past and future. *Education and Treatment of Children, 26,* 337–344.

Reschly, D. J. (2008). School psychology paradigm shift and beyond. In A. Thomas & J. Grimes (Eds.), *Best practices in school psychology V: Volume 1* (pp. 3–15). Washington, DC: National Association of School Psychologists.

Skinner, B. F. (1953). *Science and human behavior.* New York: Free Press.

Spectrum K-12 School Solutions. (2011). *Response to intervention adoption survey 2011.* Townson, MD: Author.

Wilczynski, S. M., Thompson, K. F., Beatty, T. M., & Sterling-Turner, H. E. (2002). The role of behavior analysis in school psychology. *The Behavior Analyst Today, 3,* 198–202.

Behavior Analysis: A Primer for School Psychologists

2

This chapter is an introduction to key behavior analytic principles. These principles were derived from basic behavioral research and then studied in applied settings. This chapter in no way offers readers a comprehensive review of these principles and readers wanting more detailed accounts are referred to introductory texts on ABA. However, a summary of relevant principles is provided and, where appropriate, readers will find details regarding how these principles might be applied to problems in school settings or in the context of working with children.

Conditioning

An introduction to ABA principles must begin with *conditioning*. Conditioning is defined as increasing or decreasing the probability behavior will occur in the future (see Vargas, 2013). For example, giving a child a small piece of candy after he completes a chore is likely to increase the probability that he completes that chore again in the future. The terms response and stimulus are often used in psychology textbooks when describing conditioning (see, for example, Kalat, 2013). A response is simply a behavior and a stimulus is simply an object or event. In the example above, completing the small chore is the response and the request to complete the chore is the stimulus. In the context of an academic skill, an addition problem written on a piece of paper (e.g., 2+2) is a stimulus for a response (e.g., writing the number 4).

Basic research has led to the study of conditioning from two perspectives. The first, initially conceived by Ivan Pavlov while studying the salivary reflex in dogs, is called *classical conditioning*. Classical conditioning occurs when a previously neutral stimulus elicits a reflexive response (Thorpe & Olson, 1997). In Pavlov's experiments, the neutral stimulus, a tone, was repeatedly paired with food eventually leading to the dog associating the tone with food and, after more time, salivating when hearing the tone even when the tone was no longer paired with the food. The second perspective, described by Skinner, is called *operant conditioning*. Operant conditioning describes discriminating properties of consequences on behavior (Cooper, Heron, & Heward, 2007). The following sections describe classical and operant conditioning in more detail and provide examples of how these concepts have been applied to working with children and adolescents.

Classical Conditioning

Classical conditioning is a rather straightforward process. As an example, consider Watson and Raynor's (1920) use of classical conditioning to evoke a fear response in their almost one-year-old subject, Albert. Watson and Raynor conducted a series of experiments to see how paring the loud, scary noise with a stimulus that previously failed to evoke a fear response, a white rat, might affect Albert's behavior. When presented together, Albert exhibited fear. After repeated exposure to both stimuli (i.e., the scary, loud noise and the white rat), he was exposed to the white rat alone, which resulted in a fear response. Watson and Raynor's experiments demonstrated that certain fears could be learned through repeated pairing of a neutral stimulus with a fear-producing stimulus (Thorpe & Olson, 1997).

For those interested in understanding the rather superfluous language associated with classical conditioning, consider the following example. Mike is afraid of snakes (unconditioned stimulus). At the sight of a snake, Mike screams, jumps on a table, and yells for help (unconditioned response). Mike is not afraid of drinking chocolate milk. In fact, he loves chocolate milk. To stop Mike from drinking all the chocolate milk in the refrigerator, Mike's son lets a long, black, creepy-looking snake out of a bag and into the kitchen every time Mike begins drinking chocolate milk. Over time and after enough repetitions, Mike will begin to display a fear response (conditioned response) when drinking chocolate milk (conditioned stimulus) even when that chocolate milk is no longer paired with the snake. Consider the example of Albert above:

- Loud noise = unconditioned stimulus
- Crying when exposed to the loud noise = unconditioned response
- White rat = conditioned stimulus
- Crying when exposed to the rat, by itself = conditioned response

School psychologists and other educational professionals rarely rely on classical conditioning when developing interventions. However, classical conditioning can be used to explain reflexive behavior (e.g., fear responses) and has been conceptually used to treat anxiety disorders (Thorpe & Olson, 1997). Engaging in relaxation exercises or calming activities while, at the same time, being exposed to a fear-producing stimulus is considered a primary component of cognitive behavior therapy (CBT; see Farmer & Chapman, 2008). Specifically, the relaxation exercises or calming activities are repeatedly paired with the fear-producing stimulus to eliminate the conditioned fear by producing "a counterconditioning effect that weakens the relationship between the stimuli and the fear response" (von der Embse, Barterian, & Segool, 2012, p. 67). As an example, relaxation strategies paired with exposure have been cited as an effective treatment for test anxiety of children and adolescents (see Ergene, 2003; von der Embse et al., 2012).

Operant Conditioning

Conditioning can also be conceptualized as learning. In the earlier example of the child and candy, the child is learning, through conditioning processes, to complete the chore when asked. Conditioning and, therefore, learning relies on the functional relationships developed over time between stimuli, responses, and consequences. (Skinner, 1953). Learning is actually a function of these three terms operating together. Using other parlance, the stimulus is the antecedent, the response is the behavior, and, well, the consequence is just the consequence. Vargas (2013), among others, described this relationship (i.e., antecedent-behavior-consequence [A-B-C]) as the *three-term contingency*. It can be used to understand behavior and is essential when designing intervention and instructional programs.

Skinner (1953) introduced the world to operant conditioning via his work with animal models. Conducting experiments with pigeons and rats, Skinner determined that organisms emitted behavior that is then shaped by the environment through the environment's delivery of consequences. In his classic experiments using the Skinner Box and rats, Skinner paired food, a consequential event, with the accidental hitting of a lever. Over time, the rats began hitting the lever to receive food. The food or the consequence for hitting the lever reinforced or strengthened the rats' lever-hitting behavior. Essentially the rats 'learned' that hitting the lever produced food. In a second series of experiments, Skinner sent an aversive electrical shock through the cage. He rigged the device so that the electrical shock, another consequential event, would be turned off only when the rat hit the lever. Over time, the rats began hitting the lever to turn off the electrical shock. Turning off the electrical shock or the consequence for hitting the lever reinforced or strengthened the rats' lever-hitting behavior. Again, the rats 'learned' that hitting the lever produced something good but instead of producing food, hitting the lever produced an escape from the aversive electrical shock.

POSITIVE AND NEGATIVE REINFORCEMENT

These experiments helped illustrate the two types of reinforcement. The first type, *positive reinforcement*, involves the organism receiving something (food) following engagement in a specific behavior (hitting the lever). Said differently, the food positively reinforces the lever-hitting behavior because it increases the rats' future engagement in the lever-hitting behavior. Moving away from rats, consider a classroom where students frequently engage in off-task behavior (e.g., talking with peers, playing with toys, looking out the window). The teacher might consider implementing a strategy that relies on positive reinforcement to address these problems. For example, an intervention referred to as the Star Chart might be used, where students earn 'stars' for turning in assignments. After ensuring the students' work meets an acceptable standard for accuracy and neatness, the teacher posts students' names on the Star Chart and, at a predetermined time, those students earn extra free time in the classroom (for a more thorough description of the intervention see Rathvon, 2008). Page and Edwards (1978) found that a similar procedure increased the desirable behavior of middle school students with below average reading skills. The reward of extra free time served to positively reinforce students' on-task behavior and work completion because the delivery of extra free time (i.e., the consequence) was dependent on students turning in assignments (i.e., the behavior or response), leading to an increase in desirable behavior and a decrease in disruptive behavior.

Positive reinforcement is frequently used to increase an appropriate behavior (Piazza, Roane, & Karsten, 2011). Teachers' social attention is an example of a powerful positive reinforcer that can effectively improve students' behavior (Alberto & Troutman, 2013; Cooper et al., 2007). In fact, teacher attention as a reinforcer for appropriate behavior is cited in many reviews of the literature on effective classroom management (see Simonsen, Fairbanks, Briesch, Myers, & Sugai, 2008; Sutherland, Lewis-Palmer, Stichter, & Morgan, 2008). To illustrate, Sutherland, Wehby, and Copeland (2000) demonstrated that increasing a teacher's behavior-specific praise of on-task behavior (e.g., 'Mike, I really like that you are looking at me when I speak') could increase students' on-task behavior. Conversely, they found that a students' on-task behavior decreased when the teacher's use of behavior-specific praise decreased. Other forms of positive reinforcement have been shown to be effective at improving behavior including using rewards and incentives (Alberto & Troutman, 2013). Fabiano and Pelham (2003) showed how adding a reward (i.e., opportunities to play a computer game) to a behavior management plan could profoundly improve a student's on-task behavior and decrease disruptive behavior.

Positive reinforcement is a consequential event that increases the likelihood that a behavior will occur in the future (Alberto & Troutman, 2013). While the principle of positive reinforcement is frequently used as a mechanism within an intervention to increase a behavior, the concept can also be used to help explain behavior. Consider, for example, a seventh grade boy acting up in class. He is disruptive, off-task, and disrespectful toward the teacher. A quick assessment of this student and a school psychologist might instantly conclude that Attention Deficit Hyperactivity Disorder (ADHD) or Oppositional Defiant Disorder (ODD) are responsible for this student's behavior. However, further observation finds the boy is frequently teasing the girls and clowning around with the boys. The two most frequent consequential events of those behaviors involve the student being reprimanded by the teacher and laughed at by classmates. Understanding ABA and, more specifically, positive reinforcement, the school psychologist can now hypothesize that the student's behaviors are positively reinforced by, perhaps, the attention received from peers. Furthermore, now the school psychologist can recommend a course of action that teaches the student more socially appropriate ways to access attention from peers while, at the same time, rewards peers for ignoring the student's inappropriate behavior. Recognizing that positive reinforcement helps explain relationships between stimuli and responses is important when identifying functions of behavior or planning interventions that address variables in the environment that are likely maintaining behavior.

Negative reinforcement is the second type of reinforcement. Negative reinforcement involves the organism avoiding or escaping something aversive or bad following the display of a specific behavior. In Skinner's (1953) example above, the electric shock was removed immediately following the pressing of the lever. Said another way, the removal of the electric shock (escape from the aversive stimuli) served to negatively reinforce the lever-hitting behavior because it increased the rats' engagement in the lever-hitting behavior. How might this be relevant to humans? Consider the power of avoiding or escaping something aversive. Men and women all over the United States are afraid of spiders. If, at the sight of a spider, a man screamed and his wife came into the room, scooped up the spider with a paper towel, and left, and imagine this happened repeatedly, the removal of an unpleasant stimulus (i.e., the spider) by the man's wife has strengthened his response (i.e., screaming) to the stimulus.

A wonderful example of how negative reinforcement, as a principle, can be used in practice comes from a study done by DiGennaro, Martens, and McIntyre (2005) where the avoidance of performance feedback regarding an intervention's integrity (i.e., the degree to which an intervention's procedures are implemented correctly) served to negatively reinforce the teachers' accurate implementation of the intervention. Four teachers received daily written performance feedback about their integrity implementing a behavioral intervention plan for select students' off-task behavior. When the researchers observed less than 100% integrity, written feedback and performance graphs were left in teacher school mailboxes and a meeting was scheduled for the next day. No meetings were held the day following a 100% accurate implementation of the intervention. DiGennaro and colleagues found that using principles associated with negative reinforcement "may be a viable, time-efficient technique for increasing the integrity of plan implementation by teachers in the classroom" (p. 220). This example illustrates how negative reinforcement can be used in practice to increase a desirable behavior.

Applied to student problems, interventions relying on negative reinforcement can be powerful. Teaching students appropriate ways to avoid or escape aversive stimuli or communicate the need for assistance or a task break have been found to be effective instructional strategies (Alberto & Troutman, 2013). Regarding the former, studies have shown that aberrant behavior maintained by negative reinforcement (i.e., escape) can be improved when the intervention involves escape contingent on appropriate or desirable behavior. Broussard and Northrup (1995) found that providing a student with five minutes of free time for completed academic tasks increased the percentage of intervals of academic work completed to 100% and decreased the percentage of intervals of disruptive behavior to 0%. Hawkins and Axelrod (2008) demonstrated how providing five-minute breaks, sitting alone, contingent on ten minutes of on-task behavior increased on-task behavior for three adolescents completing homework. Regarding the latter, functional communication training (FCT) focuses on teaching students alternative responses that lead to similar reinforcing consequences (Carr & Durand, 1985; Durand & Carr, 1991). For example, a student engaging in disruptive behavior resulting in avoidance or escape of a challenging academic task might be taught to ask for assistance by raising a hand and saying, 'I don't understand.'

Like positive reinforcement, negative reinforcement can help explain behavior. For example, negative reinforcement can help explain behavioral responses associated with fear. Skinner (1953) spoke about the emotional reaction one experiences when threatened and the role conditioning plays in negatively reinforcing behavioral responses that involve escape from or avoidance of aversive stimuli. Related, Friman, Hayes, and Wilson (1998) stated that experiential avoidance is often functionally related to anxiety. Using panic disorder as an example, Friman and colleagues suggested that people with phobias of public places (i.e., panic disorder with agoraphobia) do not necessarily fear being in those public places but, rather, fear having a panic attack in one of those public places. Behaviors associated with avoidance of public places are then negatively reinforced when the individual avoids those public places.

Thinking more about students' classroom behavior, school psychologists and teachers often encounter students engaging in aberrant behavior either immediately preceding or during a challenging academic task. While school professionals might describe these behaviors as pathological, representing some symptoms of a larger disorder or disability, thinking about using negative reinforcement to explain behavior might generate simple solutions. For example, McComas, Goddard, and Hoch (2002) empirically compared three different conditions—(1) free access to play items and adult attention regardless of behavior, (2) adult attention immediately following destructive or off-task behavior, and (3) removal of academic task immediately following disruptive or off-task behavior—to assess a student's problematic behavior. Results indicated that the disruptive and off-task behavior most often occurred when the academic task was removed demonstrating a functional relationship between the behavior and removal of the academic task. Next, McComas and colleagues developed an intervention that allowed the student to take a five-minute break from academic tasks when, and only when, he had finished a worksheet. The student's academic task completion behavior was negatively reinforced by the five-minute academic task breaks, as the student was now able to avoid and escape the academic task demands but only when he engaged in appropriate behavior.

POSITIVE AND NEGATIVE PUNISHMENT

Most people think 'discipline' when thinking about punishment. In fact, most people equate punishment with harsh disciplinary practices that do unpleasant things to people. But while punishment can be a part of discipline and certainly harsh or punitive, a behavior analytic perspective conceptualizes punishment as a consequential

Table 2.1   Operant Conditioning Examples

	Definition	Example	Strategies
Positive Reinforcement	Receiving something seemingly good following a behavior increases the probability the behavior will occur in the future	B: Student works quietly on assignment C: Teacher praises student and allows for 5 mins of extra recess	• Behavior-specific praise • Token economy • Contingency contract
Negative Reinforcement	Removing something seemingly bad following a behavior increases the probability the behavior will occur in the future	B: Student works quietly on assignment C: Teacher requires student to complete only half the assignment	• Decrease task demands • Contingent breaks • Teach help-seeking behavior
Positive Punishment	Receiving something seemingly bad following a behavior decreases the probability the behavior will occur in the future	B: Student throws paperclip at peer during assignment C: Teacher requires student to complete additional assignment	• Increasing task demands • Verbal reprimands
Negative Punishment	Removing something seemingly good following a behavior decreases the probability the behavior will occur in the future	B: Student throws paperclip at peer during assignment C: Teacher takes away 5 mins of recess	• Response cost • Timeout from positive reinforcement

(B=behavior; C=consequence)

event that has certain properties, like reinforcement. But unlike reinforcement, this consequential event leads to decreases in behavior or responses following repeated exposure to a stimulus (Alberto & Troutman, 2013). Consider the following example, a man repeatedly hits his thumb with a hammer while trying to put a nail in a wooden board. Hitting your thumb with a hammer is painful and doing so repeatedly is even more painful. Consequently, the pain (i.e., the stimulus) results in the man not using a hammer (i.e., the behavior or response). Wondering how punishment is different than reinforcement? Thinking that the man is just avoiding the pain by not using the hammer? Remember, reinforcement increases the likelihood of a response or behavior and punishment decreases the likelihood of a response or behavior. In this example, the behavior of hammering a nail decreases, so this is an example of punishment.

Like reinforcement, punishment can be positive or negative. It sounds strange to say 'positive punishment' but, remember, punishment, from an ABA perspective, is just a consequential event that decreases the probability that a behavior will occur in the future. *Positive punishment* is when the consequential event involves the addition of a stimulus, typically something aversive. For example, adding additional math word problems to a student's homework assignment after the student refused to take the math book out of the desk would involve adding something presumably aversive. However, the additional math word problems are only considered punishment if the consequential event results in a decrease in the behavior. *Negative punishment* is when the consequential event involves the taking away of a stimulus. However, this time the stimulus is something presumably good. A frequently used example of negative punishment is timeout from reinforcement. A child ignoring a request to put his or her shoes in the closet results in the parent putting the child in timeout. Again, this is only an example of punishment if the problem behavior (i.e., ignoring a parental request) decreases and the timeout, itself, is only a punisher if it results in a decrease in the problem behavior. If, for example, the child can access reinforcement during the timeout (e.g., a sibling's attention), then the timeout might reinforce the problem behavior not punish it. In this case, the parent is likely to become frustrated using the timeout and declare it ineffective, rather than recognize the behavior was actually being reinforced.

Keeping with timeout from reinforcement as a strategy to decrease aberrant behavior, research has found the procedure, which is based on a behavior analytic view of punishment, to be highly effective (see Kaminski, Valle, Filene, & Boyle, 2008; Vegas, Jenson, & Kircher, 2007). For example, Fabiano and colleagues (2004) examined the effects of timeout from reinforcement on the aggression, disruptive behavior, and noncompliance of 71 students with ADHD participating in an intensive summer program. Results indicated timeout was significantly more effective than no timeout. Applied to classrooms, timeout from reinforcement can also help reduce problem behavior. Barton, Brulle, and Repp (1987) implemented timeout from reinforcement in a classroom setting for three students with intellectual disabilities. The researchers targeted students' maladaptive behavior such as physical aggression and noncompliance. Their results demonstrated timeout from reinforcement could decrease the maladaptive behavior of students in a classroom setting.

Like reinforcement, punishment can be used to explain behavior. For example, teachers can inadvertently punish hand-raising behavior by ignoring instances of hand-raising. The teacher's ignoring of the hand-raising behavior serves as punishment if, and only if, a decrease in hand-raising behavior is observed. Similarly, the teacher might call on those students calling out. While punishing hand-raising behavior, the teacher is simultaneously reinforcing calling out behavior if, and only if, an increase in calling out behavior is observed. Essentially, the teacher's behavior can be both reinforcing and punishing depending on its effect on students' hand-raising and calling out behavior.

Schedules of Reinforcement and Punishment

The schedules at which reinforcement and punishment are delivered greatly affect behavior and learning. Consider a teenager losing car privileges only once every four times he or she is late for curfew. The punishment (losing car privileges) is delivered intermittently resulting in the teenager engaging in the misbehavior, being late for curfew, at a higher rate because he or she has come to understand that the parents will only punish the behavior 25% of the time. Now consider a fifth grade student earning extra recess time only once every four times a challenging math worksheet is completed. The reinforcement, extra recess time, is delivered intermittently resulting in the student engaging in the appropriate behavior, completing a math worksheet, at a higher rate, knowing the teacher will only reward the behavior 25% of the time. In both examples, the schedule of the delivery of reinforcement or punishment influences the frequency at which the targeted behavior is displayed. The latter example illustrates the powerful effect intermittent reinforcement has on human behavior. In fact, slot machines capitalize on the power of intermittent reinforcement. Jackpots are delivered on a very thin schedule leading people to sit at a machine for hours, pulling the lever, hoping to become the next millionaire. The science of ABA provides explanations of different patterns of responding given different schedules of consequential events and how to use different schedules of consequential events effectively in teaching (Alberto & Troutman, 2013; Domjan, 2015; Mace, Pratt, Zangrillo, & Steege, 2011).

CONTINUOUS SCHEDULES OF REINFORCEMENT

A *continuous schedule of reinforcement* refers to the delivery of a reinforcer following every time a targeted behavior or skill is displayed. Intuitively, a continuous schedule of reinforcement is the most obvious choice when planning to teach students a skill or target a behavior for intervention. Consider teaching a student to comply with adult requests. To do this, we might provide a superhero sticker each time the student complies with a request. Yet when considering a continuous schedule of reinforcement, it is important to note when and why this schedule might fail to produce desired outcomes. Imagine the student becoming tired of earning the superhero sticker (called satiation, described later in the chapter), or consider the poor teacher who must continuously reinforce this student's compliance with every request. Furthermore, we can predict that there might be a rapid decrease in compliant behavior should the teacher immediately move from a continuous schedule of reinforcement to no reinforcement at all (Alberto & Troutman, 2013).

INTERMITTENT SCHEDULES

In the example above, the teacher might gradually thin the reinforcement schedule so that the student is no longer reinforced every time he engages in compliant behavior but, perhaps, every other time. Reinforcing a target behavior every other time or every fourth time or every minute or five minutes means reinforcing on an *intermittent schedule*. Skinner (1953) suggested that intermittent reinforcement decreased the possibility that a reinforcer might lose its reinforcing qualities. He also noted that behavior reinforced intermittently is less prone to the effects of extinction (discussed later in this chapter). The complete removal of a reinforcer after the behavior has been continuously reinforced for a length of time might produce dramatic decreases in the frequency of the behavior. For example, a teacher continuously reinforcing compliance might observe a significant decrease in compliance following the total withdrawal of reinforcement. However, the teacher is less likely to witness a decrease in compliance following the withdrawal of reinforcement if reinforcement is thinned to an intermittent schedule. Finally, intermittent reinforcement requires the student to delay gratification and self-manage behavior that is not continuously reinforced (Alberto & Troutman, 2013). These behaviors are important for the development of independence and self-control, as planned reinforcement cannot always follow students' behavior.

Skinner (1953) and Ferster and Skinner (1957) described two categories of basic intermittent reinforcement schedules, ratio and interval, and suggested behavior that is reinforced on these two types of schedules could be predicted. Moreover, interventions derived from these two basic categories have been found to enhance skills and improve behavior in various contexts (see Mace et al., 2011).

Ratio schedules of reinforcement correspond to the number of responses required before delivery of the reinforcement. For example, compliance with teacher requests might be reinforced after every fifth time a student displays the behavior. There are two types of ratio schedules. A *fixed ratio*, illustrated in the previous example, is a schedule for reinforcing the first behavior after a fixed number of behaviors. Fixed ratio schedules often lead to higher rates of the behavior being reinforced because the behavior is subjected to frequent reinforcement the more it is displayed (Alberto & Troutman, 2013; Mace et al., 2011; Skinner, 1953). However, fluency skills are more prone to mistakes when reinforced on a fixed ratio schedule. Errors are more likely when a student attempts to complete math problems too quickly when the number of problems correct is being reinforced on a fixed ratio schedule. In addition, pauses in responding are common when moving from a dense fixed ratio schedule (reinforcing the behavior after every other occurrence of the behavior) to a thinner ratio schedule (reinforcing the behavior after every 15 occurrences of the behavior; Alberto & Troutman, 2013; Mace et al., 2011). This pause describes the student's failure to engage in the behavior for a period of time following the delivery of the reinforcement.

A *variable ratio* is a schedule for reinforcing a behavior after a variable number of behaviors. For example, we might reinforce appropriate conversation skills after the student has engaged in the behavior two, four, or six times following the delivery of the last reinforcer. The average number of responses required for reinforcement defines the variable ratio and a range is also provided. In the above example, the variable ratio schedule would be four (VR 4) with a range of two to six. The problems associated with fluency and the post-reinforcement pause are negated when using a variable ratio schedule.

Table 2.2 Schedules of Reinforcement

Schedule		Definition	Example	Uses	Limitations
Continuous		Reinforcement is delivered after every occurrence of the behavior	Teacher praises student every time student engages in appropriate peer interactions	Appropriate when teaching a new skill, as each correct response is reinforced	Requires high degree of teacher effort, student might satiate on same reinforcer
Intermittent Ratio	Fixed	Behavior is reinforced after a fixed number of that behavior has occurred	Teacher praises student after every 4th time student identifies a letter sound correctly	Appropriate when teaching a new skill but continuous reinforcement is not possible or the goal is to begin thinning the schedule	Decreases or pauses in accurate responding following reinforcement, errors are more likely when targeting fluency
	Variable	Behavior is reinforced after a variable number of that behavior has occurred	Teacher praises student after every 2nd, then 6th, then 4th time student identifies a letter sound correctly	Appropriate when targeting fluency or when decreases in accurate responding have occurred following reinforcement using fixed schedule	
Intermittent Interval	Fixed	Behavior is reinforced after a fixed time interval	Teacher praises student following compliance with request, waits 5 mins, then praises student for next compliant response	Appropriate for teacher in large group setting, appropriate when aim is to gradually increase time between reinforcement	Appropriate behavior might not be reinforced often, decreases or pauses in accurate responding following reinforcement
	Variable	Behavior is reinforced after a variable time interval	Teacher praises student following compliance with a request, waits 1 min, then praises student, waits 10 mins, then praises student	Appropriate when decreases in accurate responding have occurred following reinforcement using fixed schedule	

An *interval schedule of reinforcement* corresponds to the delivery of reinforcement following the display of the behavior after a predetermined period. A *fixed interval* schedule of reinforcement describes reinforcement following the first response after a fixed time period. For example, a teacher might reinforce compliance, wait five minutes, and then reinforce compliance again once it has been displayed. As with fixed ratio schedules, fixed interval schedules pose some problems when attempting to increase a response or improve behavior. Low rates of behavior are likely to be observed, especially when the fixed interval increases from a low interval (e.g., one minute) to a longer interval (e.g., ten minutes; Skinner, 1953). In addition, a post-reinforcement pause, like that of a fixed ratio, might occur (Alberto & Troutman, 2013; Mace et al., 2011; Skinner, 1953). This is especially true should students begin to accurately predict when the reinforcement might be delivered (Alberto & Troutman, 2013).

A *variable interval* schedule of reinforcement involves using different time intervals to reinforce a behavior. For example, a student's behavior might initially be reinforced after two minutes then after ten minutes, then after four minutes, and then after six minutes. Like the variable ratio schedule, the average time interval defines the schedule and a range is provided. The problems with low rates of behavior and the post-reinforcement pause are negated when using a variable interval schedule.

Research considering different schedules of reinforcement has provided some guidance for practitioners. Specifically, applied research has shown that variable schedules are favored over fixed schedules when attempting to improve behavior. Saudergas, Madsen, and Scott (1977) found that variable interval feedback on academic performance delivered to parents of third grade students at the end of the week was more effective at improving students' work completion than fixed interval feedback. Van Houten and Nau (1980) demonstrated that variable ratio schedules were more effective than fixed ratio schedules when reinforcement was delivered for appropriate behavior displayed by students with hearing impairments. However, fixed schedules of reinforcement can be effective as well. Rasmussen and O'Neill (2006) showed that a fixed interval schedule of reinforcement in the form of social attention (e.g., verbal praise, physical contact) had a profound effect on the compliant behavior of three elementary school students identified with emotional and behavioral disorders.

SCHEDULES OF PUNISHMENT

Punishment, as recognized from a behavior analytic perspective (i.e., consequential events that lead to a decrease in behavior), can also be delivered on different schedules. However, the schedules at which the punishment is delivered affects behavior differently than reinforcement schedules. Research with animal subjects suggests that punishment must be delivered on a continuous or near continuous schedule for it to produce decreases in a behavior when reinforcement is not available (see Lerman & Vorndran, 2002). Research with human subjects is inconclusive. According to Lerman and Vorndran, some studies have found decreases in problem behavior when intermittently punished, while other studies have demonstrated schedules of punishment that are close to continuous (i.e., dense) are ineffective.

To illustrate the complexity that exists regarding the findings on schedules of punishment with children, consider the following examples. Clark, Rowbury, Baer, and Baer (1973) studied the differential effects of using continuous and intermittent schedules of timeout to punish the disruptive behavior of a preschool child. They found an inverse relationship between the frequency of responses punished and the frequency of the disruptive behavior. That is, the frequency of the disruptive behavior decreased the more often timeout was used when the disruptive behavior was displayed. Clark and his colleagues concluded some schedules of punishment, especially as the frequency approaches a continuous schedule, might be effective at reducing problem behavior. Lerman, Iwata, and DeLeon (1997) studied the effects of continuous and intermittent timeout on the self-injurious behavior (SIB) of five adults all with intellectual disabilities. Not surprising, the authors found that a continuous schedule of punishment resulted in significant decreases in SIB. However, results were inconsistent across subjects when punishment was delivered intermittently following SIB. One participant's SIB remained low when the schedule of punishment was shifted from continuous to intermittent, while the other four participants exhibited levels of SIB that were consistent with baseline levels. For these four participants, the schedule of punishment was gradually shifted from continuous to intermittent. For two of those participants, the gradual shift resulted in decreases in SIB but, for the other two, the gradual shift produced no changes in SIB. Finally, Barton and colleagues (1987) found that punishment in the form of timeout, delivered intermittently, did improve the maladaptive behavior (e.g., biting and scratching others) of three students with intellectual disabilities. The researchers implemented the timeout on a fixed interval schedule but warned the students within the interval when the target behavior was displayed. They suggested issuing warnings and not timeouts within the intervals might have allowed the students to develop self-control skills.

Lerman and Vorndran (2002) cautioned practitioners about using punishment as a behavior change procedure. They stated the research has identified clear advantages (e.g., effectiveness of punishment to decrease aberrant behavior) and disadvantages (e.g., unpredictable side effects), and recommended that further research be done to better understand punishment before it is used systematically as a behavioral reduction strategy. This is particularly true for populations where punishment strategies have historically been used to control behavior (e.g., individuals with developmental disabilities or severe behavior problems) and in settings where punishment might be overused. Furthermore, repeated punishment fails to teach students skills and can lead to students engaging in behavior to avoid or escape the adult delivering the punishment (e.g., teacher), especially when not paired with frequent delivery of reinforcement (Alberto & Troutman, 2013).

Differential Reinforcement

One way to effectively reinforce behavior is to do so differentially. Take, for example, a mother who leaves her three-year-old son unattended in the family room while she goes off to the kitchen to prepare dinner. The three-year-old is initially quiet and 'handled' but, after just a few minutes, recognizes that he is not receiving attention from his mother and begins crying. At first, the crying is low in volume and limited to a few whimpers. However, the child's crying intensifies after the low volume whimpering is ignored by mom. Hearing the loud cries, the mother goes into the family room to respond to the child's behavior. Over time, the crying becomes whining and then is quickly placed by the mother and other family members in the category of 'annoying.' All the while, the mother attends to the crying and whining but not the quiet and 'handled' behavior. As Skinner (1953) said about a similar example, the mother has effectively taught the child to be annoying. She has differentially reinforced the child's behavior by positively reinforcing the 'annoying' behavior and ignoring (i.e., withholding reinforcement of) the appropriate behavior.

Several authors have described *differential reinforcement* as a technique to increase a desired behavior, teach a new skill, or refine an already learned skill (Alberto & Troutman, 2013; Hanley & Tiger, 2011; Skinner, 1953; Vargas, 2013), although one can differentially reinforce inappropriate or unwanted behavior as illustrated in the example above. Differential reinforcement simply means reinforcing one class of behaviors while withholding reinforcement for another class of behavior. Using compliance as a target behavior, a teacher utilizing differential positive reinforcement would provide praise to a student when the student complies with an adult request, and repeat the request when compliance is not obtained. Assuming adult attention in the form of praise is positively reinforcing, the student's compliance with adult requests should increase over time. Miller (2006) provides another example of how differential reinforcement can work to effectively improve a desired behavior. A parent can provide praise and other forms of social attention to the child when the child eats vegetables and ignore the child when bread or potato chips or some other undesirable food item is eaten. Considering differential reinforcement, eating vegetables and eating Halloween candy are two physically different behaviors.

According to Simonsen and colleagues (2008), differential reinforcement can be effectively used to improve appropriate behavior and decrease inappropriate behavior in the context of a school or classroom. Wheatley and colleagues (2009) used a school-wide Praise Note System to differentially reinforce the school cafeteria behavior of approximately 200 elementary students. The Praise Note System involved school staff (e.g., teachers, custodian, administrators) delivering slips of paper to students for appropriate cafeteria behavior (e.g., sitting appropriately at a table, throwing trash in the garbage can). During the day, students returned the slips of paper to the office. At the end of the day, the principal drew five slips of paper from a jar and read the names over the school's loudspeaker. Students whose names were called went to the office and selected a small reward (e.g., pencil, eraser, sticker). All slips of paper were stapled to a board in the school's main hallway. Students earned a larger group reward when a certain number of Praise Notes were accumulated. After about one month, students' littering, sitting inappropriately at the lunch table, and running in the cafeteria decreased by 98%, 65%, and 75%, respectively. The researchers concluded that differentially reinforcing behavior incompatible with inappropriate cafeteria behavior was highly effective. Austin and Bevan (2011) used differential reinforcement to decrease the frequency of requests for attention of three elementary school girls referred for engaging in disruptive behavior by excessively seeking the teacher's attention. The girls earned teacher-delivered rewards following sessions in which they requested the teacher's attention at a lower rate than baseline. The procedure resulted in noteworthy reductions in requesting teacher attention.

Differential reinforcement can be implemented in several ways. Wheatly and colleagues (2009) employed *differential reinforcement of incompatible behavior* (DRI), while Austin and Bevan (2011) utilized *differential reinforcement for lower rates of behavior* (DRL). Miller's (2006) example of the parent reinforcing vegetable eating is an illustration of DRI or *differential reinforcement of alternative behavior* (DRA). *Differential reinforcement of other behavior* (DRO) describes reinforcement delivered when students fail to engage in the target behavior regardless of what he or she does instead. Alberto and Troutman (2013) stated that DRO reinforces the absence of a targeted behavior. For example, a teacher wishing to target calling out behavior using DRO must reinforce all other behavior including any on-task behavior (e.g., taking notes, asking relevant questions, keeping eyes on the teacher while the teacher talks) but also any inappropriate behavior such as off-task behavior that does not include calling out including talking with a peer, reading a book, or texting a friend. Table 2.3 provides additional detail on differential reinforcement.

Learning: A Function of Contingencies and Consequences

Learning has been described as the process of permanent behavior change, typically happening because of some interaction between the organism and its environment (see Skinner, 1953; Thorpe & Olson, 1997; Vargas, 2013). Textbooks in education and psychology often vary in how learning is defined. For example, Kalat's (2013) *Introduction to Psychology* emphasizes classical and operant conditioning when covering learning. Ormrod (2013) discusses learning more broadly in *Educational Psychology: Developing Learners*, conceptualizing it from multiple perspectives including classical and operant conditioning, cognitive, knowledge construction, and social learning lenses. Not surprising, textbooks specifically on learning and behavior stress the concepts associated with classical and operant conditioning including stimulus and response, consequential events, and prior experience (see Domjan, 2015).

Behavior analysts consider *contingencies* when describing learning. That is, they analyze the behavior and what happens immediately following the behavior. This relationship between the behavior and its consequence describes a two-term contingency (see Vargas, 2013). There is a behavior and then a consequential event that effects the probability that behavior will occur in the future. Catania (2011) stated, "an organism is said to come into contact with a contingency when its behavior produces some consequences of the contingency" (p. 34). Remember, consequences can either reinforce (i.e., increase the probability that behavior will

Table 2.3 Differential Reinforcement

Differential Reinforcement Type	Definition	Example	Advantages	Disadvantages
Incompatible Behavior	Reinforcement occurs for behavior that is topographically incompatible with the target behavior	Teacher reinforces walking down the hallway, which is incompatible with running	Very effective at reducing undesirable behavior, especially when incompatible and undesirable behaviors are functional equivalents	Some behaviors might not have an incompatible response
Lower Rates of Behavior	Reinforcement occurs only for a reduced number of responses	Teacher reinforces student's behavior when the frequency of disruptions is below 5/hr	Reduces the frequency or rate of an undesirable behavior; the target frequency or rate can be altered based on student responding; reinforcement happens without requiring immediate and significant reductions of undesirable behavior	Does not reduce frequency or rate quickly—should not be used for behavior that requires rapid changes (e.g., physical aggression)
Alternative Behavior	Reinforcement occurs for a behavior, which decreases the occurrence of an undesirable behavior	Teacher reinforces collaborative work habits, which is an alternative to off-task behavior	Many alternative behaviors are likely available for reinforcement; generalization is more likely	Gradual thinning of reinforcement might be necessary
Other Behavior	Reinforcement occurs for any behavior other than the target behavior	Teacher reinforces all behavior except aggression	Appropriate for students engaging in a high intensity, undesirable behavior (e.g., aggression) but many appropriate behaviors	Reinforcement must occur for any behavior other than the target behavior including other undesirable behavior; reinforcement might be limited for students who do not engage in high rates of desirable behavior

occur in the future) or punish (i.e., decrease the probability that behavior will occur in the future) behavior. So, contingent reinforcement is reinforcement dependent on the display of a behavior and contingent punishment is punishment dependent on the display of a behavior.

Toilet training toddlers offers a great illustration of contingency as a concept. A parent provides the toilet training toddler a small piece of candy following every time he or she either urinates or defecates in the toilet. A behavior analyst would say that the delivery of candy is contingent upon the toddler going potty in the toilet. Said differently, the reinforcer is contingent upon the engagement of the behavior. If there is no behavior, there is no reinforcer. Educators and parents often use contingent attention to reinforce behavior they want increased or maintained. For example, a teacher might reinforce students' on-task behavior with a simple praise statement (e.g., 'nice job') or nonverbal attention (e.g., a smile) when students ask relevant questions or complete math problems without being disruptive. This simple form of acknowledgment represents contingent reinforcement. But remember, reinforcement is only reinforcement if the behavior increases in the future.

Contingent reinforcement has been described extensively in the literature as a method to improve or teach behavior. In 1969, Cantrell, Cantrell, Huddleston, and Wooldridge observed that evidence was accumulating supporting "the efficacy of structuring reinforcement contingencies to shape or maintain adaptive behavior in children" (p. 215). Since 1969, research on classroom management strategies and interventions for problem behavior has identified contingent reinforcement as an evidence-based practice (see Simonsen et al., 2008; Wong et al., 2014). A specific example of using contingent reinforcement to improve behavior involves setting up contracts with students. Known as contingency contracting, the strategy relies on the two-term contingency described by Vargas (2013) that includes a behavior and a consequence. A contingency contract is set up between the student and teacher (or some other staff member) whereby a pre-identified consequence (i.e., reward) is delivered to the student following the student's engagement in some pre-identified behavior (e.g., task completion, appropriate play, walking rather than running down the hall). Essentially, the consequence, or reward, is contingent on the display of the behavior.

Other research supports the use of contingency contracts. Allen, Howard, Sweeny, and McLaughlin (1993) demonstrated that using a contingency contract could increase the on-task behavior of three elementary students. Individual contracts were written specifying the required level of on-task behavior, the consequences for achieving the specified levels, and the duration of the contract. The teacher and each individual student reviewed the performance goals set at the beginning of the day and consequences in the form of rewards were delivered if students met their pre-identified goals. All three students exhibited immediate and dramatic increases in on-task behavior when the contingency contract was employed. In another study, Mruzek, Cohen, and Smith (2007) showed how a contingency contract could improve the behavior of two students with Autism Spectrum Disorder (ASD) in a school setting. Contingency contracts were developed identifying each student's target behaviors (e.g., using appropriate language with teachers and peers, gentle touching of people and objects, compliance with teacher instructions), a time frame (e.g., each hour of the day), and the consequences delivered following the meeting of the performance goals. The students met with teachers twice during the day to review the contract and students' overall behavior. Both students displayed substantial and immediate improvements in targeted behaviors relative to baseline.

Premack's Principle

In his paper 'Toward empirical behavior laws: I. Positive reinforcement,' Premack (1959) describes how a high probability behavior can serve to positively reinforce a low probability behavior. That is, a low probability behavior can be increased if a high probability behavior becomes contingent upon the occurrence of the low probability behavior. This sounds like a tongue twister. Well, consider a rule many parents use at dinner: 'You can't have dessert until you've finished your broccoli.' Eating dessert is presumably a high probability behavior and eating broccoli is presumably a low probability behavior. Stated differently, most children would gladly skip eating broccoli and go right to dessert. Yet, Premack's principle helps us to arrange consequences so that a contingent relationship can be established between the high probability and low probability behaviors.

Premack's principle is very useful for teachers wanting to increase students' appropriate behavior. Research has consistently found that having a high probability behavior be contingent upon the display of a low probability behavior is an effective behavior management tool (Alberto & Troutman, 2013). For example, Homme, deBaca, Devine, Steinhorst, and Rickert (1963) showed how Premack's principle could be used to increase the desirable behavior of three preschool children. The authors observed that the children often ignored verbal instructions (i.e., the low probability behavior) and, instead, ran around the classroom, screaming, pushing chairs, and working on puzzles (i.e., the high probability behaviors). Homme and his colleagues devised a plan whereby the teacher would ring a bell signaling to the children that is was okay to run around the room and scream when, and only when, the students had been sitting quietly in their seats, looking at the blackboard. Later, the students earned tokens for on-task behavior that could be exchanged for opportunities to play or engage in other high probability behaviors. The children's compliance and on-task behavior improved only after a few days. Other research has demonstrated how Premack's principle can be applied in educational contexts. Hosie, Gentile, and Downing Carroll (1974) employed Premack's principle to improve the behavior of fifth and sixth grade students. Following several observation sessions to identify high probability behaviors, the authors made access to those high probability behaviors, painting and playing with clay, contingent on completing a written report on dinosaurs. In another study, Geiger (1996) used Premack's principle to improve the prosocial classroom behavior and academic productivity of middle school students by using free play in an outdoor recess to reinforce the targeted behavior. Interestingly, all three studies presented intervention procedures that appear easy to implement in a classroom setting. Furthermore, interventions based on Premack's principle likely have high acceptability among teachers.

Discrimination and Stimulus Control

Humans make discriminations every day. Did you drink coffee or clam juice this morning? On your way to work, did you go on green and stop on red? At lunch, did you pay $5.50 for the sandwich or $55,000? When going through your daily routine, you make hundreds, maybe thousands of discriminations. In fact, virtually everything you do across the day involves making discriminations (Spradlin & Simon, 2011). Students also make discriminations, of course. For example, a student might discriminate between two teachers, Mr. Miller who verbally attends to appropriate behavior and punishes (in the behavioral analytic sense) disruptive behavior and Mr. Howard who ignores disruptive behavior. In fact, that discrimination might help explain the student's disruptive behavior. Alberto and Troutman (2013) defined discrimination as the "ability to tell the difference between environmental events or stimuli" (p. 296). In the above examples, you and I, and that student have learned to differentiate between environmental events or stimuli. The environmental event of drinking a beverage involved drinking coffee and not clam juice. The stimulus 'red light' signaled me to stop my car at the intersection and the stimulus 'green light' signaled me to drive my car through the intersection. Buying a sandwich signaled me to hand the cashier $5.50 and not $55,000. And for that student, the presence of Mr. Miller, the science teacher, serves as a discriminative stimulus for a set of desirable behaviors, while Mr. Howard, the math teacher, serves as a discriminative stimulus for a set of undesirable behaviors.

Discriminating between two or more stimuli is an essential component of learning (Alberto & Troutman, 2013; Domjan, 2015; Spradlin & Simon, 2011). For example, recognizing that adding two digits and subtracting two digits are two different processes is important when learning basic calculation. The student makes a discrimination between the signs (i.e., stimuli) to proceed with completing calculation problems and, consequently, learning basic math operations. Identifying that an instruction to complete an academic task is a prompt to begin working on the task is a discrimination made by students all the time. In this case, the instruction serves as the sign or stimulus and the behavior is the response.

How do people learn to make discriminations? Are these discriminations learned automatically or through some mystical force? Or are these discriminations a function of exposure to consequential events? Consider a simple task—finger tapping. Imagine wanting to teach someone to finger tap every time a green light flashed. To do this, we might positively reinforce the individual's finger tapping when and only when the finger tap follows the flash of green light. Reinforcement becomes contingent on the behavior being displayed following the green light but the green light also signals that reinforcement is available. Behavior analysts call both the green and red lights discriminative stimuli and would say that the stimuli have gained control over the finger tapping behavior (which is where the term 'stimulus control' comes from).

So, to answer the questions posed above, people learn to make discriminations through relationships that are formed over time between stimuli and behaviors, and the consequential events that follow those behaviors.

The practical applications of these principles of behavior are widespread. At one level, stimulus control can be thought of as a primary component of learning. For example, the letters c–a–t can be a discriminative stimulus for a verbal response 'cat.' The teacher delivers reinforcement in the form of a verbal response, 'correct,' and a smile (i.e., nonverbal response) following the student's verbal response 'cat.' The teacher does not provide reinforcement for any response except the verbal response 'cat.' Another example involves a teacher frustrated that the class is disruptive after coming inside from recess. The teacher decides that turning the classroom lights off will be a discriminative stimulus for quiet behavior and, subsequently, reinforces the class with five minutes of free time when they are quiet immediately following the lights being turned off.

Stimulus and Response Generalization

Most teachers want their students to settle down anytime they or another teacher asks for quiet, whether that happens in a classroom, in a cafeteria, or on a playground. Consider the example above where students learn to quiet down following the lights being turned off. The stimulus is specific, which means the behavior being reinforced following the stimulus will only be exhibited in the presence of that stimulus. That is, we need the lights to go off in the specific classroom and with the specific teacher for the students to quiet down. Fortunately, behaviors that have been reinforced following a specific stimulus can occur in the presence of other, similar stimuli (see Alberto & Troutman, 2013). This phenomenon is referred to as *stimulus generalization* and is frequently a goal of teaching and intervention programs. For example, teaching a student with ASD how to start a conversation with another person by using that person, such as a teacher, as a discriminative stimulus might be recommended. After modeling appropriate conversation starters, appropriate initiation of a conversation with the discriminative stimulus (i.e., the teacher) is reinforced. Over time, we are likely to see the student's conversation initiation skills improve when in the presence of the discriminative stimulus (i.e., the teacher), especially if the reinforcer is potent. However, we would eventually want the student to generalize the skill of initiating conversation skills to other stimuli such as other teachers or peers.

Education and psychology have continually worked to strengthen the stimulus generalization of teaching and intervention procedures (see Frey, Elliott, & Miller, 2014). Consequently, stimulus generalization has become a focus of applied research. Studies have not only demonstrated stimulus generalization can be done with challenging behaviors and populations but how stimulus generalization can be programmed. Marholin and Steinman (1977) found that stimulus generalization could be obtained by simply providing contingencies for academic task completion rather than on-task behavior for students with chronic behavior problems. They exposed eight fifth and sixth graders to conditions involving an unreinforced baseline, reinforcement for on-task behavior, and reinforcement for accuracy and rate of completed math problems. To assess stimulus generalization, the classroom teacher was out of the classroom for a portion of each session. Not surprising, students' on-task behavior decreased and disruptive behavior increased when the teacher left the classroom. However, researchers found that students' on-task behavior was highest and disruptive behavior lowest when reinforcement was contingent on accuracy and rate of completed math problems suggesting students' behavior was most appropriate and productive when under control of the academic materials rather than the teacher's presence. In a study targeting the perspective-taking skills of three students with ASD, Charlop-Christy and Daneshvar (2003) used video modeling to teach perspective-taking or the ability to understand others' viewpoints to explain or predict behavior. The video modeling procedure involved students viewing instructional videos showing known adults engaging in perspective-taking and social problem-solving tasks. After video modeling was implemented, all three students correctly answered perspective-taking questions associated with what was shown in the video (e.g., 'Where will James look for the cookie?' when a cookie was featured in the video). However, all three students also correctly answered questions involving scenarios that were not depicted in the video (e.g., 'Where will James look for the apple?' when a cookie was featured in the video) suggesting generalization across stimuli.

Sometimes educators change a behavior in hopes that they might see a change in other, related behaviors. For example, a teacher might improve a student's completion of math worksheets by reinforcing his or her completion of math worksheets. However, the student also improves the completion of social studies work-sheets without the behavior (i.e., completion of social studies worksheets) being specifically reinforced. Behavior analysts refer to this as *response generalization*. Response generalization describes a change observed in a behavior that is not specifically taught or reinforced (see Alberto & Troutman, 2013). Response general-ization differs from stimulus generalization in that a similar behavior (i.e., a behavior that is in the same response class), one that has not been previously reinforced, is displayed rather than the behavior occurring in the presence of a stimulus that has not been previously reinforced (stimulus generalization).

The literature is replete with examples showing how response generalization can occur. In another study investigating the use of video modeling, Plavnick and Ferreri (2011) found that three boys with ASD and significant language impairments viewing brief (e.g., 15–27-second) video clips of typically developing peers gesturing for attention or to obtain preferred items could acquire appropriate communicative responses. The study also found that the video modeling procedures led to children displaying gestures not shown on the video when attempting to obtain attention or a preferred item. However, response generalization only occurred when video modeling of the gesture was functionally related to the communicative response. That is, the children generalized the communicative responses only when the video depicted a gesture that matched the function of each individual child's behavior (e.g., attention, access preferred item).

PROGRAMMING FOR GENERALIZATION

Experts in the fields of ABA and education advocate thoughtfully planning for generalization rather than hoping it might occur (see Alberto & Troutman, 2013; Frey et al., 2014; Noell, Call, & Ardoin, 2011). However, educators often find planning for generalization challenging. Fortunately, ABA offers guidance on planning for generalization. In 1977, Stokes and Baer published a paper in the *JABA* outlining nine general procedures, gleaned from the literature, that promote generalization:

1.   **Train and Hope**: Following the teaching of a skill or change of a behavior, any generalization across responses or stimuli occur but were not planned for (e.g., Sally was taught to enter a conversation with the school psychologist, let us hope that she will enter conversations with her peers).

2.   **Sequential Modification**: Generalization is planned by applying the same approach or approaches that taught a skill or changed a behavior to target responses or stimuli (e.g., Sally was taught to enter conversations with the school psychologist by modeling the skill following by praise when she appropriately entered a conversation with the school psychologist; now the classroom teacher will model the skill and praise her when she enters conversations with the teacher).

3.   **Use Natural Maintaining Consequences**: Teach skills and change behaviors that will naturally encounter reinforcing consequential events (e.g., Sally's behavior of entering conversations with peers should be reinforced by those peers through the delivery of positive verbal and nonverbal attention).

4.   **Train Sufficient Exemplars**: Teach using multiple settings, stimuli, and tasks, and target similar responses until generalization occurs (e.g., Sally is taught to enter conversations with the school psychologist, other staff, and peers; she is taught several ways to enter conversations with others by saying 'hello' or asking a question; she is taught to enter conversations in class, during recess, in line for the bus, at lunch).

5.   **Train Loosely**: Teach so that accurate responses are broadly defined (e.g., Sally is taught that there are many ways of entering conversations with others including saying 'hello,' asking a simple question relevant to the conversation, or listening and then saying something relevant to the conversation).

6.   **Use Indiscriminable Contingencies**: Intermittently reinforce the targeted responses or fade reinforcement over time (e.g., Sally's behavior of entering conversations is reinforced every third or fourth time she engages in appropriate conversation entering behavior).

7.   **Program Common Stimuli**: Include stimuli that are common to both the training and natural environments (e.g., the school psychologist teaches Sally to enter conversations by practicing in the cafeteria and on the playground).

8.   **Mediate Generalization**: Teach the student to accurately report on their own display of a skill or behavior with a teacher or other staff member observing to corroborate (e.g., Sally reports to her teacher every time she appropriately

enters a conversation with a peer, Sally's accurate reporting is reinforced; have peers report on Sally's behavior every time she appropriately enters a conversation with a peer).

9. **Train to Generalize**: Reinforce generalization by reinforcing the targeted skill or behavior when is displayed in another setting or with other stimuli (e.g., Sally's behavior of entering conversations is reinforced when it occurs with peers in the cafeteria, on the playground, or in the classroom).

Generalization, either stimulus or response, remains a primary target for school psychologists and educators. Speaking specifically about social skills, Frey and colleagues (2014) stated interventions should purposefully plan to promote generalization and Bellini (2016) suggested the goal of any social skills training program should be response and stimulus generalization. Speaking more generally about academic skills, Noell and colleagues (2011) provided several examples, using the literature, of how generalization might be systematically programmed. They suggested (1) providing students with abundant opportunities to practice, master, and become fluent with a skill, (2) promoting generalization through practice of the skill in many different situations and environments, and (3) teaching students to reinforce their own behavior. Regardless of how one approaches generalization, the fact remains that generalization is an essential target for teaching and should be planned for when designing interventions.

Shaping

Imagine teaching a five-year-old to tie a shoe without teaching each successive step. Teaching the child to go from never tying a knot to tying the shoe would be miraculous. A more efficient way to teach shoe tying is to first provide the child with social praise when the laces are grabbed properly. The child would be provided more social praise when the laces are looped correctly and even more social praise when the laces are tucked correctly to make the knot. And so on and so on. Teaching shoe tying in this manner illustrates the process of *shaping*. Skinner (1953) observed that the final form of a response (e.g., behaviors, skills) is rarely initially reinforced and that teaching especially complex skills and behaviors requires reinforcement of successive approximations of the final behavior or skill.

Shaping is best described as the process of applying differential reinforcement to a series of steadily chained responses as the responses more closely approximate the target behavior or skill (Cooper et al., 2007; Miller, 2006). Shaping differs from ordinary conditioning in that shaping involves a response that is being reinforced as it continually moves closer to the final response being targeted for teaching (Vargas, 2013). Hanley and Tiger (2011) wrote that shaping contains (1) the identification of a response that approximates the skill or behavior being taught, (2) the differential reinforcement of that response, and (3) the reinforcement of responses that begin to more closely resemble the skill or behavior being taught.

Shaping procedures have been used to solve applied problems. Ferguson and Rosales-Ruiz (2001) trained horses to load onto a horse trailer by reinforcing each horse's movement toward a target. The target was moved closer and closer to the front end of the trailer until the horses were finally reinforced for moving toward the target and onto the trailer. This simple procedure resulted in the horses quickly entering the trailer without the need for aversive stimuli. Furthermore, the effects were observed to generalize to novel stimuli such as a different trailer and trainer. Smeets, Lancioni, Ball, and Olivia (1985) shaped the self-initiated toileting behavior of four infants by initially teaching their mothers to recognize the relationship between the infants' body signals (e.g., straining) and defecation. Next, the mothers established a temporal relationship between the body signals and the elimination by bringing the infants to the toilet. Finally, the mothers reinforced (e.g., smiling, cuddling, presenting preferred objects to the infant) prompted and then unprompted toilet reaching/grabbing responses, and then fecal and urinary eliminations in the toilet. All four infants could self-initiate toileting or signal to their mothers the need to have an elimination by one year of age.

In the context of children and schools, shaping has been used extensively to teach skills to children with ASD (Rogers, 2000), increase fluency, rate, or speed of responding (Alberto & Troutman, 2013), and as part of instruction to teach academic skills (Vargas, 2013). Specific to ASD, shaping as part of a larger behavior treatment within a school setting has been shown to be significantly more effective than commonly used school-based approaches that involve eclectic treatments (see Eikeseth, Smith, Jahr, & Eldevik, 2002), and large-scale reviews of interventions for children with ASD have identified shaping, again as part of a larger behavioral treatment package, to be an evidence-based practice (Wong et al., 2014). For example, Nichols (2014) shaped the verbal approximations of children's social interactions with peers to increase verbalizations and social interactions with peers. However, shaping has been widely used to treat other school-related problems. For example, Walker and Buckley (1968) demonstrated that gradually increasing the interval of the attending behavior being reinforced had a profound effect on the attention span of an elementary student referred because of high rates of off-task and disruptive behavior.

Chaining

Chaining describes a specific sequence of responses in which the completion of each response serves as a cue for the next response (Alberto & Troutman, 2013; Vargas, 2013). Getting dressed in the morning is a classic example of chaining. First, getting out of the shower serves as a discriminative stimulus for the next step in your morning routine—getting dressed. To get dressed, you begin by putting on underwear, which cues your putting on socks. Having the socks and underwear on then cues you to put on a shirt, which cues you to button the shirt, which cues you to put on pants, button the fly, and pull up the zipper. This process continues until you are finally dressed.

Educators often use chaining to teach behaviors or skills that involve multiple steps. In a classroom, chaining can be used to establish a sequence resulting in waiting quietly for instructions (e.g., sit in chair, put books in desk, look at teacher). Each step following the initial response reinforces the previous step while, at the same time, cues the next step in the chain. Chaining can also be used to teach complex skills. Tarbox, Madrid, Aguilar, Jacobo, and Schiff (2009) taught two children with ASD and one child with a developmental delay to echo adults using vocal modeling. The researchers used a chaining procedure that divided words into syllables. The first syllable of a word served as a cue for the second syllable (e.g., 'mun' functioned as a cue for 'day'). Moreover, chaining is effective for teaching academic skills. Jones Falkenstine, Collins, Schuster, and Kleinert (2009) used chaining to teach students with moderate intellectual disabilities (e.g., IQ below 50) various academic skills including reading sight words and identifying state abbreviations. Finally, chaining has been used in the context of parent training for families of children with ADHD. Danforth, Harvey, Ulaszek, and McKee (2006) taught parents to follow a behavior management flowchart using chaining. Initial parent responses to their child's inappropriate behavior served to cue next steps in the flowchart.

Extinction

Extinction describes the discontinuation of reinforcement of a previously reinforced response. According to Cooper and colleagues (2007), extinction produces a decrease in the frequency of the response until either the response returns to pre-reinforcement levels or terminates altogether. Parents frequently use ignoring to extinguish a problem behavior by trying to initially ignore their child's whining behavior when faced with an unfavorable decision. The reinforcer is parental attention and the response being extinguished is the child's whining behavior. However, many parents fail to follow through with ignoring because their child's whining does not always decrease, especially when the parent's attention is initially withdrawn. Often referred to as an extinction burst, rates of responding often initially increase when reinforcement for responding is withdrawn, which is why parents observe high rates of misbehavior and give up ignoring. Extinction bursts are most often observed in situations where the response was continuously or nearly continuously reinforced (Alberto & Troutman, 2013). Skinner (1953) noted that reinforcement history is critical to understanding an organism's reaction to extinction. He found that intermittently reinforced responses were more difficult to extinguish when compared to continuously reinforced responses and responses that have a long-standing history of reinforcement were less prone to extinction than responses that had only been reinforced a few times. Vollmer and Athens (2011) described other effects of extinction including response variation (e.g., the organism's tendency to display new or varied forms of the behavior), extinction-induced aggression, extinction-induced emotional behavior, and spontaneous recovery (e.g., reemergence of the response).

Interventions built on extinction have been studied extensively for a variety of problems. For example, Friman and Piazza (2011) described using extinction and gradual extinction procedures to treat healthy children's bedtime resistance.

Bedtime resistance is often maintained or positively reinforced by parental attention. Ignoring the child's requests for the parent (i.e., going cold turkey) or systematically increasing the response requirement for parental attention have been shown to be effective at decreasing bedtime resistance, including the child leaving the bedroom and crying at bedtime. Janney, Umbreit, Ferro, Liaupsin, and Lane (2012) used extinction procedures (e.g., redirect and ignore responses) as part of a larger intervention package that included positive reinforcement contingent on appropriate behavior to improve the on-task behavior of three elementary school students. Stahr, Cushing, Lane, and Fox (2006) also found that combining ignoring with contingent praise was effective at improving on-task behavior. Not surprising, research on the use of extinction plus reinforcement for appropriate behavior (i.e., differential reinforcement) is considered more effective than utilizing extinction procedures alone. Vollmer and Athens (2011) suggested two possible reasons for this finding. First, they cited the *matching law* (Herrnstein, 1974), which states that the relative rate of responding matches the relative rate of reinforcement. If there is ample reinforcement for an appropriate alternative behavior and no reinforcement for an inappropriate behavior, we would expect to observe only appropriate behavior. Second, extinction, by itself, is difficult to implement and we would likely observe low rates of treatment fidelity (i.e., the degree to which the procedures are implemented as intended) with an intervention that relies solely on ignoring. For example, parents and teachers often stop ignoring misbehavior following the extinction burst. Friman and Piazza (2011) described another procedure for bedtime resistance called the 'bedtime pass,' used in response to parent difficulties ignoring their children's crying at bedtime. The bedtime pass allows the child one (or some other predetermined number) pass out of the bedroom. All subsequent attempts to leave the bedroom are met with parental redirection (i.e., gently guiding or carrying the child) and no verbal attention. The positive reinforcement occurs immediately after the use of the pass. Research on the bedtime pass has found it to be successful without the presence of an extinction burst and the intervention has high treatment acceptability with parents.

Deprivation and Satiation: Effects on Reinforcement

Skinner (1953) described two situations in which the availability of reinforcement in the environment influenced the effectiveness of the reinforcement. The first, termed *deprivation*, describes a condition where reinforcement is scarcely or not at all available in the environment. Depriving a reinforcer increases the value of that reinforcer. An organism deprived of something reinforcing would likely go to great lengths to access that something. The second, called *satiation*, describes a condition where reinforcement is readily available in the environment. Satiation decreases the value of a reinforcer. An organism that has unlimited access to something would be less likely to engage in behavior to access that something. The importance of deprivation and satiation for school professionals lies in how these two states affect positive reinforcement and behavior.

Researchers have studied the effects of deprivation and satiation on positive reinforcement with children in applied settings (Piazza et al., 2011). For example, Gewirtz and Baer (1958) found that brief social deprivation significantly impacted the social reinforcement given to preschool children by a teacher. Specifically, they discovered that the children's socially reinforced responses increased following exposure to a brief period of no social reinforcement. Rispoli and colleagues (2016) studied the effects of satiation on the challenging behavior of three children with ASD. The authors began by exposing participants to a condition involving free access to a preferred item functionally related to the challenging behavior and then removing the preferred item entirely during the normal classroom routine. The authors found that the frequency of challenging behavior was low immediately following the pre-session condition but gradually increased as time progressed suggesting that pre-session access affected responding.

Understanding *motivating operations* (see Michael, 1982) is important when assessing the effects of reinforcement. For example, a teacher might find that the use of positive reinforcement in the form of social attention fails to improve a student's behavior and conclude that positive reinforcement, as an intervention, does not work. However, the teacher's conclusions fail to consider the effects satiation might have had on the social reinforcement. Social reinforcement might have lost its reinforcing value if the student had constant social reinforcement from the teacher. Vollmer and Iwata (1991) warned of this and suggested that programming schedules and environments be done strategically. For example, a teacher might schedule independent seatwork, where a student's appropriate behavior is positively reinforced by social attention, after an activity where the teacher and student have little to no contact. Such a schedule should increase the reinforcing qualities of the teacher's attention by placing the student in a condition of deprivation. Free access to a preferred item, activity, or person might devalue its reinforcing qualities. Using candy to positively reinforce on-task behavior might not work when students have free access to candy. Similarly, using escape from an academic task to reinforce on-task behavior might not work when students have free access to breaks. Understanding these motivating operations is central to understanding the relationship between behavior and the environment. Furthermore, gaining control over available reinforcers improves the effectiveness of interventions relying on reinforcement. School psychologists hearing from teachers and other school professionals that reinforcement-based interventions do not work might consider assessing the availability of reinforcers in the student's environment, and using deprivation and satiation to change the relative value of reinforcers.

Conclusion

Becoming fluent with the fundamental principles of ABA allows school psychologists to better function within a scientific framework. Evidence-based assessment, instructional, and intervention practices typically rely on the principles discussed in this chapter. Furthermore, these principles apply to adults and organizations. School psychologists called on to consult with resistant teachers, provide professional development to colleagues, or address system-wide problems are likely to find principles of behavior helpful. Finally, clinical innovation only happens when creativity is applied to scientifically proven principles. To master the concepts presented in this chapter and become skilled in their application, consider thinking about behavior in the context of conditioning (e.g., reinforcement, punishment), contingencies, discriminations, and motivating operations. In addition, watching everywhere for consequences of behavior and the schedules at which those consequences are delivered might help someone less familiar with ABA become more fluent with its core principles.

References

Alberto, P. A., & Troutman, A. C. (2013). *Applied behavior analysis for teachers* (9th ed.). Upper Saddle River, NJ: Pearson.

Allen, L. J., Howard, V. F., Sweeny, W. J., & McLaughlin, T. F. (1993). Use of contingency contracting to increase on-task behavior with primary students. *Psychological Reports, 72,* 905–906.

Austin, J. L., & Bevan, D. (2011). Using differential reinforcement of low rates to reduce children's requests for teacher attention. *Journal of Applied Behavior Analysis, 44,* 451–461.

Barton, L. E., Brulle, A. R., & Repp, A. C. (1987). Effects of differential scheduling of timeout to reduce maladaptive responding. *Exceptional Children, 53,* 351–356.

Bellini, S. (2016). *Building social relationships—2: A systematic approach to teaching social interaction skills to children and adolescents with autism spectrum disorders and other social difficulties.* Shawnee Mission, KS: Autism Asperger Publishing.

Broussard, C. D., & Northrup, J. (1995). An approach to functional assessment and analysis of disruptive behavior in regular education classrooms. *School Psychology Quarterly, 10,* 151–164.

Cantrell, R. P., Cantrell, M. L., Huddleston, C. M., & Wooldridge, R. L. (1969). Contingency contracting with school problems. *Journal of Applied Behavior Analysis, 2,* 215–220.

Carr, E., & Durand, M. (1985). Reducing problem behavior through functional communication training. *Journal of Applied Behavior Analysis, 18,* 111–126.

Catania, A. C. (2011). Basic operant contingencies: Main effects and side effects. In W. W. Fisher, C. C. Piazza, & H. S. Roane (Eds.), *Handbook of applied behavior analysis* (pp. 34–54). New York: Guilford.

Charlop-Christy, M. H., & Daneshvar, S. (2003). Using video modeling to teach perspective taking to children with autism. *Journal of Positive Behavior Interventions, 5,* 12–21.

Clark, H. B., Rowbury, T., Baer, A. M., & Baer, D. M. (1973). Timeout as a punishing stimulus in continuous and intermittent schedules. *Journal of Applied Behavior Analysis, 6,* 443–455.

Cooper, J., Heron, T., & Heward, W. (2007). *Applied behavior analysis* (2nd ed.). Upper Saddle River, NJ: Merrill/Pearson Education.

Danforth, J. S., Harvey, E., Ulaszek, W. R., & McKee, T. E. (2006). The outcome of group parent training for families of children with attention-deficit hyperactivity disorder and defiant/aggressive behavior. *Journal of Behavior Therapy and Experimental Psychiatry, 37,* 188–205.

DiGennaro, F. D., Martens, B. K., & McIntyre, L. L. (2005). Increasing treatment integrity through negative reinforcement: Effects of teacher and student behavior. *School Psychology Review, 34,* 220–231.

Domjan, M. P. (2015). *Principles of learning and behavior* (7th ed.). Stamford, CT: Cengage.

Durand, V. M., & Carr, E. (1991). Functional communication training to reduce challenging behavior: Maintenance and application in new settings. *Journal of Applied Behavior Analysis, 24*, 251–264.

Eikeseth, S., Smith, T., Jahr, E., & Eldevik, S. (2002). Intensive behavioral treatment at school for 4- to 7-year-old children with autism: A 1-year comparison controlled study. *Behavior Modification, 26*, 49–68.

Ergene, T. (2003). Effective intervention on test anxiety. *School Psychology International, 24*, 313–328.

Fabiano, G. A., & Pelham, W. E. Jr. (2003). Improving the effectiveness of behavioral classroom interventions for attention-deficit/hyperactivity disorder: A case study. *Journal of Emotional and Behavioral Disorders, 11*(2), 122–131.

Fabiano, G., Pelham, W. E., Manos, M. J., Gnagy, E. M., Chronis-Tuscano, A. M., & Onyango, A. N. (2004). An evaluation of three time-out procedures for children with attention-deficit/hyperactivity disorder. *Behavior Therapy, 35*, 449–469.

Farmer, R. F., & Chapman, A. L. (2008). *Behavioral interventions in cognitive behavior therapy: Practical guidelines for putting theory into action*. Washington, DC: American Psychological Association.

Ferguson, D. L., & Rosales-Ruiz, J. (2001). Loading the problem loader: The effects of target training and shaping on trailer-loading behavior of horses. *Journal of Applied Behavior Analysis, 34*, 409–424.

Ferster, C. B., & Skinner, B. F. (1957). *Schedules of reinforcement*. New York: Appleton-Century-Crofts.

Frey, J. R., Elliott, S. N., & Miller, C. F. (2014). Best practices in social skills training. In P. L. Harrison & A. Thomas (Eds.), *Best practices in school psychology: Student level services* (pp. 213–224). Bethesda, MD: National Association of School Psychologists.

Friman, P. C., Hayes, S. C., & Wilson, K. G. (1998). Why behavior analysts should study emotion: The example of anxiety. *Journal of Applied Behavior Analysis, 31*, 137–156.

Friman, P. C., & Piazza, C. C. (2011). Behavioral pediatrics: Integrating applied behavior analysis with pediatric medicine. In W. W. Fisher, C. C. Piazza, & H. S. Roane (Eds.), *Handbook of applied behavior analysis* (pp. 433–450). New York: Guilford.

Geiger, B. (1996). A time to learn, a time to play: Premack's principle applied in the classroom. *American Secondary Education, 25*, 2–6.

Gewirtz, J., & Baer, D. M. (1958). Deprivation and satiation of social reinforcers as drive conditions. *Journal of Abnormal and Social Psychology, 57*, 165–172.

Hanley, G. P., & Tiger, J. H. (2011). Differential reinforcement procedures. In W. W. Fisher, C. C. Piazza, & H. S. Roane (Eds.), *Handbook of applied behavior analysis* (pp. 229–249). New York: Guilford.

Hawkins, R. O., & Axelrod, M. I. (2008). Increasing the on-task homework behavior of youth with behavior disorders using functional behavior assessment. *Behavior Modification, 32*, 840–859.

Herrnstein, R. J. (1974). Formal properties of the matching law. *Journal of the Experimental Analysis of Behavior, 21*, 159–164.

Homme, L. E., deBaca, P. C., Devine, J. V., Steinhorst, R., & Rickert, E. J. (1963). Use of the Premack principle in controlling the behavior of nursery school children. *Journal of the Experimental Analysis of Behavior, 6*, 544.

Hosie, T. W., Gentile, J. R., & Downing Carroll, J. (1974). Pupil preferences and the Premack principle. *American Education Research Journal, 11*, 241–247.

Janney, D. M., Umbreit, J., Ferro, J. B., Liaupsin, C. J., & Lane, K. L. (2012). The effect of the extinction procedure in function-based intervention. *Journal of Positive Behavior Interventions, 15*, 113–123.

Jones Falkenstine, K., Collins, B. C., Schuster, J. W., & Kleinert, H. (2009). Presenting chained and discrete tasks as non-targeted information when teaching discrete academic skills through small group instruction. *Education and Training in Developmental Disabilities, 44*, 127–142.

Kalat, J. W. (2013). *Introduction to psychology* (10th ed.). Belmont, CA: Wadsworth.

Kaminski, J. W., Valle, L. A., Filene, J. H., & Boyle, C. L. (2008). A meta-analytic review of components associated with parent training program effectiveness. *Journal of Abnormal Child Psychology, 36*, 567–589.

Lerman, D. C., Iwata, B. A., & DeLeon, I. G. (1997). Effects of intermittent punishment on self-injurious behavior: An evaluation of schedule thinning. *Journal of Applied Behavior Analysis, 30*, 187–201.

Lerman, D. C., & Vorndran, C. M. (2002). On the status of knowledge for using punishment: Implications for treating behavior disorders. *Journal of Applied Behavior Analysis, 35*, 431–464.

Mace, F. C., Pratt, J. L., Zangrillo, A. N., & Steege, M. W. (2011). Schedules of reinforcement. In W. W. Fisher, C. C. Piazza, & H. S. Roane (Eds.), *Handbook of applied behavior analysis* (pp. 55–75). New York: Guilford.

Marholin II, D., & Steinman, W. M. (1977). Stimulus control in the classroom as a function of the behavior reinforced. *Journal of Applied Behavior Analysis, 10*, 465–478.

McComas, J. J., Goddard, C., & Hoch, H. (2002). The effects of preferred activities during academic work breaks on task engagement and negatively reinforced destructive behavior. *Education and Treatment of Children, 25*, 103–112.

Michael, J. (1982). Distinguishing between discriminative and motivational functions of stimuli. *Journal of the Experimental Analysis of Behavior, 37*, 149–155.

Miller, L. K. (2006). *Principles of everyday behavior analysis* (4th ed.). Stamford, CT: Cengage.

Mruzek, D. W., Cohen, C., & Smith, T. (2007). Contingency contracting with students with autism spectrum disorders in a public school setting. *Journal of Developmental and Physical Disabilities, 19*, 103–114.

Nichols, S. M. (2014). The effects of naturalistic behavior strategies on the quality of social interactions of children with autism (Unpublished doctoral dissertation). Denton, TX: University of North Texas.

Noell, G. H., Call, N. A., & Ardoin, S. P. (2011). Building complex repertoires from discrete behaviors by establishing stimulus control, behavioral chains, and strategic behavior. In W. W. Fisher, C. C. Piazza, & H. S. Roane (Eds.), *Handbook of applied behavior analysis* (pp. 250–269). New York: Guilford.

Ormrod, J. E. (2013). *Educational psychology: Developing learners* (8th ed.). Upper Saddle River, NJ: Prentice-Hall, Inc.

Page, D. P., & Edwards, R. P. (1978). Behavior change strategies for reducing disruptive classroom behavior. *Psychology in the Schools, 15*, 413–418.

Piazza, C. C., Roane, H. S., & Karsten, A. (2011). Identifying and enhancing the effectiveness of positive reinforcement. In W. W. Fisher, C. C. Piazza, & H. S. Roane (Eds.), *Handbook of applied behavior analysis* (pp. 151–164). New York: Guilford.

Plavnick, J. B., & Ferreri, S. J. (2011). Establishing verbal repertoires in children with autism using function-based video modeling. *Journal of Applied Behavior Analysis, 44*, 747–766.

Premack, D. (1959). Toward empirical behavior laws: I. Positive reinforcement. *Psychological Review, 66*, 219–233.

Rasmussen, K., & O'Neill, R. E. (2006). The effects of fixed-time reinforcement schedules on problem behavior of children with emotional and behavioral disorders in a day treatment classroom setting. *Journal of Applied Behavior Analysis, 39*, 453–457.

Rathvon, N. (2008). *Effective school interventions: Evidence-based strategies for improving student outcomes* (2nd ed.). New York: Guilford.

Rispoli, M., O'Reilly, M., Lang, R., Machalicek, W., Kang, S., Davis, T., & Neely, L. (2016). An examination of within-session responding following access to reinforcing stimuli. *Research in Developmental Disabilities, 48*, 25–34.

Rogers, S. J. (2000). Interventions that facilitate socialization in children with autism. *Journal of Autism and Developmental Disorders, 30*, 399–409.

Saudergas, R. W., Madsen, C. H., & Scott, J. W. (1977). Differential effects of fixed- and variable-time feedback on production rates of elementary school children. *Journal of Applied Behavior Analysis, 10*, 673–678.

Simonsen, B., Fairbanks, S., Briesch, A., Myers, D., & Sugai, G. (2008). Evidence-based practices in classroom management: Considerations for research to practice. *Education and Treatment of Children, 31*, 351–380.

Skinner, B. F. (1953). *Science and human behavior.* New York: Free Press.

Smeets, P. M., Lancioni, G. E., Ball, T. S., & Olivia, D. S. (1985). Shaping self-initiated toileting in infants. *Journal of Applied Behavior Analysis, 18,* 303–308.

Spradlin, J. E., & Simon, J. L. (2011). Stimulus control and generalization. In W. W. Fisher, C. C. Piazza, & H. S. Roane (Eds.), *Handbook of applied behavior analysis* (pp. 76–91). New York: Guilford.

Stahr, B., Cushing, D., Lane, K., & Fox, J. (2006). Efficacy of a function-based intervention in decreasing off-task behavior exhibited by a student with ADHD. *Journal of Positive Behavior Interventions, 8*, 201–211.

Stokes, T. F., & Baer, D. M. (1977). An implicit technology of generalization. *Journal of Applied Behavior Analysis, 10*, 349–367.

Sutherland, K. S., Lewis-Palmer, T., Stichter, J., & Morgan, P. L. (2008). Examining the influence of teacher behavior and classroom context on the behavioral and academic outcomes for students with emotional and behavioral disorders. *Journal of Special Education, 41*, 223–233.

Sutherland, K. S., Wehby, J. H., & Copeland, S. R. (2000). Effect of varying rates of behavior-specific praise on the on-task behavior of students with EBD. *Journal of Emotional and Behavioral Disorders, 8*, 2–8.

Tarbox, J., Madrid, W., Aguilar, B., Jacobo, W., & Schiff, A. (2009). Use of chaining to increase complexity of echoics in children with autism. *Journal of Applied Behavior Analysis, 42*, 901–906.

Thorpe, G. L., & Olson, S. L. (1997). *Behavior therapy: Concepts, procedures, and applications* (2nd ed.). Upper Saddle River, NJ: Allyn & Bacon.

Van Houten, R., & Nau, P. A. (1980). A comparison of the effects of fixed and variable ratio schedules of reinforcement on the behavior of deaf children. *Journal of Applied Behavior Analysis, 13*, 13–21.

Vargas, J. S. (2013). *Behavior analysis for effective teaching.* New York: Routledge.

Vegas, K. C., Jenson, W. R., & Kircher, J. C. (2007). A single-subject meta-analysis of the effectiveness of time-out in reducing disruptive classroom behavior. *Behavioral Disorders, 32*,109–121.

Vollmer, T. R., & Athens, E. (2011). Developing function-based extinction procedures for problem behavior. In W. W. Fisher, C. C. Piazza, & H. S. Roane (Eds.), *Handbook of applied behavior analysis* (pp. 317–334). New York: Guilford.

Vollmer, T. R., & Iwata, B. A. (1991). Establishing operations and reinforcement effects. *Journal of Applied Behavior Analysis, 24*, 279–291.

von der Embse, N., Barterian, J., & Segool, N. (2012). Test anxiety interventions for children and adolescents: A systematic review of treatment studies from 2000–2010. *Psychology in the Schools, 50*, 57–71.

Walker, H. M., & Buckley, N. K. (1968). The use of positive reinforcement in conditioning attending behavior. *Journal of Applied Behavior Analysis, 1*, 245–250.

Watson, J. B., & Rayner, R. (1920). Conditioned emotional reactions. *Journal of Experimental Psychology, 3*, 1–14.

Wheatley, R. K., West, R. P., Charlton, C. T., Sanders, R. B., Smith, T. G., & Taylor, M. J. (2009). Improving behavior through differential reinforcement: A praise note system for elementary school students. *Education and Treatment of Children, 32*, 551–571.

Wong, C., Odom, S. L., Hume, K., Cox, A. W., Fettig, A., Kucharczyk, S., . . . Schultz, T. R. (2014). *Evidence-based practices for children, youth, and young adults with Autism Spectrum Disorder.* Chapel Hill: The University of North Carolina, Frank Porter Graham Child Development Institute, Autism Evidence-Based Practice Review Group.

The Measurement of Behavior in School Settings

3

Historically, behavioral assessment has involved evaluating constructs (e.g., personality) or internal states (e.g., anger, sadness) through indirect, highly inferential methods. However, greater accountability in education requires assessment be grounded in science, which necessitates taking a different perspective on evaluating behavior in school settings. This chapter focuses on measuring behavior (broadly defined as academic and social behavior) using a behavior analytic perspective. Specifically, this chapter addresses limitations to current behavioral assessment methods by presenting direct behavioral observation approaches that have been applied in school settings. These approaches have high standards regarding measurement accuracy, reliability, and validity.

Assessment and the Measurement of Behavior

Assessment serves many functions and the function of an assessment can differ depending on its intended purpose. In educational settings, assessments typically serve to screen, diagnose or determine eligibility for special education, monitor progress, establish a baseline and evaluate instructional or intervention effectiveness, identify a cause, or solve a problem (Salvia & Ysseldyke, 1995; Sattler, 2001; Thompson & Borrero, 2011). Traditional assessment models involve the measurement of constructs, like intelligence or personality, or a skill, such as reading fluency or engaging in appropriate peer relations, and assume that traits are stable, behavior represents an underlying pathology, and behavior is consistent regardless of context or time (Hintze, Volpe, & Shapiro, 2008). However, these assumptions are inconsistent with a behavior analytic perspective, which emphasizes direct measurement and quantification of observable behavior (Hartmann, Barrios, & Wood, 2004). Moreover, assessment within an ABA framework minimizes inferences reducing error and places great importance on the role the environment plays as a casual variable of behavior. Applied to schools, this means taking a more scientific view of measurement by focusing on behavior that is observable and countable, eliminating speculation and conjecture when formulating conclusions based on data, and underscoring the environment's part in producing behavior.

What is Measurement?

How is measurement conceptualized within a school context using an ABA framework? Simply stated, measurement is the process of quantifying some phenomenon of importance and relevance. As Vargas (2013) noted, measurement "is a process of assigning numbers for equivalent units" (p. 95) and numbers are important in education. For example, assigning numbers to a student's performance on a math test allows a teacher to make comparisons between that student's performance and some standard or the performance of similar peers (e.g., classmates who took the same math test). These comparisons allow educators to determine discrepancies between the student's performance and some classroom norm. Furthermore, comparisons help identify deficient skills that should be mastered or are important for success. For example, multiplication fact fluency is critical for mastery of long division. Finally, comparisons let teachers track changes in students' performance over time. Pre- and post-tests might assist in assessing students' responses to instruction and guided or independent practice.

Measurement involves three equally important components: accuracy, validity, and reliability, with each of these components contributing to the measurement instrument's value as a tool (Groth-Marnat, 2009; Sattler, 2001; Vannest, Davis, & Parker, 2013). Within an educational context, we want to know if an assessment produces a true value of the construct being measured (accuracy), measures what the assessment is designed or intended to measure (validity), and produces consistent results over time (reliability). A ruler is no good if the construct being measured is temperature (validity), if measurements yield different distances each time (reliability), or if the distance between each marking (that is supposed to measure an inch) is slightly more or slightly less than an inch (accuracy). Invalid, unreliable, and inaccurate measurements result in error. Test developers have longed to create assessments that are void of measurement error. In doing so, an effort is made to "maximize the similarity between test response and criterion measure" (Goldfried & Kent, 1972, p. 419). Said differently, the objective is to create a measure that is accurate, reliable, and valid.

Assessing Behavior

School psychologists frequently assess student behavior as part of a more comprehensive assessment. Perhaps the referral question involves the student's academic skills and understanding the student's behavior within the classroom might provide insight on the student as a learner. The student might be distracted and off-task during instructional time, noncompliant when asked to practice academic skills, or both on-task and compliant suggesting something else might be responsible for poor academic performance. In assessing the student's behavior, interviewing the teacher to obtain information about the student's behavior, while possibly helpful in understanding the behavior, fails to produce a quantifiable measurement of behavior. School psychologists might also use behavior rating scales, such as the Behavior Assessment System for Children or the Conners Rating Scale, to obtain information about the student's behavior. Again, while potentially helpful in understanding the referral concerns, behavior rating scales do not count actual behavior but, rather, offer informants' perceptions of a student's behavior. Furthermore, interviews (with teachers, parents, and students) and behavior rating scales are both prone to rater biases. Finally, we might consider conducting observation of the student. Direct behavioral observation, more than any other assessment method, is consistent with a science of behavior.

From a behavior analytic perspective, *direct behavioral assessment* makes several important assumptions about the measurement of behavior. First, direct behavioral assessment allows for the precise measurement of behavior despite its fluidity and continuous nature (Alberto & Troutman, 2013; Mace, 1994). For example, attempting to measure the behavior of someone playing the guitar might seem near impossible. However, utilizing a structured format for observing sequences can lead to precise measurement (Hartmann et al., 2004). Second, the behavior being observed is, itself, important (Cooper, Heron & Heward, 2007). That is, the behavior being observed represents nothing more than the behavior. This perspective limits inference and error. School psychology is plagued by the indirect measurement of constructs and assessing constructs, like intelligence, requires some degree of inference (Whitcomb & Merrell, 2013). Inference in measurement suggests that the phenomenon is being measured indirectly. That is, the construct being measured cannot be measured directly. When something cannot be measured directly, error is introduced. Cronbach (1956) described interferences as "hazardous," (p. 174) suggesting conclusions or predictions based on the interpretation of constructs are highly problematic. Consequently, direct behavioral assessment measures behavior and nothing else. Third, direct behavioral assessment assumes behavior is context specific (Mash & Terdal, 1988). Behavioral analysis seeks to understand the environment and its effect on behavior. Finally, direct behavioral assessment allows for comparisons to be made between and within individuals (Hintze et al., 2008) As described above, comparisons are important assessment outcomes.

What to Measure? Using Direct Behavioral Observation in School Settings

Directly observing behavior within the context of a school setting requires several considerations, the first of which is answering the question, 'what should I observe?'

With so many available behaviors to observe, narrowing down options is a priority. The following section helps school psychologists consider the selection of behaviors to observe (including when to observe those behaviors) and how to operationally define target behaviors. Furthermore, the selection of target behaviors is placed within the context of understanding antecedents and consequences.

Selecting Behaviors to Observe

Identifying socially important target behaviors is the first task in planning for the direct observation of behavior. Because resources, such as time, prevent the school psychologist from addressing every concern, the prioritization of those concerns is of utmost importance. Cooper and colleagues (2007) noted that the selection of a target behavior should ultimately benefit the student, not someone else. Furthermore, the target behavior should not be selected simply because it is interesting. Rather, school psychologists should begin by selecting target behaviors with behavior change in mind (Cooper et al., 2007). That is, target behaviors should be behaviors considered for future intervention or change. For example, physical aggression might be an appropriate target behavior because of the likelihood intervention will be required.

Cooper and colleagues (2007) provided the following guidelines for practitioners when prioritizing identified behaviors:

- Which behaviors are dangerous or pose threats to the safety of the student and others?
- How long has the behavior been a problem?
- How frequently does the behavior occur?
- Does the behavior result in frequent problems for the student?
- Will changing the behavior expose the student to consequential events that might strengthen appropriate behavior?

In addition, practitioners might consider identifying behaviors that are most concerning to the referral source, are relatively simple to change, could lead to response generalization, and are part of a larger behavioral response chain (Nelson & Hayes, 1979). Answers to these questions can be obtained from standard interviews with teachers, administrators, and other school staff, as well as with parents. Furthermore, informal observations of the student (i.e., narrative or A-B-C observations) will likely yield data helpful when selecting target behaviors. Once these data are collected, a formal ranking matrix might assist the school psychologist to identify priority behaviors to directly observe (Cooper et al., 2007).

A behavior's social significance, as it relates to the referral concerns, should also be considered. Appropriate target behaviors need to be crucial for the student's success. Barnett (2005) described these behaviors as *keystone variables* or behaviors that involve narrowly defined response classes (i.e., sets of behaviors that have similar functions), are likely to lead to favorable outcomes across other behaviors and domains (e.g., academic, social), encompass foundational skills necessary for the learning of more complex skills, and include skills needed to adapt to different contexts or settings. For example, completing a math assignment independently in class requires prerequisite skills such as following multistep instructions independent of an adult's supervision, maintaining a high degree of on-task behavior when distractions are present, and certain academic skills that are necessary for the assignment to be completed accurately and without help. Consequently, school psychologists might consider focusing on these foundational skills when selecting a behavior to observe. Related, Rosales-Ruiz and Baer (1997) defined a *behavioral cusp* as a behavior that, when changed, has far-reaching positive consequences for the individuals. Changing these behaviors might allow the student to access reinforcement in new ways or in new environments. For example, sharing with peers is a behavioral cusp, as mastery of the skill will likely lead to contingencies that shape other adaptive social behaviors, and many more naturally occurring and positively reinforcing consequences delivered by peers.

SELECTING THE SETTING OR SETTINGS TO OBSERVE

Following the selection of an appropriate target behavior, the school psychologist should ask, 'in what setting or settings should observations occur?' Such a decision requires some strategy, as the context in which the behavior occurs is essential to fully understand the behavior. Furthermore, selecting appropriate settings helps ensure that a true measurement of the behavior is taken. Selecting the setting or settings to observe involves more than simply identifying a location. The school psychologist should also identify when during the school day is best to observe. Consider the following questions when planning observations:

- When and where does the behavior occur most frequently?
- When and where is the behavior most problematic?
- Where might the observer best see individual responses (e.g., discrete behaviors)?
- Where might the observer best see interactions between the student and some other person (e.g., teacher, peer)?

Defining the Target Behavior

Clear and unambiguous definitions of the target behavior are critical to collecting accurate, valid, and reliable observational data (see Alberto & Troutman, 2013; Cooper et al., 2007; Hartmann et al., 2004). Often referred to as an *operational definition*, such descriptions ensure that the behavior being observed truly represents the selected target behavior. Furthermore, clearly understanding behavioral definitions helps observers accurately record the occurrence and nonoccurrence of the target behavior. Finally, the definition of a target behavior should only include the observable elements of the behavior (Hawkins & Dobes, 1977). Including constructs and ambiguous terms requires others to make inferences about the behavior, thus decreasing the observation's accuracy, validity, and reliability. For example, 'upset' or 'angry' requires the observer to infer an internal state, which is prone to error. Rather, one might consider what these constructs look like in the context and setting in which the observation is to occur. The definition should describe both examples and non-examples of the target behavior, decreasing the need for observer judgment (Hawkins & Dobes, 1977). For example, both on- and off-task behavior should be clearly defined for the observer. Finally, consideration of how the target behavior has been previously defined might clear up misconceptions of what behavior is currently being targeted for observation.

Hartmann and colleagues (2004) suggested refining the behavioral definition by "writing a draft and sending it out for review and feedback to knowledgeable critics" (p. 111). Refinement might also include answering the following questions posed by Morris (1985) to determine the strength of the behavioral definition:

- Can the behavior be measured? Can the frequency be counted? Can the length of time the student exhibits the behavior be calculated? Can the length of time between when the student was given a task and when the task was initiated or completed be computed?
- Can the behavior be seen by an observer? Can a person unfamiliar to the student accurately identify the target behavior when given the definition?
- Does the target behavior represent the smallest, most specific component of the behavior?

Considering Antecedents and Consequences

Identifying antecedents and consequences allows for a thorough understanding of variables that effect the behavior. Developing a picture of what occurs before and after a behavior can have a profound impact on intervention planning. Specific to consequences of behavior, observations can assist in developing hypotheses regarding the *function of behavior* (e.g., positive or negative reinforcement; Alberto & Troutman, 2013; Cooper et al., 2007; Wacker, Berg, Harding, & Cooper-Brown, 2011). While functional assessment and analysis is presented in Chapter 5, the following questions from Hintze and colleagues (2008) provide guidance to practitioners looking to use observational data to develop functional hypotheses:

- Does the student engage in behavior that leads to task avoidance or escape?
- Does the type of task demand impact the behavior?
- Does the student engage in behavior that leads to social attention from peers or teachers?
- Are there contextual or setting characteristics associated with the behavior?

In addition, asking if the student can access tangible items, activities, or free time after engaging in the behavior might identify non-social consequences that reinforce the behavior.

Measuring Behavior Using Direct Behavioral Observation Methods

Direct observation involves measuring a behavior directly, through observation. Direct observation is contrasted with *indirect observation*, which often includes using behavior rating scales, interviews, and surveys to obtain data on the target behavior. However, indirect observation requires the observer to make inferences about the target behavior leading to possible concerns about the accuracy and validity of the data (Kahng, Ingvarsson, Quigg, Seckinger, & Teichman, 2011). Direct observation, on the other hand, is less inferential resulting in more accurate and valid data (Cooper et al., 2007). The remainder of this chapter focuses on direct behavioral observation methods.

Direct observation of behavior can be generally categorized as either naturalistic or systematic. Naturalistic observations involve an unbiased observer recording descriptions of behavior as the behavior occurs in a natural setting during real time (Hintze et al., 2008). For example, a natural observation might assist the school psychologist obtain a general description of contextual variables that co-occur with the target behavior and identify consequential events that follow the behavior. Naturalistic observations most often involve writing a narrative description of the scene. On the other hand, systematic observational methods encompass a set of specific procedures that quantify behavior (Kratochwill, Alper, & Cancelli, 1980). While each observational approach differs regarding its purpose and procedures, both involve observing behavior directly.

Narrative Observations

Narrative observation involves running records of behavioral events within a naturalistic setting. Employing a narrative observational approach simply means recording behaviors and events chronologically. Special attention is paid to contextual events that might be of interest to understanding the target behavior. For example, a school psychologist might be interested in knowing when or with whom a target behavior is most likely to occur and what happens immediately before and after the target behavior.

While narrative procedures are easy to use and require minimal training (Hintze et al., 2008), there are two notable limitations. First, narrative observations are less reliable than more systematic observational approaches (Hartmann & Wood, 1990). Two individuals observing the same classroom might attend to different events and variables. Second, the descriptive nature of the observational system limits the degree to which one can make interpretations about the data. Having only a running record of what occurred during the observation does not allow conclusions to be drawn about the behavior. Furthermore, narrative observations rarely provide a measure or count of the behavior, which can be problematic when making comparisons or establishing interobserver reliability. Accordingly, narrative observations should only be considered during the initial stages of an assessment (Hartmann & Wood, 1990; Sattler, 2001). Specifically, narrative observations should focus on understanding a target behavior and its impact on student functioning, contextual variables relevant to the referral concerns, and informal recordings of frequency, duration, and latency.

Several authors have recommended narrative observations take a more specific form to improve the reliability and interpretive quality of the data. For example, Hintze and colleagues (2008) suggested utilizing an A-B-C recording scheme to better identify antecedent and consequent events that surround the behavior. An *A-B-C narrative observation* involves the observer briefly noting what came before the target behavior, a description of the target behavior, and what happened following the target behavior. For example, the school psychologist would record the antecedent (teacher requests student to complete worksheet), behavior (student tears worksheet), and consequence (teacher provides verbal reprimand to student). Of course, specific details about the antecedent and consequence are favored and a running record of the behavioral chain that began with the teacher's initial request is probably most helpful when developing hypotheses about the behavior's function.

Systematic Observational Methods

Systematic observational schemes allow for the quantification of behavior, which is a hallmark of behavior analysis. The importance of quantifying behavior cannot be stressed enough. An accurate, reliable, and valid measurement of behavior assumes quantification, which is important given school psychology's emphasis on measuring behavior to assess discrepancies between typical and atypical behavior, comparing different conditions or interventions, and evaluating change over time. Each of these tasks requires the school psychologist to do more than simply describe behavior.

Behavior analysts have traditionally categorized recording methods as either *continuous* or *discontinuous*. Continuous methods measure all instances of a behavior observed during a session (see Table 3.1). Discontinuous methods measure a sample of all instances of behavior observed during a session (see Table 3.2). While continuous recordings will yield the most complete documentation of behavior (i.e., every single instance), such observational approaches can be problematic (Kahng et al., 2011). For example, the behavior might not be discrete (i.e., have a clear beginning and end) or continuous observation might not be possible in the context of a school setting. Consequently, the observer must consider a discontinuous method or one that utilizes intermittent sampling of behavior. Obtaining an intermittent sample of behavior involves dividing the observational session into short, pre-determined intervals (e.g., 15 seconds) and recording whether a behavior or set of behaviors occurred during the interval.

Table 3.1   Continuous Recording Methods

Method	Description	Examples	Comments
Frequency Count or Event Recording	Counts with number of occurrences of behavior	• John hit his peer 4 times during circle time • Sarah followed the teacher's instructions 8 times during the morning • Kris said 'hello' to her peer 2 times during recess	• Appropriate for behaviors that have a discrete beginning and end • Good for behaviors that are consistent in terms of how long they might take to occur • Good for infrequent behaviors
Rate of Behavior	Frequency count per unit of time (Rate = count of occurrences divided by some unit of time (e.g., minute))	• Henry read 45 words correct per min • Tanika completed 30 problems in 30 mins • Mary had 4 vocal tics in 10 mins	• Can be used for the measurement of both academic and non-academic behavior
Duration	Length, in time, from when the behavior began and when it finished (i.e., how long a behavior lasts)	• Molly's tantrum lasted 14 mins • Max played appropriately with his peer for 30 mins	• Good for behaviors where changing the duration is a socially important target • Comparisons across observations can be made when sessions are of the same length
Latency	Measurement of the elapsed time between the onset of a stimulus and the initiation or completion of a specified behavior	• Lucy took 5 mins to complete the task • Will took 25 secs to begin the task after being given the instruction	• Good for compliance tasks or measuring the time it takes to start an action once a signal has been given

Table 3.2 Discontinuous Recording Methods

Method	Description	Examples	Comments
Partial-Interval	Records whether the behavior occurred during any part of the interval	• An occurrence is recorded if Kate was observed on-task during any part of the 10-sec interval	• Can overestimate occurrence of long-duration behavior • Can underestimate occurrence of instantaneous or high-rate behavior
Whole-Interval	Records whether the behavior occurred during the entire interval	• An occurrence is recorded if Kate was observed on-task during the entire 10-sec interval	• Can accurately estimate occurrence of long-duration behavior • Can underestimate occurrence of instantaneous or high-rate behavior
Momentary Time Sample	Records whether the behavior occurred at the end of the interval	• An occurrence is recorded if Kate was observed on-task at the end of the 10-sec interval	• Least biased estimate of behavior

Considering how to include others' (e.g., peers, teachers) behaviors using the methods described above is also important. Observing a target student, the target behaviors of that student, and specific teacher or peer behavior might provide helpful data when analyzing behavior and developing interventions. For example, a school psychologist might target a student's on-task behavior and, at the same time, the teacher's use of explicit instructions and behavior-specific praise. Doing so within a continuous or discontinuous recording method would be easy if teacher behavior was clearly defined. Examples of observable teacher behavior include positive academic and behavioral feedback, asking questions, ignoring student behavior, and verbal redirection of misbehavior.

Final Considerations

Interobserver Agreement

Reporting *interobserver agreement* (IOA) data is standard to ABA practice and research (Kahng et al., 2011). IOA has many benefits including assessing an observer's skill,

FREQUENCY RECORDING RECORDING FORM
Tally the behavioral occurrences for each student and record the total number

Student(s) observed: _____

Grade: _____

Teacher: _____   Observer: _____

Date: _____

Time begin: _____   Time end: _____

Target behavior: _____

Behavioral definition: _____

Student	Occurrences	Total Number
Student 1		
Student 2		
Student 3		

Additional Observation Notes:

Figure 3.1 Example of Frequency Recording Form

detecting observer drift and reactivity, and ensuring the target behavior's operational definition was clear (Cooper et al., 2007; Whitcomb & Merrell, 2013). Furthermore, IOA data provide a measure of the observation's reliability. That is, IOA allows for the evaluation of the data's quality. To obtain IOA data, two observers independently mark the occurrence of the same behavior and agreement between the observers is noted. For IOA data to be reliable, the observers must observe the same events (e.g., student, time, setting) and use the same measurement system. While there are numerous ways to compute IOA, perhaps the easiest involves dividing the number of agreements by the number of agreements plus disagreements and multiplying by 100%. This calculation obtains a percentage agreement (readers are referred to Cooper et al. (2007) for a more thorough review of methods of calculating IOA). Practitioners should consider the feasibility of conducting IOA checks. Ideally, IOA data would be obtained regularly (i.e., at least 25% of sessions); however, practitioners will likely be constrained by time and other resources (e.g., availability of a second observer, time to train other observers), so careful consideration of when to conduct IOA checks might be necessary. Regarding the interpretation of IOA data, best practices suggest reliable observational data when IOA scores are above 80–90% (Johnston & Pennypacker, 1993).

LATENCY RECORDING FORM

Student observed: _____

Grade: _____

Teacher: _____ Observer: _____

Date: _____

Time begin: _____ Time end: _____

Target behavior: _____

Behavioral definition: _____

Setting characteristics: _____

Time Instruction Given	Time Behavior Starts	Length of Time for Behavior to Start

Figure 3.2 Example of Latency Recording Form

Using Observational Data to Make Comparisons

Observational data can be used to make comparisons between and within individuals (Hartmann et al., 2004; Hintze et al., 2008). *Between-individual comparisons* are made by selecting a nonreferred peer within the same setting (e.g., classroom, playground, cafeteria) and observing both the target student and the peer using the same target behaviors. With peer comparison data, a school psychologist can assess the degree to which the target student's behaviors differ from those of a same-age peer within specific settings. For example, observing the on-task behavior of a peer can aid in determining if a discrepancy exists between the target student's behavior and some

BEHAVIOR DURATION RECORDING FORM

Student observed: _____

Grade: _____

Teacher: _____   Observer: _____

Date: _____

Time begin: _____   Time end: _____

Target behavior: _____

Behavioral definition: _____

Setting characteristics: _____

Start Time	Stop Time	Duration (min)

Figure 3.3   Example of Behavior Duration Recording Form

classroom norm. Moreover, peer comparison data can identify deficient skills that require mastery and behaviors crucial for success in specific settings. Without between-individual comparison data, the inappropriateness of a behavior or the deficiency of a skill may be over- or understated (Whitcomb & Merrell, 2013).

Within-individual comparisons differ conceptually from between-individual comparisons but are equally valuable in behavioral assessment. Within-individual comparisons involve the direct observation of the same target behaviors over time in one or multiple settings. Such an approach is valuable for several reasons. First, collecting observational data over time allows for the validation of results. Observing the same student over several days enhances the reliability of the data collected and

INTERVAL RECORDING FORM

Student observed: _____

Grade: _____

Teacher: _____   Observer: _____

Date: _____

Time begin: _____   Time end: _____

Target behavior: _____

Behavioral definition: _____

Setting characteristics: _____

Observation length: _____

Interval type: Partial–Whole–Momentary   Interval length: _____

Begin Time																Total %

Begin Time																Total %

Figure 3.4   Example of Interval Recording Form

improves its predictive capabilities. For example, finding that a student engages in frequent off-task behavior (e.g., off-task at least 50% of observed intervals) across several observations allows the observer to state, with confidence, that the student's behavior is consistent across time and that future observations are likely to yield similar data. Second, collecting observational data over time also allows school psychologists to assess change. Initial observations might serve as a baseline that is then used to track changes during an intervention phase. Third, collecting observational data in different settings provides important clues regarding how the target student's behavior differs depending on the context. For example, a school psychologist might observe a middle school student during multiple classroom periods or an elementary school student during different unstructured periods (e.g., recess, lunch) to assess variables that might be contributing to the occurrence and nonoccurrence of the target behavior. Recognizing that a target behavior occurs or does not occur in different settings and with different people (e.g., peers, teachers) offers insight into environmental variables operating on the behavior.

Minimizing Observer Error by Ensuring Proper Training

While school psychologists will often directly observe the student, other school professionals might be needed for assistance (e.g., to serve as a substitute observer, to conduct a second observation to calculate IOA). Inadequate observer training is often cited as a threat to measurement accuracy and reliability, and observational data collected by poorly trained observers are likely to produce unreliable information (Cooper et al., 2007; Whitcomb & Merrell, 2013). Training someone to conduct a reliable behavioral observation should be based on principles of effective instruction. Formal didactic teaching, modeling, many opportunities for practice, and behavioral-specific feedback are all components of a recommended model for training observers. Techniques involving sample vignettes, video examples, role playing, and practice sessions in the setting in which most observations will take place have been used to enhance training (Cooper et al., 2007). For example, Axelrod, Zhe, Haugen, and Klein (2009) trained assistant house parents at a residential treatment facility to collect observational data. Their training process included a one hour formal presentation on direct behavioral observation and multiple practice sessions in the natural environment. The assistant house parents were deemed proficient after achieving agreement rates (i.e., comparisons between the observation of the trainees and trainers) with the authors of at least 95%. Predetermined criteria should be set; however, the level of agreement should be determined based on factors such as the behavior being observed (complex behaviors might require a lower set agreement rate), and the level of experience and education of the trainee.

Using Technology as an Aid

With recent advances in mobile technology, there are an abundance of applications and software available to assist school psychologists conducting direct behavioral observations. As expected, the usability and dependability of these aids varies considerably. Many have the capability of collecting frequency count and interval data, and allow for the observation of multiple target behaviors and students. Furthermore, several applications can synchronize observational data to commercially available spreadsheets or collate data for graphing. School psychologists are encouraged to explore technology as a support for conducting direct behavioral observations.

Conclusion

Federal legislation and educational policy groups have recommended greater educator accountability, which requires valid, reliable, and accurate measurement of student outcomes. For social behavior, direct behavioral observation is most appropriate as it quantifies behavior, minimizes inferences, and identifies relationships between environmental variables and behavior. This chapter presents fundamentals of the measurement and assessment of behavior, perspectives on selecting and defining target behaviors, and features of narrative and systematic observational methods. School psychologists, charged with conducting behavioral assessment and evaluating behavioral outcomes, will likely find themselves needing a model consistent with the methodologies offered in this chapter. Quantifying behavior is necessary for schools to meet accountability demands and support students struggling with behavioral challenges.

References

Alberto, P. A., & Troutman, A. C. (2013). *Applied behavior analysis for teachers* (9th ed.). Upper Saddle River, NJ: Pearson.

Axelrod, M. I., Zhe, E. J., Haugen, K. A., & Klein, J. A. (2009). Self-management of on-task homework behavior: A promising strategy for adolescents with attention and behavior problems. *School Psychology Review, 38*, 325–333.

Barnett, D. (2005). Keystone behaviors. In S. W. Lee (Ed.), *Encyclopedia of school psychology* (pp. 279–280). Thousand Oaks, CA: SAGE Publications.

Cooper, J., Heron, T., & Heward, W. (2007). *Applied behavior analysis* (2nd ed.). Upper Saddle River, NJ: Merrill/Pearson Education.

Cronbach, L. J. (1956). Assessment of individual differences. *Annual Review of Psychology, 7*, 173–196.

Goldfried, M. R., & Kent, R. N. (1972). Traditional versus behavioral personality assessment: A comparison of methodological and theoretical assumptions. *Psychological Bulletin, 77*, 409–420.

Groth-Marnat, G. (2009). *Handbook of psychological assessment* (5th ed.). Hoboken, NJ: Wiley & Sons.

Hartmann, D. P., Barrios, B. A., & Wood, D. D. (2004). Principles of behavioral observation. In M. J. Hilsenroth, D. L. Segal, & M. Hersen (Eds.), *Comprehensive handbook of psychological assessment* (pp. 108–127). Hoboken, NJ: Wiley & Sons.

Hartmann, D. P., & Wood, D. D. (1990). Observational methods. In A. S. Bellack, M. Hersen, & A. E. Kazdin (Eds.), *International handbook of behavior modification and therapy* (2nd ed.) (pp. 107–138). New York: Plenum.

Hawkins, R. P., & Dobes, R. W. (1977). Behavioral definitions in applied analysis: Explicit or implicit? In B. C. Etzel, J. M. Leblanc, & D. M. Baer (Eds.), *New developments in behavioral research: Theory, methods, and applications* (pp. 167–188). Hillsdale NJ: Lawrence Erlbaum.

Hintze, J. M., Volpe, R. J., & Shapiro, E. S. (2008). Best practices in the systematic direct observation of student behavior. In A. Thomas & J. Grimes (Eds.), *Best practices in school psychology V: Volume 2* (pp. 319–336). Washington, DC: National Association of School Psychologists.

Johnston, J. M., & Pennypacker, H. S. (1993). *Strategies and tactics for human behavioral research* (2nd ed.). Hillsdale, NJ: Erlbaum.

Kahng, S., Ingvarsson, E. T., Quigg, A. M., Seckinger, K. E., & Teichman, H. M. (2011). Defining and measuring behavior. In W. W. Fisher, C. C. Piazza, & H. S. Roane (Eds.), *Handbook of applied behavior analysis* (pp. 113–131). New York: Guilford.

Kratochwill, T. R., Alper, S., & Cancelli, A. A. (1980). Nondiscriminatory assessment in psychology and education. In L. Mann & D. A. Sabatino (Eds.), *Fourth review of special education* (pp. 229–286). New York: Grune & Stratton.

Mace, F. C. (1994). The significance and future of functional analysis methodologies. *Journal of Applied Behavior Analysis, 27,* 385–392.

Mash, E. J., & Terdal, L. G. (1988). Behavioral assessment of child and family disturbance. In E. J. Mash & L. G. Terdal (Eds.), *Behavioral assessment of childhood disorders* (2nd ed.) (pp. 3–68). New York: Guilford.

Morris, R. J. (1985). *Behavior modification with exceptional children: Principles and practices.* Glenview, IL: Scott, Foresman.

Nelson, R. O., & Hayes, S. C. (1979). Some current dimensions of behavioral assessment. *Behavioral Assessment, 1,* 1–16.

Rosales-Ruiz, J., & Baer, D. M. (1997). Behavioral cusps: A developmental and programmatic concept for behavior analysis. *Journal of Applied Behavior Analysis, 30,* 533–544.

Salvia, J., & Ysseldyke, J. E. (1995). *Assessment* (6th ed.). Boston: Houghton Mifflin.

Sattler, J. M. (2001). *Assessment of children: Cognitive applications* (4th ed.). San Diego, CA: Jerome M. Sattler Publishing.

Thompson, R. H., & Borrero, J. C. (2011). *Direct observation.* In W. W. Fisher, C. C. Piazza, & H. S. Roane (Eds.), *Handbook of applied behavior analysis* (pp. 191–205). New York: Guilford.

Vannest, K. J., Davis, J. L., & Parker, R. I. (2013). *Single case research in schools: Practical guidelines for school-based professionals.* New York: Routledge.

Vargas, J. S. (2013). *Behavior analysis for effective teaching.* New York: Routledge.

Wacker, D. P., Berg, W. K., Harding, J. W., & Cooper-Brown, L. J. (2011). Functional and structural approaches to behavioral assessment of problem behavior. In W. W. Fisher, C. C. Piazza, & H. S. Roane (Eds.), *Handbook of applied behavior analysis* (pp. 165–181). New York: Guilford.

Whitcomb, S. A., & Merrell, K. W. (2013). *Behavioral, social, and emotional assessment of children and adolescents.* New York: Routledge.

Evaluating Outcomes in Education

4

School psychologists and other educational professionals are now, more than ever, documenting educational outcomes, as legislation (e.g., the Elementary and Secondary Education Act (2015), the Individuals with Disabilities Education Act (2004)) requires schools to monitor academic progress to ensure students are meeting specific learning objectives. Furthermore, the National Association of School Psychologists' *Model for Comprehensive and Integrated School Psychological Services* (NASP, 2010) calls for school psychologists to work collaboratively with teachers and other school professionals to collect and interpret outcome data as a method for evaluating student progress (see Armistead & Smallwood, 2014). Finally, best practices in data-based decision making maintain accountability by documenting student growth over time (see Brown, Steege, & Bickford, 2014). Consequently, school psychologists and other school professionals need to consider appropriate methodologies for evaluating educational outcomes.

This chapter presents a template for evaluating the effectiveness of interventions or instructional approaches. First, an idiographic (i.e., single case design methodology) perspective on evaluating change highlighting experimental control, repeated measurements of the target behavior, verification and replication, and collection of baseline data is presented. Second, commonly used single case experimental designs (SCED) are introduced, emphasizing advantages and limitations. In addition, the chapter offers examples of how these different designs might be used in school settings with common academic and behavior problems. Finally, important considerations when using SCED to evaluate the effectiveness of educational practice are discussed.

Idiographic Approaches to Evaluating Change and Single Case Experimental Design

Traditional research designs (i.e., group designs) found in education and psychology are hardly appropriate when evaluating the effectiveness of an intervention for a single student. Such designs typically collect group performance data and average results across groups, evaluating effects using statistical analyses (Kazdin, 1998). However, these designs might not be appropriate when wanting to evaluate change for a single student. In this case, the unit of analysis is at the individual level, not the group level, as the intention is to understand how the intervention affects the individual. Group designs fail to identify individual differences or how different students respond differently to an intervention (Cooper, Heron, & Heward, 2007). There are two other features of group research designs that make them incongruent with our primary aim. First, we are most concerned with directly observing student behavior over time to evaluate change or growth. Bailey and Burch (2002) said, paraphrasing Sidman (1960), "the use of larger numbers of participants (in group statistical designs) virtually wipes out any hope of this type of understanding because individual differences are obscured by the averaging process that is required by statistical design" (p. 143). Second, group designs emphasize external validity or how well the results generalize to a larger population. We are clearly not interested in generalizing our results to some larger population. Rather, we are interested in knowing whether the introduction of an intervention produced a change in some behavior or skill for one student.

Group designs are poorly matched to the process of evaluating change at the individual level. A more fitting methodology, idiographic designs or SCED allow for the thorough evaluation of effects of an intervention on individuals and within specific contexts (Axelrod, Tornehl, & Fontanini-Axelrod, 2014). Some SCED emphasize experimental control, meaning changes observed in the measured behavior or skill (the dependent variable) was likely a result of the introduction of an intervention (the independent variable). Said differently, experimental control allows us to assert that the independent variable caused a change in the dependent variable (see Cooper et al., 2007; Horner et al., 2005; Kazdin, 1998). Unmistakably, establishing a causal relationship between the intervention and outcome variable is important when wanting to know about an intervention's effectiveness.

There are two other important features of SCED that highlight their appropriateness for evaluating student growth or progress. First, SCED requires active manipulation of the independent variable. Intentionally manipulating the independent variable allows for the systematic introduction of different interventions at strategic times (e.g., when the intervention is ineffective) but also helps establish experimental control (Horner et al., 2005). For example, a teacher might actively change (or alternate) the difficulty level of addition problems from easy to hard (independent variable) while measuring a student's on-task behavior (dependent variable). If the student is more on-task when completing easy problems, then the teacher can confidently conclude that changing the level of difficulty of addition problems caused some change in the student's on-task behavior. These active manipulations, going from one condition to another, enable us to conclude causal relationships exist between the independent (i.e., intervention) and dependent (i.e., behavior) variable. Second, SCED are flexible, allowing practitioners to make case-by-case decisions about both the independent and dependent variable. Regarding the former, a teacher might find that behavior-specific praise is only partially effective at improving a student's on-task behavior and decide to either implement some other intervention or add a component to the existing intervention. SCED enable us to make those decisions without compromising experimental control. Regarding the dependent variable, SCED allow for the selection of socially significant behaviors following consultation with others (e.g., parents, teachers), individualizing the dependent variable based on the needs of the student. Furthermore, SCED allow for the evaluation of the reliability of the dependent variable (i.e., IOA). Doing so ensures that we target behaviors or academic skills that are important and confidently conclude that our measurements are accurate, reliable, and valid (Cooper et al., 2007; Horner et al., 2005; Riley-Tillman & Burns, 2009).

Repeated measurement of the dependent variable is a hallmark of SCED. That is, target behaviors are measured repeatedly, over time, and across varying conditions (e.g., baseline, intervention). Repeated measurements allow us to establish paths by connecting two or more data points, and these data paths determine the level and trend of a measured behavior across time. Repeated measurement also aids in the identification of patterns, which, in turn, improves predictions of future behavior (Cooper et al., 2007; Johnston & Pennypacker, 1993; Vannest, Davis, & Parker, 2013). Look at Figure 4.1. Can you, with a high degree of confidence, say where the next data point might fall? The data path provides insight into that prediction. Finally, repeated measurements of the same dependent variable for the same student facilitate comparisons among conditions (Riley-Tillman & Burns, 2009; Vargas, 2013). Identifying patterns involves assessing trends over time, permitting comparisons to be made between different conditions (e.g., baseline, intervention). For example, a student's reading fluency or words read correct per minute might look stable during baseline (i.e., no intervention) but appear as increasing following the introduction of some intervention. Observing this after repeated measurements allows us to conclude the intervention did something to the targeted skill.

Prediction is also important when assessing the effectiveness of an intervention or instructional practice. Logically, we need to compare measurements taken of the dependent variable before the introduction of the intervention and also during the intervention. Baseline is established through the measurement of some behavior or academic skill in the absence of some procedure. Understanding how the data behave (i.e., patterns, trends) if nothing were done is one reason for collecting baseline data. Collecting data on the target behavior before introducing an intervention allows us to make predictions about what might happen if an intervention were introduced. For example, we might observe a student engage in frequent noncompliant behavior during baseline condition. We would then predict or expect the frequency of noncompliant behavior to decrease following the introduction of some intervention or procedure known to decrease noncompliance.

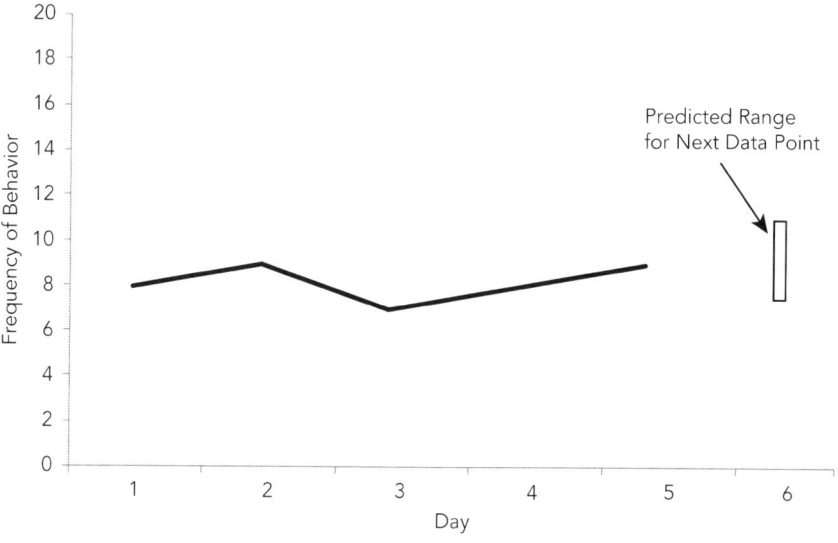

Figure 4.1 Using Stable Data Points to Predict Future Measurements

Baselines are also used to establish patterns of behavior when taking initial measurements. There are four patterns: stable, increasing, decreasing, and variable (see Figure 4.2). Predictions about what might happen next if we continued to do nothing are easiest with a stable baseline. In these cases, it is most appropriate to introduce the intervention when baseline data are stable. When baseline trends in a favorable direction (e.g., increasing when we want to see more of a target behavior or skill), there might be no need to intervene, as the student's current program appears to be producing favorable results. When the baseline trends in an unfavorable direction (e.g., decreasing when we want to see more of a target behavior or skill), the decision to intervene is made obvious. Variable baseline data points might suggest the dependent variable is poorly defined or not being reliably observed, the student is exhibiting a behavior or skill inconsistently and further assessment is warranted, or there are variables in the environment that might be contributing to the variability (e.g., different teachers on different days, student illness).

Verification and replication are two features of SCED's *baseline logic* (Cooper et al., 2007; Riley-Tillman & Burns, 2009). *Verification* involves demonstrating that baseline measurements would have remained unchanged had the intervention not been implemented. This is done by withdrawing the intervention and returning to baseline when some level of stability in the data is achieved. Observing the dependent variable return to baseline levels verifies the independent variable had some effect (see Figure 4.3), allowing us to state, affirmatively, that the independent variable controls responding (i.e., behavior) and that baseline conditions control responding both then and now (Cooper et al., 2007). *Replication* is achieved via additional reversals in conditions (Morgan & Morgan, 2001). For example, we might find that the

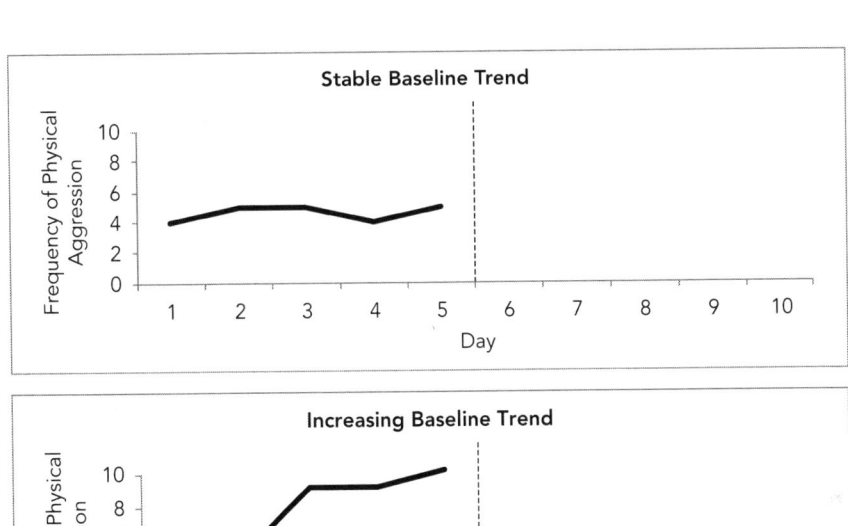

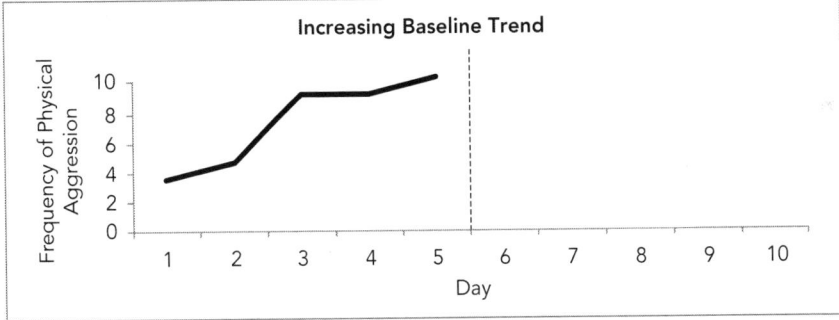

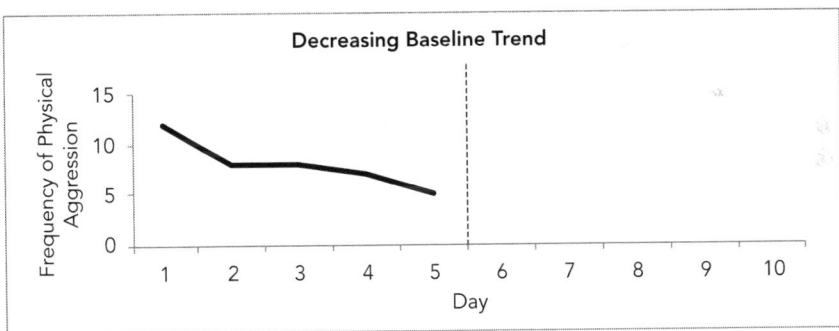

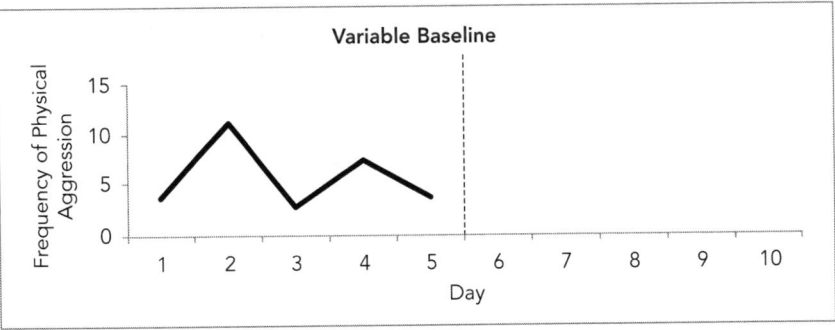

Figure 4.2   Four Baseline Patterns

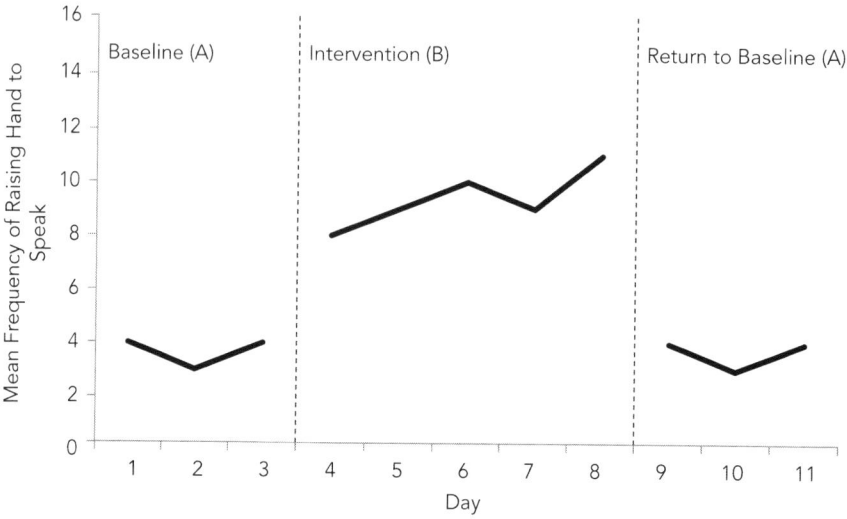

Figure 4.3   Example of an A-B-A Design with Return to Baseline Levels

frequency of compliance improved from baseline to the intervention condition, went back to baseline levels when the intervention was withdrawn, and then increased again when the intervention was reintroduced. Why is this important? Replication lessens the probability that some other variable contributed to the detected differences between baseline and the intervention condition (Cooper et al., 2007). Said differently, replication helps establish that the active manipulation of the independent variable caused a change in the dependent variable.

Types of Single Case Experimental Designs (SCED)

The following section highlights several commonly used SCED. Each of these designs are appropriate in a school setting, using target behaviors that are most likely to be encountered in schools, and for interventions likely to be implemented by educational professionals. First, however, it is important to review the notation system commonly used with SCED. This notation system, described in Table 4.1, provides a means of interpreting various conditions or phases (Tawney & Gast, 1984). For example, A-B represents a SCED involving a baseline phase followed by an intervention and A-B-A-C describes a baseline phase, followed by an intervention, a return to baseline, and some other intervention.

A-B Design

A-B designs involve a baseline phase followed by an intervention (see Figure 4.4). This design allows for comparisons between a behavior repeatedly measured during an

Table 4.1 SCED Notation System

Notation	Explanation
A	Baseline phase
B	Intervention phase
$B^1, B^2, \ldots B^x$	Minor change to the intervention phase
C, D, ... Z	Intervention phases different than B
- (hyphen)	Denotes phase change (e.g., A-B, A-B-A, A-B-A-C)

intervention and the same behavior repeatedly measured during baseline. It is important to remember that collection of baseline data allows us to do two things. First, we can take measurements of a behavior when nothing is done to establish some pattern (e.g., stable, increasing, decreasing). Second, we can now make a prediction about what might happen when some intervention is introduced. This is precisely what the A-B design is able to do, determine a pattern before an intervention is introduced so that we can evaluate our prediction that the behavior will change when the intervention is introduced. In addition, the A-B design can identify the nature of the effect (e.g., level, trend). The level of the effect can be lower, higher, or the same as baseline and the trend can increase, decrease, or remain stable.

The A-B design is popular in education probably because it is uncomplicated and does not require more than collection of data during baseline and intervention conditions. This design also does not require the removal of the intervention, which might pose problems in a school setting. For example, we might observe a student's

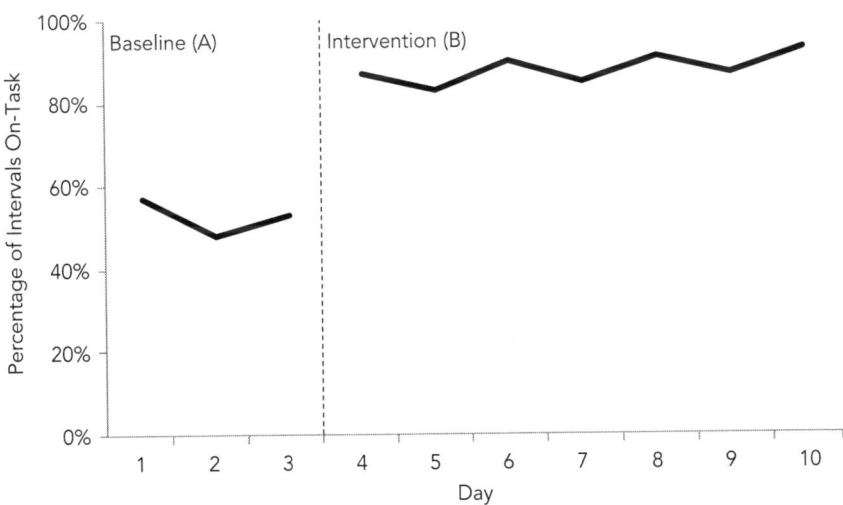

Figure 4.4 Example of an A-B Design

physically aggressive behavior decrease with the introduction of an intervention. Attempting to exert experimental control to establish a causal relationship between the target behavior and intervention by withdrawing the intervention (i.e., verifying through reversal) might not be prudent or acceptable to staff. On the other hand, the A-B design cannot conclude a causal relationship exists between the intervention (i.e., independent variable) and the target behavior (i.e., dependent variable). In fact, we cannot say, when using an A-B design, that an observed change to the dependent variable was because of the independent variable. The A-B design only suggests a correlation between the independent and dependent variable (Tawney & Gast, 1984).

A-B-A Design

By taking the A-B design and withdrawing the intervention (i.e., returning to baseline), we create the A-B-A design. This design allows us to verify our prediction that the target behavior would have remained unchanged if not for the introduction of the intervention. We begin by collecting baseline data demonstrating a stable trend (the first A) and then introduce some intervention we predict will increase the frequency of the target behavior (the B). Once we can say that the target behavior was different than when measured during the baseline phase, we withdraw the intervention and observe the target behavior return to baseline levels (the second A; see Figure 4.3, p. 62). The return to baseline provides additional evidence (i.e., a second time) that a measureable difference exists between baseline and the intervention. We have now confirmed our prediction, that the intervention had some effect on the target behavior and, as Tawney and Gast (1984) suggest, a tentative statement can be made indicating a causal relationship between the independent and the dependent variables. However, we are unable to definitively say that the intervention caused an increase or decrease in the target behavior.

One limitation of the A-B-A design, especially in applied settings like a school, is that often the target behavior partially or completely fails to return to baseline (Riley-Tillman & Burns, 2009). In school settings, we rarely expect a full return to baseline when the target behavior involves a skill we want to teach (e.g., sharing with peers, reading fluency) or the intervention leads to some enduring or semi-enduring change in behavior (e.g., compliance with adult instructions). In fact, a goal of many interventions is to maintain change long after the intervention has been withdrawn. While a partial or complete failure to return to baseline problematically affects our ability to demonstrate experimental control, we are sometimes able to conclude that the target behavior is different (i.e., higher or lower) during the second baseline phase than the first baseline phase (see Figure 4.5). In a school setting, this is often more important than establishing experimental control, especially in circumstances where a student's behavior or academic performance is now more consistent with that of his or her peers. A second limitation is that the A-B-A design requires the intervention to be withdrawn. There are clear practical and, perhaps, ethical considerations when withdrawing an intervention that otherwise appears to be working. Practitioners are urged to

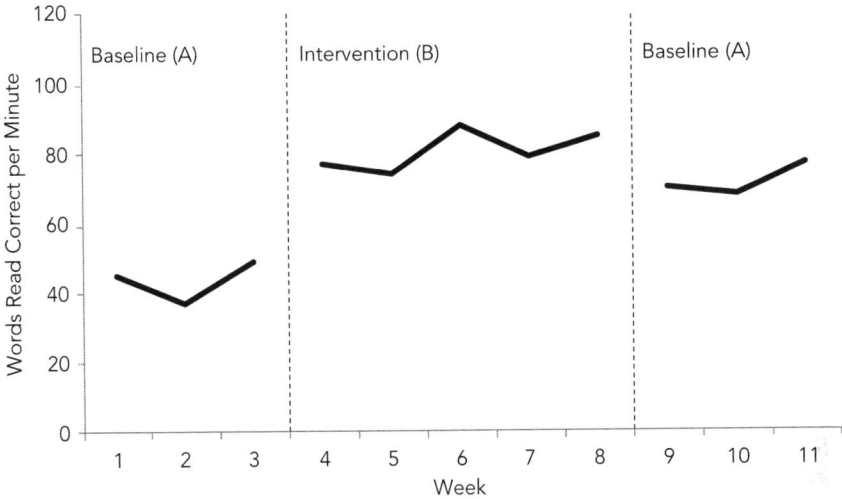

Figure 4.5 Example of an A-B-A Design with No Return to Baseline Levels

weigh the importance of establishing experimental control with these concerns to determine the appropriateness of the design in measuring intervention outcomes.

A-B-A-B Design

The A-B-A-B design (see Figure 4.6) establishes experimental control through both verification and replication. As in the A-B-A design, we can confirm our prediction by the second demonstration that something is different in the target behavior when we move from baseline to intervention and then from intervention back to baseline (i.e., withdraw the intervention). However, the A-B-A-B design introduces replication or a second demonstration that moving from baseline to the intervention leads to a change in the target behavior. This is important, as it helps affirm that the change was not as a result of some irrelevant or unrelated variable but, rather, because the intervention was implemented. Furthermore, we are able to observe a change in the dependent variable following three active manipulations of the independent variable during the phase changes. It is through this replication (i.e., A to B, B to A, and A to B) that experimental control is established. As in the A-B-A design, limitations include the possibility that the target behavior will not fully return to baseline levels and the need to withdraw a potentially effective intervention.

Other Variations of the A-B Design

In some cases, it might be important to consider either minor or full-scale changes to an intervention or add some component to boost the intervention's potency. For

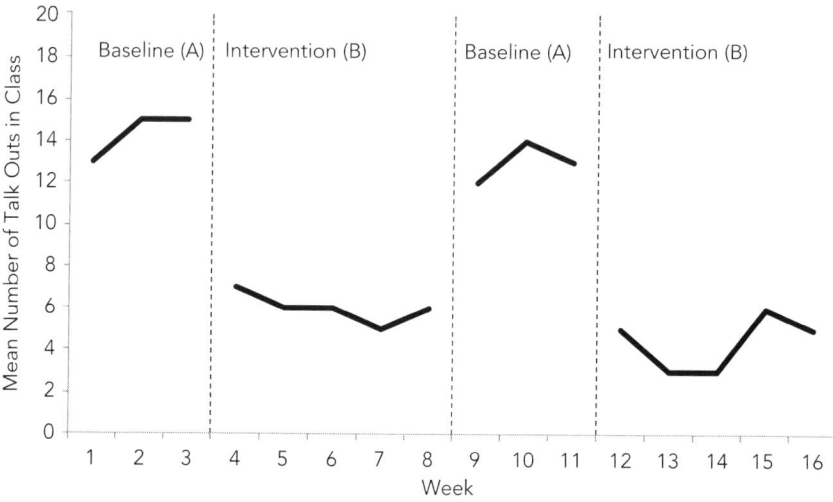

Figure 4.6 Example of an A-B-A-B Design

example, a teacher might implement an intervention that provides a student with behavior-specific praise for appropriate behavior. After collecting baseline data that are stable, the teacher begins the intervention only to find that it marginally improves the student's compliance with instructions. Upon consultation with a colleague, the decision is made to introduce an intervention that provides the student with a small reward for completing independent seatwork on time. In this case, an A-B-A-C-A design might be used where the first A represents the initial baseline phase, the B represents the behavior-specific praise, the second A represents the return to baseline, and the C is the combination of behavior-specific praise and the small reward (see Figure 4.7). Introducing a new component to an already implemented intervention is commonplace in education and this variation of the A-B-A design allows for an assessment of this change. Another example involves slightly adjusting or modifying an intervention that is already implemented. Imagine a teacher implementing a repeated reading intervention (i.e., having the student read the same passage multiple times with the teacher or some other interventionist providing feedback) where the student reads the passage twice. After collecting stable baseline data, the teacher implements the intervention, finds that it has not produced a change, and decides to have the student read the passage four times instead of twice. Here we have an $A-B^1-B^2-A$ design, if the teacher returned to baseline following the implementation of the slight modification to the repeated reading intervention.

Another example of a SCED is the B-A-B or B-A-B-A design. In this design, the intervention is implemented without the collection of initial baseline data. Implementation of an intervention before collecting baseline data might be necessary for several reasons. For example, the collection of baseline data might have been neglected or overlooked, or the student's behavior was so extreme that

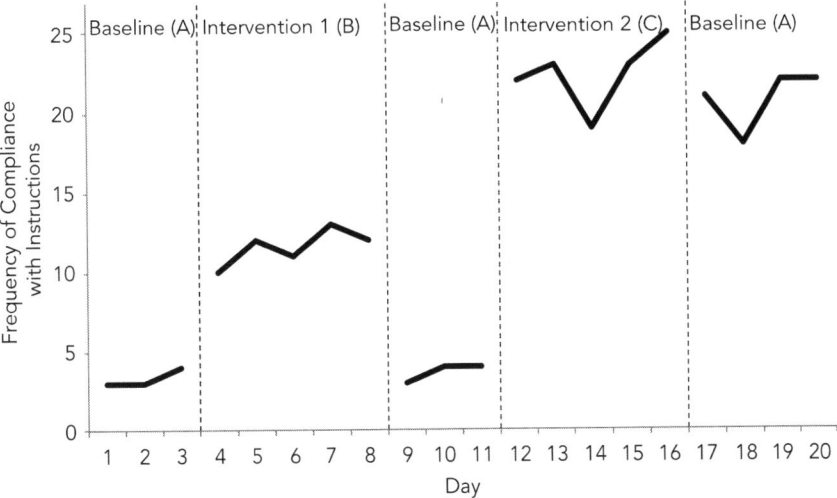

Figure 4.7 Example of an A-B-A-C-A Design

immediate intervention was required. When this happens, the first phase of the SCED is the intervention, followed by baseline, followed by intervention, and so on. Verification, by demonstrating that a return to baseline produced a change in the target behavior when compared to intervention phase levels, increases our confidence that the intervention had some effect on the target behavior. However, we are unable to establish a causal relationship nor are we able to determine the true effect of the intervention on the target behavior without collecting initial baseline data.

Multiple-Baseline Designs

While the A-B-A-B design is the most straightforward SCED, the multiple-baseline design (MBD) is useful when a return to baseline is not appropriate or feasible but demonstrating experimental control is important (Roane, Ringdahl, Kelley, & Glover, 2011). In a MBD, experimental control is established by conducting a series of A-B designs whereby the introduction of the intervention (B) is staggered at different points in time across people, places, or skills. For example, a teacher might implement a reward system with three students in the class. Using a MBD, the teacher would begin collecting baseline data for all three students. The intervention would then be implemented in a staggered fashion across the three students, with each student beginning the intervention on different days when data become stable during baseline (see Figure 4.8, p. 69). The MBD's logic is that our prediction that a change in the target behavior will occur when the intervention is introduced is now replicated multiple times but with different students. Another example involves implementing an intervention across different skills. A spelling intervention might be implemented with one student but with three separate spelling lists. In this case, the teacher implements the intervention with one spelling list, then the second, followed by the third. Again, our prediction that a change will occur in the student's performance is replicated but using different lists of words. According to Horner and colleagues (2005), observed inter-subject effects allow us to imply a causal relationship between the independent and dependent variable. However, several mechanisms must be in place for a causal relationship to be established. First, the conditions (i.e., baseline, intervention) must be similar across people, places, and skills. Ensuring similarity is essential when stating the intervention effected the target behavior and by maintaining similarity we are controlling for extraneous variables that might be impacting the conditions. That is, we want to be able to say that extraneous variables impacted each person equally. Second, the people (i.e., students) must be similar as well. Having students of different ages or developmental levels introduces an important variable that lessens our ability to make causal statements. Perhaps any differences between students in observed changes to the target behavior are because of their differing skill or developmental levels. Finally, we must consider possible contagion effects. For example, we might be using an incentive program to improve two students' compliance with teacher requests. If the students are in the same class, we might find that when moving one student to the intervention phase the behavior of the other student is impacted in some way—perhaps the student becomes angry at not being able to earn rewards for compliance. We might also observe contagion effects when using a MBD across settings with the same student. It is quite possible that the student's behavior in the non-intervention setting is effected by the student being exposed to the intervention in the other setting.

Figure 4.8 depicts a concurrent MBD. All three students began the baseline phase at the same time. While important when using a MBD, this practice might not be feasible in a school setting where students are often referred for intervention at different times. Waiting for additional students with the same problem who will receive the same intervention might be both impractical and unethical. A nonconcurrent MBD describes a series of A-B designs across behaviors, settings, or students started at different points in time (Cooper et al., 2007). Both the baseline and intervention conditions might not occur concurrently, which poses problems when applying MBD's experimental reasoning to establish a causal relationship between the intervention and outcome data. However, in his review of concurrent and nonconcurrent MBDs, Christ (2007) concluded that both were equally acceptable at limiting threats to internal validity and maintaining experimental control. Consequently, school psychologists are encouraged to use nonconcurrent MBDs to help establish experimental control when assessing intervention effects.

Multiple-Treatment Designs

Occasionally, we are interested in evaluating the differential effects of two or more interventions on a student's academic performance or behavior. While a traditional

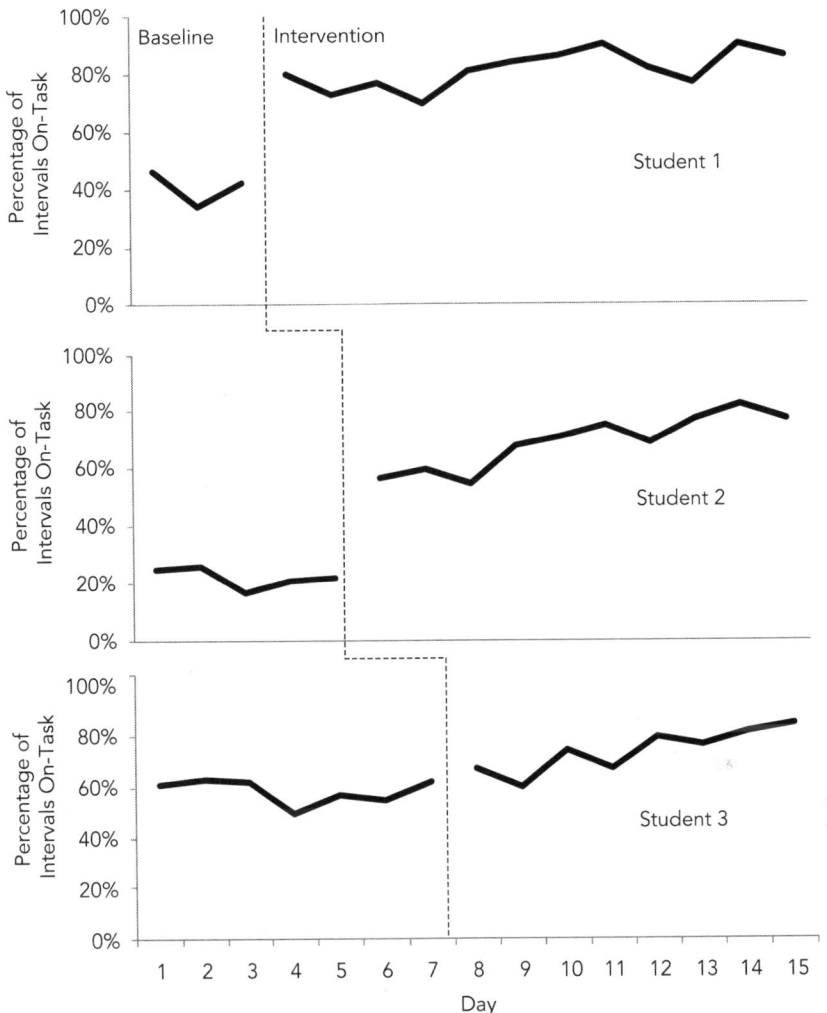

Figure 4.8   Example of a Multiple-Baseline Design Across Three Students

A-B-A-C design might be considered, certain limitations preclude us from making definitive statements about our findings. Specifically, the A-B-A-C design or its variations (e.g., A-B-A-C-D, A-B-C-A) is limited in that the number of data points needed to establish verification and replication is quite large (i.e., 60 data points are required to obtain three repetitions of an A-B-A-C design where five data points are collected during each phase). Furthermore, the first intervention (i.e., B) might influence the student's responses during the second intervention (i.e., C). Said differently, a student's history with the first intervention might affect the student's behavior during the second intervention. Fortunately, we are able to use a multiple-treatment design, or what is

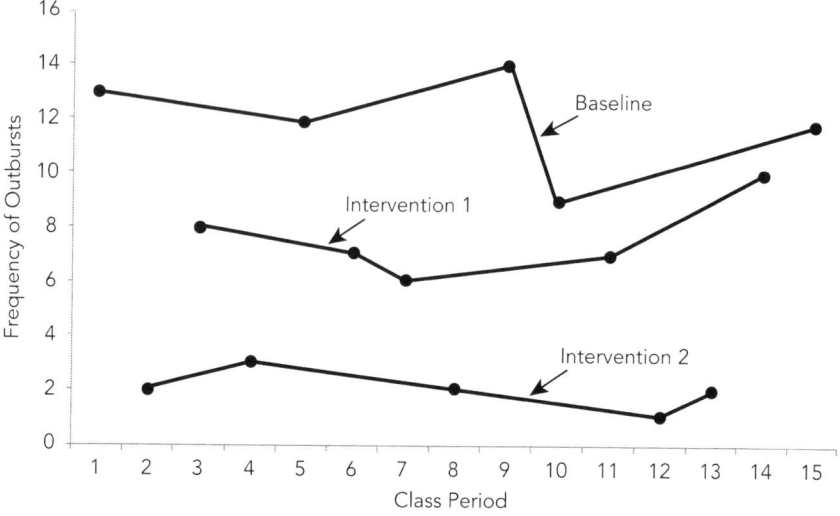

Figure 4.9   Example of a Multiple-Treatment Design with a Baseline and Two Intervention Conditions

also called a multi-element or alternating treatment design, to compare the two intervention conditions. Within a multiple-treatment design, we are also able to compare the intervention conditions to a baseline condition (see Figure 4.9).

Utilizing the multiple-treatment design involves presenting each condition (e.g., baseline or a control, intervention 1, intervention 2) in an alternating fashion across observations (e.g., morning and afternoon) or days in a randomized manner. Randomization is important so that each condition is not associated with a particular time of day, setting, or person. The effects are assessed by connecting the data points for each condition and then making comparisons between the data paths. Experimental control is established through the rapid alternation between conditions or the sequence of several mini-reversals. More confident statements about the causal relationship between the independent and dependent variable are made when clear differentiation between the data paths occurs (i.e., the data paths for each condition are noticeably separated). The multiple-treatment design has some unique advantages over the more traditional A-B designs. First, it is convenient to rapidly alternate several intervention conditions when wanting to test different interventions against one another. Consequently, there is no need to collect multiple data points in one condition in order to make comparisons, and interventions that are clearly not effective can be dropped. Comparisons between conditions can be made almost immediately, although caution should be taken when developing conclusions prematurely. Second, the multiple-treatment design allows the testing of conditions against baseline without extending baseline, delaying an intervention, or withdrawing an intervention. As mentioned previously, one limitation of the A-B-A-B design is its reliance on collecting stable baseline data and its requirement that the intervention be withdrawn.

School psychologists might attend to the following issues when considering using the multiple-treatment design to evaluate outcomes. First, rapid alternation of interventions might not provide enough time for the dependent variable to demonstrate a noticeable change (Roane et al., 2011). For example, certain social skills, like sharing, take time to develop and the multiple-treatment design might not allow for clear differences to be detected. Practitioners are encouraged to consider the degree to which the target behavior is a skill that requires time to learn. Second, the student might become sensitive to the changing conditions. For example, the student might begin to recognize that a condition that allows rewards to be earned for appropriate behavior is always followed by a condition in which misbehavior is ignored. This carryover effect has the possibility of influencing student responding. Finally, the conditions might not be different enough from one another to demonstrate differentiation. A teacher interested in comparing two different reward conditions might find that both rewards have a similar impact on the student's behavior because the rewards are qualitatively similar.

Final Considerations

Data Points

The number of available data points is important when interpreting data paths and, more generally, SCED graphs. The number of data points is typically proportional to the confidence you can have in your predictions about a data path; more data points mean more accurate predictions. More accurate predictions lead to more valid interpretations of what the data paths mean. Ideally, data points would continue to be collected until the data path indicated a stable level had been obtained or some clear conclusions could be drawn (i.e., two phases are noticeably different from one another). However, applied settings including schools are not always able to continue collecting data and extend data paths until clarity and stability is achieved. As a result, predictions are less confidently made and decisions are more prone to error.

While there is no hard and fast rule about how many data points are needed, there is some consensus that five or more data points per phase are necessary to make valid interpretations of SCED research. For example, Kratochwill and colleagues (2010) suggested five data points per phase is acceptable, with three data points per phase meeting standards with reservations. The National Autism Center (2015) used similar criteria (i.e., five or more data points) when evaluating the research on treatments for children with ASD. School psychologists and other educational professionals utilizing SCED to evaluate educational outcomes should weigh the cost of collecting five or more data points per phase with the practical limitations of the school setting. Keep in mind, however, that fewer data points restrict the predictive power of the data path resulting in less valid conclusions about an intervention's effect.

Data Analysis and Interpreting Graphs

Unlike group design studies in which inferential statistics are used to determine effects, SCED typically only requires visual inspection to analyze data. In many cases, visual inspection of the graph provides enough evidence to determine the effects of the intervention or, at least, whether a change occurred following the introduction of the intervention. Morgan and Morgan (2001), among others, have noted that "data from an individual participant behaving under well-specified conditions should provide unequivocal evidence of an independent variable's effect and that such an effect should be visible to the naked eye" (p. 121). For example, we might observe graphically a dramatic and immediate effect when moving from the baseline to intervention phase, represented by a noteworthy difference between baseline and intervention levels, and that the effect was maintained over time. As Roane and colleagues (2011) stated, "meaningful changes in the DV should be apparent when displayed graphically" (p. 134). However, some cases will require a more careful examination of the data paths within each phase.

Many authors writing on visual analysis of SCED data graphs suggest beginning with an examination of level and trend (e.g., Cooper et al., 2007; Vannest et al., 2013; Vargas, 2013). Level indicates how high or low the data path lies on the y-axis. Figure 4.10 provides an example of a change in level depicted in an A-B-A-B SCED. The mean frequency of aggressive behavior is approximately 25 during the initial baseline and six during the first intervention phase. Trend indicates the degree to which the data path changes in a particular direction. Figure 4.11 shows two stable baseline phases but a decreasing trend during both intervention phases. Riley-Tillman and Burns (2009) suggest also examining the immediacy or latency of the change. Figure 4.12 is a demonstration of a MBD where John and Michael appear to immediately change their behavior when the intervention is introduced. However, Dan does not appear to exhibit a change until later in the intervention phase. Variability or the stability of the behavior is another way to analyze SCED data. An aim of many interventions, particular those that target behavior (e.g., on-task, compliance), is to reduce or abate the amount of variation that exists. Figure 4.13 depicts an intervention successful at minimizing the variability of the student's on-task behavior, despite a failure to significantly improve the behavior.

The process of visually analyzing graphed SCED data is akin to making predictions (Roane et al., 2011). In all the cases described above, we can say, with some degree of confidence, what might happen if the intervention continued. However, what happens when the data are less clear? Several texts (e.g., Riley-Tillman & Burns, 2009; Vannest et al., 2013) provide strategies for analyzing SCED data statistically that could offer practitioners mathematical effect sizes that go beyond just comparing mean values of the behavior in each condition. Some SCED effect sizes are rather straightforward and involve the calculation of the percentage of non-overlapping data points (i.e., the percentage of data points in one phase lying above the highest data point in another phase; PND), while others are more complicated and require some knowledge of calculating effect sizes. Readers are referred to these texts to learn more about statistical analysis of SCED data but are cautioned about

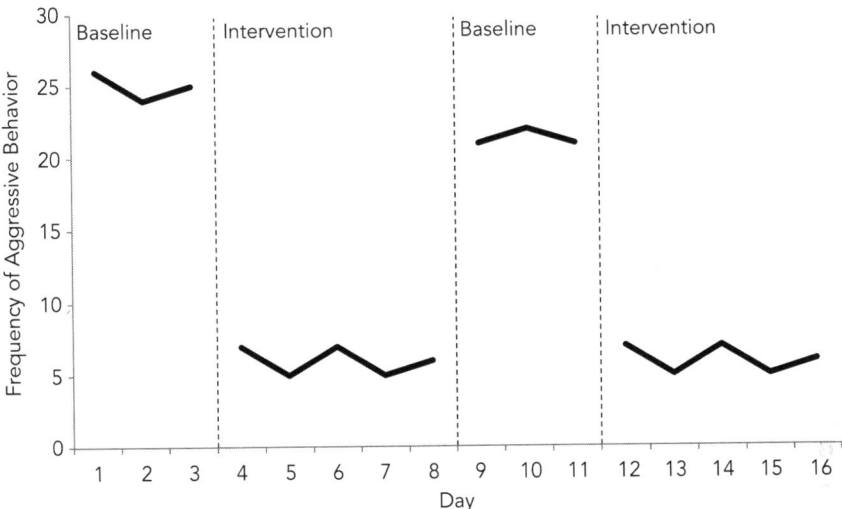

Figure 4.10   Example of Change in Level Depicted in an A-B-A-B Design

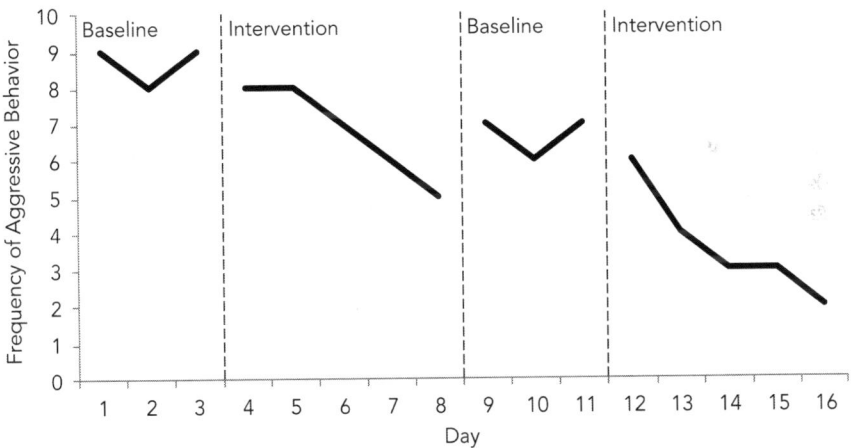

Figure 4.11   Example of a Decreasing Trend in Both Intervention Phases in an A-B-A-B Design

relying too heavily on statistical procedures. Observable changes in the dependent variable should be made apparent from a visual inspection of the graph.

Experimental Control

Considerable attention has been given to experimental control. Practicing school psychologists might wonder why experimental control is so important if all that is

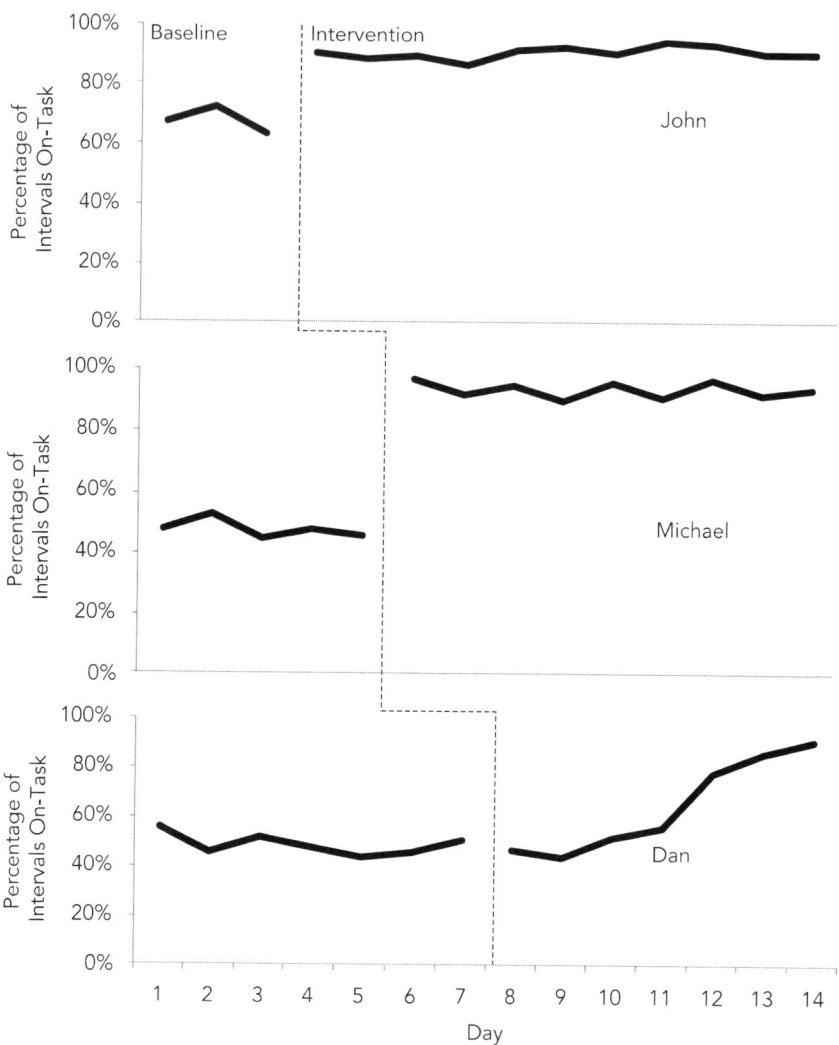

Figure 4.12 Examples of Immediacy and Latency of Changes in a Multiple-Baseline Design Across Students

needed is an evaluation of the effectiveness of an intervention. Many educators are content simply knowing if a student's academic skills or behavior improved over some period of time. An A-B design or even just implementing an intervention without considering the use of a SCED (e.g., a B design) is sufficient when wanting to document a change in a dependent variable and not needing to establish a causal relationship between the dependent and independent variables. However, increased accountability and changes in special education eligibility criteria have compelled

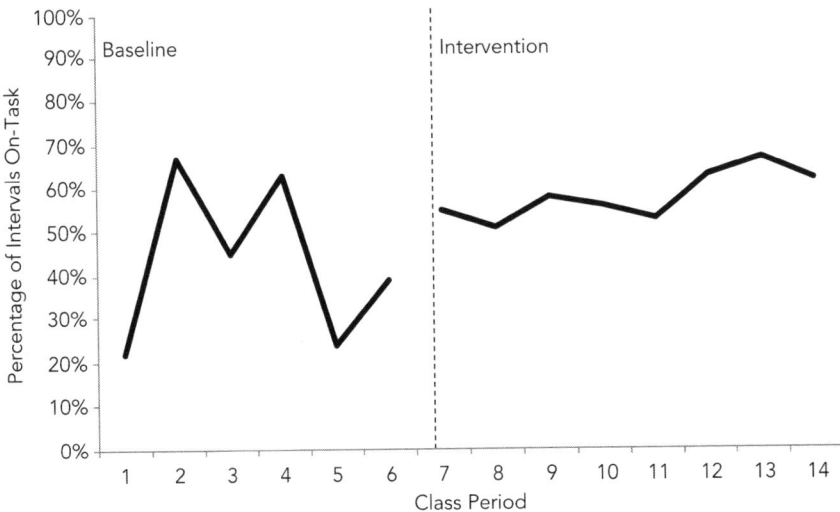

Figure 4.13 Example of a Variable Baseline Followed by a Stable Intervention Phase in an A-B Design

educators to go beyond just documenting change in the dependent variable. Determining causal relationships becomes more important when educators are asked to verify what intervention or instructional approach produced the change.

Experimental control helps assert that a causal relationship exists between the independent and dependent variable and, in an educational setting, documenting this relationship is noteworthy. Establishing experimental control allows us to conclude that the intervention had some causal effect on the target behavior. Even stating that an intervention was effective requires, to some degree, experimental control. With an emphasis on accountability in education, documenting that an intervention was effective through a formal data analysis process is preferred over anecdotal report. Furthermore, being certain that the intervention's effects were due to the intervention and not some random variable is critical when using a student's response to an intervention to help make special education eligibility decisions. As Riley-Tillman and Burns (2009) stated, "while the idea of documenting causality may seem novel, to avoid this issue with high-stakes cases is hardly defensible" (p. 9). School psychologists and other educational professionals are encouraged to consider the implications of not documenting experimental control. However, establishing experimental control must be balanced with limitations associated with employing SCED when evaluating educational outcomes.

Conclusion

Accountability in education means, in part, evaluating student outcomes and documenting change or improvements in student achievement and behavior.

Consequently, schools need an evaluation model that reliably, validly, and accurately measures student outcomes and is sensitive to change. Furthermore, schools must adopt a methodology that can determine causal relationships between interventions or instructional programs and those behaviors and skills that are important to educators. While establishing experimental control is not typically a priority for most practitioners, it might become more important under the current educational climate.

ABA provides a systematic framework for evaluating change within the context of learning and behavior, and SCED relies on repeated measurements of the target behavior, verification and replication, and the establishment of experimental control. This idiographic perspective appears ideal for evaluating student learning and behavior. Baseline logic and the SCED presented in this chapter offer a methodology to school psychologists wanting to establish causal relationships between interventions and outcomes to promote evidence-based practice and data-based decision making.

References

Armistead, R. J., & Smallwood, D. L. (2014). The national association of school psychologists model for comprehensive and integrated school psychological services. In P. L. Harrison & A. Thomas (Eds.), *Best practices in school psychology: Data-based and collaborative decision making* (pp. 9–23). Bethesda, MD: National Association of School Psychologists.

Axelrod, M. I., Tornehl, C., & Fontanini-Axelrod, A. (2014). Enhanced response using a multicomponent treatment for nocturnal enuresis. *Journal for Specialists in Pediatric Nursing, 19*, 172–182.

Bailey, J. S., & Burch, M. R. (2002). *Research methods in applied behavior analysis*. Thousand Oaks, CA: Sage.

Brown, R., Steege, M. W., & Bickford, R. (2014). Best practices in evaluating the effectiveness of interventions using single-case methods. In P. L. Harrison & A. Thomas (Eds.), *Best practices in school psychology: Foundations* (pp. 371–380). Bethesda, MD: National Association of School Psychologists.

Christ, T. J. (2007). Experimental control and threats to internal validity of concurrent and nonconcurrent multiple baseline designs. *Psychology in the Schools, 44*, 451–459.

Cooper, J., Heron, T., & Heward, W. (2007). *Applied behavior analysis* (2nd ed.). Upper Saddle River, NJ: Merrill/Pearson Education.

Horner, R. H., Carr, E. G., Halle, J., McGee, G., Odom, S., & Wolery, M. (2005). The use of single-subject research to identify evidence-based practice in special education. *Exceptional Children, 71*, 165–179.

Johnston, J. M., & Pennypacker, H. S. (1993). *Strategies and tactics for human behavioral research* (2nd ed.). Hillsdale, NJ: Erlbaum.

Kazdin, A. E. (1998). *Research design in clinical psychology* (3rd ed.). Boston: Allyn & Bacon.

Kratochwill, T. R., Hitchcock, J., Horner, R. H., Levin, J. R., Odom, S. L., Rindskopf, D. M. & Shadish, W. R. (2010). Single-case designs technical documentation. Retrieved from What Works Clearinghouse website: http://ies.ed.gov/ncee/wwc/pdf/wwc_scd.pdf.

Morgan, D. L., & Morgan, R. K. (2001). Single-participant research design. *American Psychologist, 56*, 119–127.

National Association of School Psychologists (2010). *Model for comprehensive and integrated school psychological services.* Bethesda, MD: Author.

National Autism Center (2015). *Findings and conclusions: National standards project, phase 2.* Randolph, MA: Author.

Riley-Tillman, T. C., & Burns, M. K. (2009). *Evaluating educational interventions: Single-case design for measuring response to intervention.* New York: Guilford.

Roane, H. S., Ringdahl, J. E., Kelley, M. E., & Glover, A. C. (2011). Single-case experimental designs. In W. W. Fisher, C. C. Piazza, & H. S. Roane (Eds.), *Handbook of applied behavior analysis* (pp. 132–147). New York: Guilford.

Sidman, M. (1960). *Tactics of scientific research.* New York: Basic Books.

Tawney, J. W., & Gast, D. L. (1984). *Single-subject research in special education.* Columbus, OH: Merrill.

Vannest, K. J., Davis, J. L., & Parker, R. I. (2013). *Single case research in schools: Practical guidelines for school-based professionals.* New York: Routledge.

Vargas, J. S. (2013). *Behavior analysis for effective teaching.* New York: Routledge.

Linking Assessment to Intervention

5

Experimental analysis (EA) is a methodological approach designed to experimentally manipulate variables to determine their effect on outcome measures (Fisher, Groff, & Roane, 2011). To use language from previous chapters, EA helps establish causal relationships between independent and dependent variables. The independent variable involves the systematic manipulation of different antecedent or consequent events (e.g., attending to or ignoring noncompliance, using different instructional approaches), while the dependent variable is a behavior or skill identified as socially important to the individual (e.g., compliance with adult instructions, oral reading fluency). EA can be a powerful assessment tool used to inform our choice of an intervention through the empirical selection of interventions. This chapter describes EA as an assessment method and provides a model for using assessment for intervention selection.

Experimental Analysis as an Assessment Methodology

Commonly used assessment instruments, like intelligence tests or behavior rating scales, provide little guidance regarding intervention selection. Standardized academic assessments, for example, only offer snapshots of students' current academic skills within the context of national normative data. While helpful in some ways, knowing a student's current academic functioning compared to same age peers nationally does little to help a teacher or problem-solving team determine what to do instructionally. In addition, non-traditional assessment models used to evaluate student performance and monitor student progress (e.g., curriculum-based measurement) fail to answer the question, 'how do I teach Hannah tomorrow?' In fact, teachers, often overwhelmed with the amount of data collected on students, remain unimpressed with how data are employed in schools.

Using experimental methods to demonstrate causal relationships between environmental variables and behavior is a hallmark of behavior analysis. More specifically, the science of behavior emphasizes analysis through experimentation. In practice, this experimental approach actively manipulates environmental conditions to determine changes in outcome measures. For example, Iwata, Dorsey, Slifer, Bauman, and Richman (1982/1994) used EA to assess the functional properties of the self-injurious behavior of nine children and adolescents with developmental disabilities. What was so significant about this seminal paper was that the authors empirically identified the function of each individual subject's self-injurious behavior by systematically manipulating antecedent and consequent events. Iwata and colleagues concluded that identification of environmental variables that maintain self-injurious behavior via empirical means might be important when developing individualized interventions. Subsequent research, over many years, has confirmed this point (see Fisher et al., 2011). Frequently, interventions for academic skills and social behavior require a high degree of individualization, as contextual features of the environment can vary considerably from student to student. For example, reinforcers in a classroom setting might be different for different students. One student's off-task behavior might be maintained by peer attention, while another student's off-task behavior might be maintained by escape from an academic task demand. Contrast that with the results of traditional assessments used in education. How can an IQ score inform our intervention planning? What might an oral reading fluency probe, administered to a student during an academic screening, tell us about which instructional approach is likely to be most effective? And how might a student's behavior rating scale profile be used to develop an intervention that addresses function of behavior? These traditional assessment methods, while helpful in understanding the degree to which a problem is a problem, fail to inform the intervention selection.

The practice of linking assessment to intervention, or assessing for intervention, involves hypothesis development and confirmation (Batsche, Castillo, Dixon, & Forde, 2008). In EA, hypotheses assert that one intervention or instructional approach will be more effective than another or that a specific functional property maintains a behavior. Confirmation relies on the empirical testing of that hypothesis and SCED is precisely the tool needed to establish experimental control. By actively manipulating the independent variable (i.e., intervention) and looking for changes in the dependent variable (i.e., behavior or skill), SCED provides a system of assessing the effects of interventions or the functional properties of behavior. Baseline logic, or predicting and validating via replication and reversal, offers a scientifically sound method of empirically selecting interventions. Thus, we can assess to make decisions about intervention and instructional delivery.

Selection of interventions has traditionally been arbitrary or random. Vollmer and Northrup (1996) noted that behavioral intervention procedures are often selected based on the preferred direction of the behavior change. That is, interventions for problem or aberrant behavior are typically punishment-based and interventions that target increasing appropriate behavior are typically reinforcement-based. Interventions might also be selected using a least-to-most intrusive continuum (Mace, 1994). Initial interventions would involve few, if any, disruptions to the setting. For example, behavior-specific praise might be selected because its procedures are minimally intrusive in the classroom setting. If behavior-specific praise failed to produce desirable changes in behavior, a more intrusive intervention might be considered, such as behavior-specific praise paired with a timeout procedure. Interventions are sometimes selected because of their support in the empirical literature or presence on a clearinghouse website. However, practitioners might find accessing the literature difficult and time-consuming, and interpreting the quality of the research could be challenging for those with limited training in research design. In addition, published group studies are often based on variable participant and setting characteristics that are rarely identified well enough to be of any value to the practitioner (Vollmer and Northrup, 1996). Finally, school professionals often pick interventions based on preference and past experiences, with little regard for effectiveness or match to the presenting problem. Furthermore, practitioners are drawn to intervention packages that are high on face validity but low on empirical support. Taken altogether, intervention selection is typically an uninformed process that often fails to consider assessment data, let alone link assessment data to intervention selection.

Experimental Analysis and Behavior

Imagine that two interventions, each with equal support in the research literature, are available and the school's problem-solving team wants to know which should be implemented with a student. Thinking back to Chapter 4, the team might use a multiple-treatment design to assess the differential effects of the two interventions on some outcome variable. After identifying compliance with teacher instructions as the target behavior, the team opts to test behavior-specific praise and timeout from reinforcement. To conduct an EA, the team would simply implement the two inter-ventions, along with a control condition (i.e., business as usual), in some counter-balanced or random order, observe the target behavior across time, plot the data on a graph, and determine, using visual analysis, which intervention was more effective and how the interventions compared to the control condition. Using Figure 5.1 as an example, the team might conclude both interventions were effective when compared to control but the behavior-specific praise produced higher percentage of compliance across all sessions.

The literature provides numerous examples of how EA can be used in school settings to empirically select interventions. Lalli, Browder, Mace, and Brown (1993) used an EA to identify individualized interventions for two students exhibiting SIB and one student engaging in high rates of aggressive behavior. The authors systematically presented interventions involving positive and negative reinforcement (e.g., contingent attention), ignoring, and skills training. Results indicated the EA was able to differentiate between intervention conditions and produce improvements in problem behavior, and conducting the EA in the students' natural environment contributed to valid results. Harding and colleagues (1999) used a brief experimental

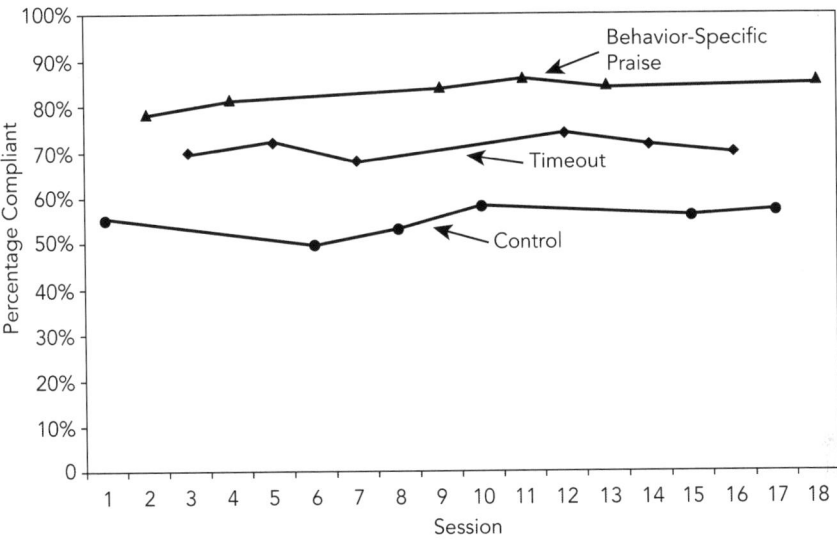

Figure 5.1 Example of an Experimental Analysis Involving Two Interventions and a Control Condition

analysis (BEA) to identify teacher-implemented antecedent and consequent strategies that improved the behavior of three pre-school children. Findings confirmed BEA as a method of empirically selecting interventions and the authors concluded that BEA might serve as a valuable assessment tool when determining how to proceed with treatment.

EA has also been used to test how different environmental variables, rather than specific interventions, might be manipulated to effect students' behavior. While the examples above demonstrated the use of EA for empirically selecting interventions, the methodology can also be used to empirically identify contextual features that might help inform intervention planning. For example, Smitham, Feller, and Horsham (2006) compared two conditions involving different positive to negative adult interaction ratios (i.e., high vs. low) provided to an adolescent with an emotional and behavioral disorder. Not surprising, the authors found that the student's percentage of compliance was higher when the interaction ratios were high. However, Williams and Schlueter (2006) found that lower adult interaction ratios produced improvements in compliance with adult instructions when compared to higher ratios for another adolescent with noteworthy problem behavior. Taken together, EA produced individualized results based, perhaps, on individual student differences and specific environmental variables. In the first study, the adolescent's appropriate behavior might have been positively reinforced by increased adult attention, whereas the adolescent's appropriate behavior in the second study might have been negatively reinforced through a reduction in adult attention. Said differently, the first student probably found adult attention reinforcing, resulting in improvements in behavior when contingent adult attention increased. The second student likely found adult attention aversive, resulting in improvements in behavior when adult attention was limited. Other studies have demonstrated that contextual features such as which teacher delivered praise or punishment to students, the form of feedback students received (e.g., public or private), and how adult instructions were delivered to students (e.g., verbally or in writing) might be manipulated experimentally to empirically identify important environmental variables that could be used in intervention planning (see Axelrod, Edwards, & Handwerk, 2006).

Experimental Analysis and Academic Skills

Daly, Witt, Martens, and Dool (1997) suggested EA could be used to empirically select interventions for students with academic skill deficits. They described a process whereby conditions based on hypotheses for academic problems could be developed and briefly tested using a multiple-treatment design. Daly and colleagues identified five reasonable hypotheses and possible interventions for those hypotheses (see Table 5.1). This procedure of 'test driving' various academic and behavioral interventions (see Witt, Daly, & Noell, 2000) has been demonstrated in the literature many times over (see Burns & Wagner, 2008). For example, Daly, Martens, Dool, and Hintze (1998) empirically identified effective interventions for three students with oral reading fluency (ORF) deficits. Specifically, the researchers tested an ORF practice strategy, an ORF modeling and practice strategy, positive reinforcement contingent on meeting ORF goals, and combinations of the three interventions by exposing students to each condition once until a clear differentiation in ORF emerged. Results indicated students responded differently to each intervention condition and that the empirically selected intervention was different for each student. The authors concluded a system of quickly testing interventions using a BEA was useful and that assessing intervention effectiveness might 'rule-out' possible ineffective interventions. Research since 1998 has confirmed the value of EA and BEA of academic skill deficits with different academic skills (e.g., math, written language, reading comprehension), student populations (e.g., different grade levels, English Learners, children with ADHD), and delivery mechanisms (e.g., parent- or peer-mediated) (Burns & Wagner, 2008).

Conducting an EA targeting academic skills is not complicated. Table 5.2 (p. 84) and Figures 5.2 and 5.3 (p. 85) provide an example of a BEA for math computation fluency. The two figures represent two separate ways of analyzing the data. Figure 5.2 displays the student's digits correct per minute (DCPM) following each intervention session. Figure 5.3 displays the student's DCPM before and after each intervention session, showing pre- and post-intervention performance for each condition. Results from the BEA indicate Copy, Cover, Compare (CCC) was the most effective intervention when compared to the other interventions and baseline. The student's DCPM following each session's intervention were higher during the CCC condition and the calculated difference between pre- and post-intervention DCPM was greatest

Table 5.1 Hypotheses Derived from an Experimental Analysis of Academic Skills, and Related Intervention Goals and Possible Interventions

Reasonable Hypothesis	Intervention Goal	Possible Interventions
Student is not motivated to complete the academic task	Enhance motivation and increase interest in academic task	1. Provide incentives and rewards for quantity and quality of academic task completion 2. Practice the academic skill using real world examples 3. Offer choice of academic tasks
Student has not practiced the skill enough	Increase practice opportunities	1. Increase practice opportunities 2. Provide immediate feedback (e.g., praise, error correction)
Student has not been adequately taught the skill	Change or modify instructional approach	1. Duet reading 2. Flashcards with feedback 3. Peer tutoring 4. Model (e.g., Listening Passage Preview) 5. Overcorrection 6. Copy, Cover, Compare 7. Use multiple examples
Student has not been required to complete the academic task that way before	Match instruction to curriculum	1. Use activities that allow student to use the skill in natural context
Academic material is too difficult for student	Match academic task demands to student skill level	1. Identify appropriate instructional level

during CCC. Consequently, we would consider implementing the CCC intervention with the student, assess progress over time, and make decisions about the intervention plan should progress stall or the student achieve some predetermined level of success. One option, should the student fail to make progress, is to conduct another BEA using similar or different academic interventions. While the literature is limited on the administration of multiple BEAs across time for the same student, there is research suggesting that it might be important to re-administer BEAs for certain students. Schounard, Sutton, and Axelrod (2012) and Butterfuss and Coolong-Chaffin (2015) found that for 9/12 and 7/10 students, respectively, the empirically selected intervention changed when BEAs were administered several months apart. These

Table 5.2 Example Protocol for a Brief Experimental Analysis of Math Fact Fluency Interventions

Condition	Description
Control	1. Teacher administers 1-min subtraction fact probe to student 2. Teacher scores probe, calculates digits correct 3. No intervention
Cover, Copy, Compare	1. Teacher administers 1-min subtraction probe to student 2. Teacher scores probe, calculates digits correct 3. Teacher provides student with CCC worksheet 4. Student studies the correct subtraction fact in the left column 5. Student writes the subtraction equation in the first blank column 6. Student covers the two subtraction equations and writes the subtraction equation in the second blank column from memory 7. Student uncovers the correct subtraction equation and checks for accuracy—if correct, move on—if incorrect, redo 8. Teacher administers same 1-min subtraction probe to student when CCC task is complete 9. Teacher scores probe, calculates digits correct
Taped Problems	1. Teacher administers 1-min subtraction probe to student 2. Teacher scores probe, calculates digits correct 3. Teacher provides student with TP worksheet and MP2 player 4. Subtraction equations are presented in recording, student listens and writes answers on worksheet 5. Student completes all problems in recording 6. Teacher administers same 1-min subtraction probe to student when TP task is complete 7. Teacher scores probe, calculates digits correct
Flashcards	1. Teacher administers 1-min subtraction probe to student 2. Teacher scores probe, calculates digits correct 3. Student reads subtraction equation on flashcard, writes answer on dry erase board 4. Student checks other side of flashcard for accuracy—if correct, places flashcard in 'finished' pile—if incorrect, places flashcard in 'to do' pile 5. Student finishes all flashcards 6. Teacher administers same 1-min subtraction probe to student when flashcard task is complete 7. Teacher scores probe, calculates digits correct

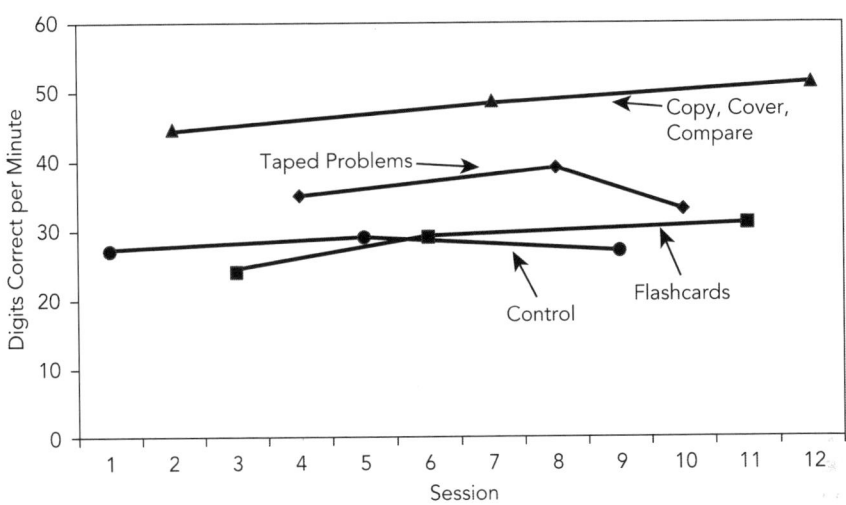

Figure 5.2 Example of a Brief Experimental Analysis of Math Computation Fluency

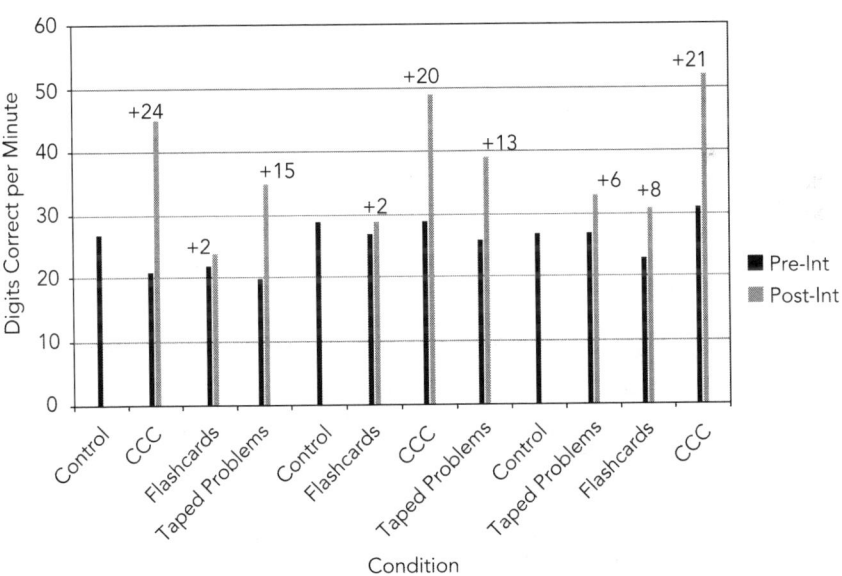

Figure 5.3 Example of a Brief Experimental Analysis Comparing Digits Correct per Minute Pre-Intervention and Post-Intervention

results suggested BEAs might need to be conducted at least every few months to ensure students are receiving effective interventions. EA or BEA data and progress monitoring information could be used concurrently to make decisions about changing students' intervention or instructional programs.

Functional Analysis of Problem Behavior

EA has also been used in school-based settings to assess the function of students' behavior. Function refers to consequential events that maintain a behavior. While there are an almost infinite number of possible consequential events, we learned in Chapter 2 that these consequential events can be generally categorized as either positive or negative reinforcement, or positive or negative punishment. Carr (1977) was one of the first scholars to promote a process of using the function of behavior to develop interventions. His review of the research on functions of SIB suggested that positive, negative, and automatic or sensory reinforcement maintained behavior. Carr also established that the function of behavior could be identified empirically via EA procedures.

Iwata and colleagues (1982/1994) extended the work of Carr and others by demonstrating a methodology for identifying the function of a behavior. Their study described a systematic process by which different environmental conditions experimentally assessed the effects positive, negative, and automatic reinforcement had on the SIB of nine individuals with developmental disabilities. A multiple-treatment design compared the frequency of SIB in four conditions: academic (escape from academic demands), social disapproval (attention for target behavior), alone (automatic or sensory reinforcement), and play (control condition). Iwata and colleagues observed the occurrence of SIB, watching specifically for conditions that might demonstrate an increase in the behavior, over many sessions. They found variability in responding across participants suggesting the function of SIB was specific to the individual participant.

Research since those early studies has confirmed the value of using functional behavior analysis (FBA) when attempting to understand the consequential events maintaining an individual's SIB (Betz and Fisher, 2011). However, FBA has been shown to be beneficial with other populations and problems. For example, the published literature on FBA includes children and adolescents with problems other than SIB and diagnoses other than developmental disability. More specific to school settings, studies have demonstrated the usefulness of FBAs for a myriad of inappropriate (e.g., aggression, disruptive behavior, off-task behavior, noncompliance) and appropriate (e.g., social skills, functional communication) behaviors (Ervin et al., 2001; Vollmer & Northrup, 1996). Moreover, students with a variety of disabilities (e.g., Intellectual Disability, ASD, learning disability, emotional/behavior disorder) have been assessed using FBA (Ervin et al. 2001; Vollmer & Northrup, 1996). Finally, procedural variations, such as conducting brief or one-trail FBAs, have found their way into the literature in response to claims that FBAs are too time intensive for school settings (see Gardner, Spencer, Boelter, DuBard, & Jennett, 2012; Ishuin, 2009).

Linking Functional Behavior Analysis to Intervention

While there is a noticeable and direct association between results from an EA and intervention development, the relationship between FBA results and intervention selection might be less intuitive. Figure 5.4 and Table 5.3 provide examples of a brief FBA with a middle school student to identify the function of off-task behavior when completing independent seatwork (e.g., worksheets). Results from the brief FBA indicate that the student's off-task behavior is maintained primarily by escape. Said differently, the most frequent consequential event when the student engaged in off-task behavior was escape of the academic task. When planning an intervention, we would not implement the condition that produced the most behavior. Remember, this FBA was designed to identify an inappropriate behavior's function and, as a result, required identifying the condition producing the most inappropriate behavior. Alternatively, we might consider using escape (the identified function) to contingently reward the display of appropriate behavior (i.e., allow escape but only following the desired behavior). For example, the intervention might involve permitting the student to complete only a portion of the worksheet contingent on compliance with, and accurate responding to, the academic task demand. While extending the intervention across an entire school year might not be advisable, the intervention could be systematically faded over time so that the student escapes fewer and fewer problems potentially resulting in an increase in both compliance and the number of problems completed. This example illustrates how knowing a misbehavior's function can inform intervention development.

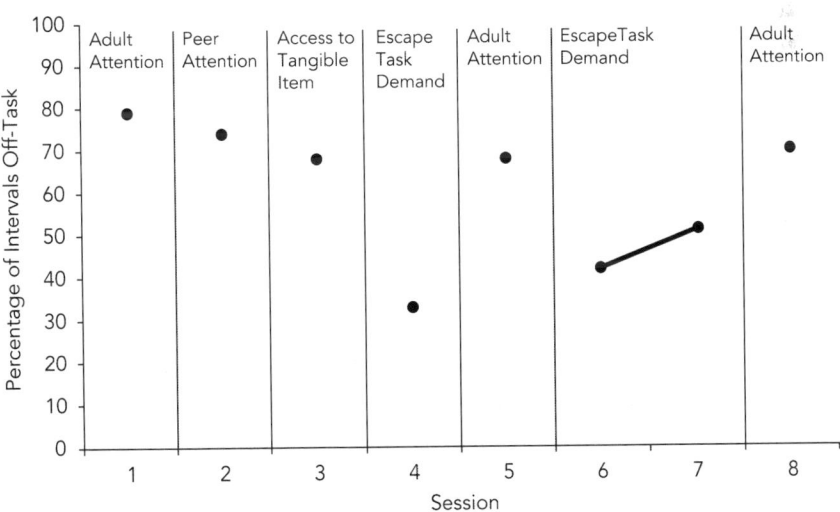

Figure 5.4 Example of a Brief Functional Behavior Analysis

Table 5.3   Example of a Brief Functional Behavior Analysis Protocol Assessing the Function of a Student's Off-Task Behavior During Independent Seatwork

Condition	Description
Adult Attention	Teacher provides 30 secs of verbal attention contingent on student's off-task behavior
Peer Attention	Confederate peer provides 30 secs of verbal and nonverbal attention contingent on student's off-task behavior
Access to Tangible Item	Teacher provides 30 secs of access to a preferred item contingent on student's off-task behavior
Escape Task Demand	Teacher removes the academic task for 2 mins contingent on student's off-task behavior

Functional Behavior Assessment

School psychologists and other school professionals often conduct functional behavior assessments with students who engage in aberrant or problematic behavior. Functional behavior assessments typically involve behavior analytic teacher interviews (e.g., interviews that focus on contextual variables, antecedents and consequences, discriminative stimuli), direct observations of student behavior (e.g., narrative, systematic), and surveys and rating scales (Steege & Scheib, 2014). While likely easier to implement than a FBA, a functional behavior assessment stops at the hypothesis development stage and because the method fails to experimentally test the hypothesis, results from functional behavior assessments are limited. However, practitioners in the school setting might be best able to conduct a functional behavior assessment given setting limitations (e.g., time).

Limitations and Considerations

Despite the potential benefits of conducting EAs and FBAs, they are not without their limitations. For example, some behaviors might not be appropriate for EAs and FBAs including low-rate, high-intensity behavior and behavior that is not often observed (e.g., stealing; see Steege & Scheib, 2014). Practitioners are encouraged to select behaviors that are exhibited at a high-rate, directly observable and measureable, and socially important. Some scholars have cited the time required to conduct a valid and reliable EA as a hurdle to more extensive use of EA procedures in school and other applied settings (e.g., Cooper, Heron, & Heward, 2007; Gresham, Watson, & Skinner, 2001). Others have suggested that implementing experimental conditions that might provoke or reinforce a potentially dangerous behavior (e.g., physical aggression, SIB) or intensify aberrant behavior (e.g., non-compliance) is problematic and possibly unethical (Cooper et al., 2007; Steege & Scheib, 2014). Specifically, the target behavior is reinforced on a continuous schedule, possibly resulting in high rates of that behavior, or FBAs could establish a functional relationship between a reinforcer and a behavior that was not present prior to the introduction of the FBA (Betz & Fisher, 2011). For example, providing tangible reinforcement in the form of a toy every time the student engages in inappropriate behavior during the FBA, when such a contingency was never present in the natural setting, could result in the student learning a new functional relationship that carries over to the natural setting.

Brief forms of EA and FBA have been developed that involve fewer sessions (e.g., one session per condition) than traditional forms (see Cihak, Alberto, & Fredrick, 2007; Wilder, Chen, Atwell, Pritchard, & Weinstein, 2006). BEA of academic skill deficits and brief FBA are both examples of how a shortened version of EA can be used to empirically select interventions or behavioral functions through exposure of students to multiple conditions once, identifying changes in the outcome variable, and using replication and reversal to confirm that changes in conditions result in changes in academic or social behaviors. While extended EAs and FBAs are preferred, the literature provides support for the use of brief versions of each approach (see Burns & Wagner, 2008; Gardner et al., 2012) and brief versions should be considered when either resources or time are scarce, or there is concern about increasing a problem behavior.

The need for well-trained staff members is also cited as a limitation, which might hinder the use of EA and FBA in school settings (see Cooper et al., 2007). Teachers' limited knowledge about experimental procedures and behavior analytic principles, the complexity of the procedures, and the limited use of EA and FBA in school settings likely contribute to a research-to-practice gap (Erbas, Tekin-Iftar, & Yucesoy, 2006; Flynn & Lo, 2016). School psychologists and other school professionals are not always well versed in the conceptual foundations of ABA, nor are they usually taught how to develop, implement, and interpret EAs and FBAs. Consequently, their ability to consult with and provide ongoing support to teachers is limited. Training programs are encouraged to emphasize the use of EA and FBA when preparing future school psychologists but should also consider other, equally important, domains. For example, ample coursework in ABA and SCED, experiences with behavioral assessment and direct observation of behavior, and skills associated with culturally competent practice should be integrated with supervised field and internship experiences (see Steege & Scheib, 2014). Furthermore, practicing school psychologists should consider seeking professional development and ongoing education in the areas of EA, FBA, and ABA.

Regarding consultation, the literature is rich with examples of how classroom teachers can be taught to conduct FBAs. Erbas and colleagues (2006) taught five special education teachers to conduct FBAs in classroom settings. Test conditions included teacher attention contingent on misbehavior (attention), removal of a task contingent on misbehavior (escape), free play (control), and access to a preferred item contingent on misbehavior (tangible). Their teaching model involved readings and a lecture on FBA, video modeling of each test condition, and regular consultation and feedback meetings. The authors found that the teachers' skills when implementing the FBA were low during baseline but improved following the training, and that teachers required intensive consultation on how to conduct the FBA. Results also indicated implementation integrity was lowest during the escape condition, which the authors attributed to the complexity of the condition. Finally, teachers' opinions of FBA became more positive after the training and implementation of the FBA. This point is perhaps most important, as teacher acceptability of FBA procedures could be associated with implementation fidelity and student outcomes. Other published research has found similar results when implementing a structured and comprehensive FBA training program that included didactic teaching of concepts and skills, modeling and practice, and ongoing consultation and feedback (see Flynn & Lo, 2016; Moore et al., 2002; Rispoli et al., 2015). School psychologists are encouraged to consider this service delivery option for students exhibiting problematic behavior.

Conclusion

Experimental manipulations of independent variables that include potential interventions or instructional approaches, or possible functions of behavior, allow school psychologists to be more efficient in the selection of interventions. While EAs and FBAs involve time and effort, untreated problems and ineffective strategies are also costly (Cooper et al., 2007). School psychologists and other school professionals are encouraged to consider EA and FBA as an assessment method, especially when wanting to empirically select interventions that are proven to produce positive outcomes with students.

References

Axelrod, M. I., Edwards, C., & Handwerk, M. L. (2006, May). Evaluating the effects of functional and experimental analysis on the behavior of typically developing adolescents. In S. Hirsch (Chair), *Utilizing functional and experimental analysis methodology to treat aberrant behavior in typically developing adolescents.* Symposium conducted at the meeting of the Association for Behavior Analysis International, Atlanta, GA.

Batsche, G. M., Castillo, J. M., Dixon, D. D., & Forde, S. (2008) Best practices in linking assessment to intervention. In A. Thomas & J. Grimes (Eds.), *Best practices in school psychology V: Volume 2* (pp. 177–193). Washington, DC: National Association of School Psychologists.

Betz, A. M., & Fisher, W. W. (2011). Functional analysis. In W. W. Fisher, C. C. Piazza, & H. S. Roane (Eds.), *Handbook of applied behavior analysis* (pp. 206–225). New York: Guilford.

Burns, M. K., & Wagner, D. (2008). Determining an effective intervention within a brief experimental analysis for reading: A meta-analytic review. *School Psychology Review, 31*, 126–136.

Butterfuss, R., & Coolong-Chaffin, M. (2015, February). *Evaluating the outcomes of brief experimental analyses at two points in time.* Poster session presented at the meeting of the National Association of School Psychologists, Orlando, FL.

Carr, E. G. (1977). The motivation of self-injurious behavior: A review of some hypotheses. *Psychological Bulletin, 84,* 800–816.

Cihak, D., Alberto, P. A., & Fredrick, L. D. (2007). Use of brief functional analysis and intervention evaluation in public settings. *Journal of Positive Behavior Interventions, 9,* 80–93.

Cooper, J., Heron, T., & Heward, W. (2007). *Applied behavior analysis* (2nd ed.). Upper Saddle River, NJ: Merrill/Pearson Education.

Daly, E. J., Martens, B. K., Dool, E. J., & Hintze, J. M. (1998). Using brief functional analysis to select interventions for oral reading. *Journal of Behavioral Education, 8,* 203–218.

Daly, E. J., Witt, J. C., Martens, B. K., & Dool, E. J. (1997). A model for conducting functional analysis of academic performance problems. *School Psychology Review, 26,* 554–574.

Erbas, D., Tekin-Iftar, E., & Yucesoy, S. (2006). Teaching special education teachers how to conduct functional analysis in natural settings. *Education and Training in Developmental Disabilities, 41,* 28–36.

Ervin, R. A., Radford, P. M., Bertsch, K., Piper, A. L., Ehrhardt, K. E., & Poling, A. (2001). A descriptive analysis and critique of the empirical literature on school-based functional assessment. *School Psychology Review, 30,* 193–210.

Fisher, W. W., Groff, R. A., & Roane, H. S. (2011). Applied behavior analysis: History, philosophy, principles, and basic methods. In W. W. Fisher, C. C. Piazza, & H. S. Roane (Eds.), *Handbook of applied behavior analysis* (pp. 3–13). New York: Guilford.

Flynn, S. D., & Lo, Y. (2016). Teacher implementation of trial-based functional analysis and differential reinforcement of alternative behavior for students with challenging behavior. *Journal of Behavioral Education, 25,* 1–31.

Gardner, A. W., Spencer, T. D., Boelter, E. W., DuBard, M., & Jennett, H. K. (2012). A systematic review of brief functional analysis methodology with typically developing children. *Education and Treatment of Children, 35,* 313–332.

Gresham, F. M., Watson, T. S., & Skinner, C. H. (2001). Functional behavioral assessment: Principles, procedures, and future directions. *School Psychology Review, 30,* 156–172.

Harding, J., Wacker, D. P., Cooper, L. J., Asmus, J., Jensen-Kovalan, P., & Grisolano, L. A. (1999). Combining descriptive and experimental analysis of young children with behavior problems in preschool settings. *Behavior Modification, 23,* 316–333.

Ishuin, T. (2009). Linking brief functional analysis to intervention design in general education settings. *Behavior Analyst Today, 10,* 47–53.

Iwata, B. A., Dorsey, M. F., Slifer, K. J., Bauman, K. E., & Richman, G. S. (1982/1994). Toward a functional analysis of self-injury. *Journal of Applied Behavior Analysis, 27,* 197–209. (Reprinted from *Analysis and Intervention in Developmental Disabilities, 2,* 3–20, 1982.)

Lalli, J. S., Browder, D. M., Mace, F. C., & Brown, D. K. (1993). Teacher use of descriptive analysis data to implement interventions to decrease students' problem behaviors. *Journal of Applied Behavior Analysis, 26,* 227–238.

Mace, F. C. (1994). The significance and future of functional analysis methodologies. *Journal of Applied Behavior Analysis, 27,* 385–392.

Moore, J. W., Edwards, R. P., Sterling-Turner, H. E., Riley, H., DuBard, M., & McGeorge, A. (2002). Teacher acquisition of functional analysis methodology. *Journal of Applied Behavior Analysis, 35,* 73–77.

Rispoli, M., Burke, M. D., Hatton, H., Ninci, J., Zaini, S., & Sanchez, L. (2015). Training head start teachers to conduct trial-based functional analysis of challenging behavior. *Journal of Positive Behavior Interventions, 17,* 235–244.

Schounard, C. A., Sutton, M. J., & Axelrod, M. I. (2012, May). *Investigating the consistency of results obtained from a brief experimental analysis of oral reading fluency.* Poster session presented at the meeting of the Association for Behavior Analysis International, Seattle, WA.

Smitham, S., Feller, G., & Horsham, S. (2006, May). Developing applied behavior analytic technology for use with typically developing adolescents. In S. Hirsch (Chair), *Utilizing functional and experimental analysis methodology to treat aberrant behavior in typically developing adolescents*. Symposium conducted at the meeting of the Association for Behavior Analysis International, Atlanta, GA.

Steege, M. W., & Scheib, M. A. (2014). Best practices in conducting functional behavior assessments. In P. L. Harrison & A. Thomas (Eds.), *Best practices in school psychology: Data-based and collaborative decision making* (pp. 273–286). Bethesda, MD: National Association of School Psychologists.

Vollmer, T. R., & Northrup, J. (1996). Some implications of functional analysis for school psychology. *School Psychology Quarterly, 11*, 76–92.

Wilder, D. A., Chen, L., Atwell, J., Pritchard, J., & Weinstein, P. (2006). Brief functional analysis and treatment of tantrums associated with transitions in preschool children. *Journal of Applied Behavior Analysis, 39*, 103–107.

Williams, K., & Schlueter, C. (2006, May). Treating aberrant behavior in typically developing adolescents: Consequent based interventions. In S. Hirsch (Chair), *Utilizing functional and experimental analysis methodology to treat aberrant behavior in typically developing adolescents*. Symposium conducted at the meeting of the Association for Behavior Analysis International, Atlanta, GA.

Witt, J. C., Daly, E. J., III, & Noell, G. H. (2000). *Functional assessments: A step-by-step guide to solving academic and behavior problems*. Longmont, CO: Sopris West.

Intervention Design and Implementation   **6**

Research on the use of evidence-based practices (EBPs) in schools is rather discouraging (see Ennett et al., 2003). Using unproven interventions or instructional practices, or using them but without fidelity is a problem. The successful implementation of school-based interventions requires more than simply identifying an EBP and, while the research literature regularly touts the latest and greatest interventions, schools and school professionals continue to find implementing EBPs challenging. Scholars have described this as the research-to-practice gap or the challenge of "translating research findings to everyday practices" (Cook & Odom, 2013, p. 138). Within the empirical research, variables such as implementation fidelity and teachers' skills implementing an intervention's procedures are likely addressed in well-designed studies. However, those same variables are under much less control when EBPs are implemented in applied settings. Fortunately, research exists describing practices that influence intervention selection, development, and implementation. Furthermore, school psychology and other professional fields (e.g., special education, clinical psychology) have begun emphasizing variables that contribute to the effective application of EBPs in their research agendas. For example, research on consultation in school settings identifies several consultant behaviors (e.g., collaboration, ongoing contact with consultee) that contribute to positive outcomes.

Researchers are placing more importance on the delivery of EBPs in applied settings by studying implementation features including developing innovative EBPs, communication between those who know about EBPs and those in applied settings, and unique features of the system (e.g., school) and intervention agent (e.g., teacher, school psychologist; Forman et al., 2013). However, these features are more universal and, while important to consider, provide little guidance to consultants recommending interventions with students right now. Instead, consultants are in need of variables to manipulate that contribute to the appropriateness, acceptability, and integrity of interventions. This chapter focuses on variables that enhance an intervention's delivery in school settings including quality indicators of effective interventions, the problem identification and validation process, and intervention acceptability and fidelity.

School-Based Interventions

When describing the environment's importance, Skinner (1953) said, "behavior must be appropriate for the occasion" (p. 129). For our purposes, this means context is significant when designing or selecting interventions. A poor match between the setting and the strategies employed will defeat even the most well-conceived, functionally driven, research-supported intervention. Within the school context, interventions are most effective when based on clearly identified and purposeful procedures that modify the environment in a way that changes behavior or improves a skill (Tilly & Flugum, 1995). The ABA literature has emphasized this framework since the late 1960s. Baer, Wolf, and Risley (1968), in their discussion of the dimensions of ABA, highlighted the importance of explicit and comprehensive intervention procedures or protocols and Bijou (1970), in speaking about how ABA can inform educational practices, underscored the significance of maintaining control over antecedents and consequences to facilitate learning. Empirical research, conducted through the decades, has confirmed that actively and intentionally manipulating antecedent and consequent events enhances student learning and behavior. Moreover, interventions or instructional procedures that are specific have a better chance of success than those that are ambiguous.

Conceptually, the importance of well-defined intervention procedures should make sense to the school psychologist. Just as ambiguous definitions of behavior lead to unreliable measurements, vague and unclear procedures lead to poorly implemented interventions. As Baer and colleagues (1968) suggested, determining the clarity of an intervention plan should be done by assessing whether someone could replicate the intervention and its effects by only using a description of the procedures. Moreover, a comprehensive intervention should include procedural guidelines for all possible contingencies. For example, a plan for managing a student's aggressive classroom behavior might state that the teacher escorts the student to the resource room but it is not exact enough if there are no descriptions of what to do should the student refuse, run out of the classroom, or bite the teacher.

More recent articles on the practice of school psychology have emphasized behavioral perspectives including the importance of addressing environmental variables that contribute to learning and behavior problems. Behavioral perspectives on human behavior submit that all behavior is learned (Alberto & Troutman, 2013). An emphasis is on the role the environment plays in shaping behavior and that changing or modifying the environment could have a profound impact on behavior and learning. As Skinner (1968) noted, the teacher teaches the student through the arrangement of contingencies of reinforcement. Related to intervention development, educators are most effective when able to influence variables that can be manipulated (e.g., schedules of reinforcement) rather than focus resources on factors that might be internal to the individual (e.g., cognition, personality).

Quality Indicators of Effective Interventions

The school psychology literature offers practitioners a comprehensive problem-solving framework. For example, the most recent edition of *Best Practices in School Psychology* (Harrison & Thomas, 2014) includes several chapters on problem-solving within a multi-systemic, tiered service-delivery model. Many of these chapters offer guidance to school psychologists and, more generally, school professionals on how to employ the problem-solving model within a school setting. Considering quality indicators of effective interventions, such as problem identification and analysis, is an important component of the problem-solving model. For example, collecting baseline data to establish a student's current level of performance and assess outcomes is essential to effective problem-solving, and intervention design and delivery.

ABA pioneered the utilization of quality indicators in its research and practice by emphasizing clarity and precision when defining problems. This is not surprising given ABA's roots and the early work done to develop a science of behavior. In the initial issue of *JABA*, Baer and colleagues (1968) outlined six qualities that differentiated ABA from comparable laboratory work: applied, behavioral, analytic, technological, conceptually systematic, and effective. These qualities stressed the applied nature of a behavioral science that strives to resemble methodologies and perspectives found in the natural sciences. Ten years later, Wolf (1978) presented ABA with a new term—social validity—which described a framework for considering the social relevance of ABA's goals, the social appropriateness of ABA's procedures, and the social importance of ABA's effects. These elements apply to developing and implementing school-based interventions within a consultative framework (e.g., conjoint behavioral consultation) in the following way:

- **Social relevance of the goals**: Agreement between the consultant and consultee or change agent (e.g., teacher, parent) on the problem to be targeted by the intervention.
- **Social appropriateness of the procedures**: Agreement between the consultant and consultee or change agent (e.g., teacher, parent) on the intervention's procedures.
- **Social importance of the effects**: Agreement between the consultant and consultee or change agent (e.g., teacher, parent) on what constitutes a successful intervention.

The remainder of this chapter highlights problem identification and verification (social relevance of an intervention's goals), intervention acceptability (social appropriateness of the intervention's procedures), and intervention fidelity (social importance of the intervention's effects).

Problem Identification and Verification

Problem identification is the first step in the intervention process and involves several features of the problem-solving model. Specifically, identifying and operationally defining the problem of concern, collecting baseline data, and validating the problem are initial stages in the problem-solving model (Upah, 2008). These processes are important because rarely do referral sources provide detailed descriptions of the problem, offer reliable information regarding the frequency and intensity of the problem, or contextualize the problem using normative references. Not surprising, best practices call on school psychologists and other school professionals to engage multiple sources (e.g., teacher, student, parent), utilize multiple approaches (e.g., interview, direct observation), and assess multiple settings when beginning to identify and define problems (Christ, 2008). A comprehensive assessment model that includes various sources, approaches, and settings holds great promise, as research confirms the general use of this framework by school psychologists engaged in consultation with teachers (see Newell & Newell, 2011). Furthermore, effective collaboration among a problem-solving team necessitates agreement of the problem and its definition.

Engaging referral sources to clearly and precisely identify problems is of upmost importance. Referral sources (e.g., school staff, parents) rarely speak about problems using behavioral-specific terminology. A teacher might refer a student to the school psychologist because of aggressive behavior without describing the behavior in detail (e.g., hits, bites). Consequently, aggressive behavior, as a behavioral definition, requires the problem identification interview to specify and refine the target. Asking questions such as 'what does aggressive behavior look like?' helps establish a visualization of what the teacher means by the term aggression. Referral sources might also suggest a student's problem is a result of some internal state. For example, a student might be referred to a problem-solving team because of anger. Anger represents an internal condition that is unobservable and measured only through self-report. Having referral sources speak to a problem in more behavior-specific terms is akin to asking them to describe the problem in a way that allows an individual unfamiliar with the student and problem to recognize the behavior when it occurs (Upah, 2008). Aggressive behavior and anger are just too ambiguous and vague to be meaningful when identifying a problem or defining an intervention's target.

Referral sources also commonly speak about a problem behavior as if the school psychologist already knows precisely what they mean. Parents and teachers might use nonspecific terms like off-task, poor social skills, or anxiety when describing the referral concerns. These terms can represent many behaviors, requiring further clarification. Teachers and other school professionals might also include their own conceptualizations of the problem when engaged in the problem identification process. For example, a teacher might suggest nonspecific internal variables (e.g., poor cognitive processing, depression) or functional hypotheses (e.g., attention-seeking behavior) that fail to adequately operationally define the problem in a way that allows multiple observers to accurately distinguish that behavior from other behavior. Again, asking referral sources to describe the problem behavior, in specific terms, helps develop an observable, measureable, and adequately detailed definition.

School psychologists are encouraged to use structured interviews that emphasize questions addressing function of behavior when defining the problem behavior (e.g., Functional Assessment Interview; O'Neill et al., 1997). These interviews typically focus on the topography of the behavior but also antecedent (e.g., 'what typically happens before the behavior occurs?') and consequent (e.g., 'what typically happens right after the behavior occurs?') events, setting events (e.g., task demands, noise, activity level of students), and previously attempted interventions (Cooper, Heron, & Heward, 2007). Furthermore, understanding the student's access to and history with reinforcement aids in evaluating motivating operations (e.g., deprivation, satiation). Erchul and Martens (2002) provide helpful questions that might be used as part of a larger problem identification interview. Specifically, they note that understanding and prioritizing behaviors, developing an operational definition, identifying target behaviors that impact students learning, and obtaining information to consider the behavior's function are all essential to the collaborative problem-solving process.

Rarely do referral sources have reliable data on the frequency, rate, duration, latency, or intensity of a problem behavior. Consequently, the school psychologist must next measure the target behavior. According to Upah (2008), there are three primary uses for baseline data. The first two involve evaluating the effects of an intervention and measuring student progress. The third aids in verifying or validating that a problem, in fact, exists. Problem behavior is frequently defined as a discrepancy between expectations and performance (Howell & Nolet, 2000). In practice, validation means identifying something as a problem by assessing the student's current behavior or skill during baseline and comparing it to some standard. Consequently, we are interested in examining the following:

1. Differences between the target student's behavior or performance and some standard set by the teacher, school, parent, etc.
2. Differences between the target student's behavior or performance and peer behavior or performance.

If differences exist, determining the magnitude of the differences becomes important. Doing so not only verifies a problem exists, but also helps the school psychologist understand how severe the problem might be in the context of others' performance or behavior. In practice, verification might involve the use of a flowchart (see Figure 6.1) to aid in intervention development.

Intervention Acceptability

Engaging in problem analysis (e.g., determining function of the behavior) and determining goals (i.e., negotiating what constitutes a successful outcome) follows problem identification, the collection of baseline data, and problem validation

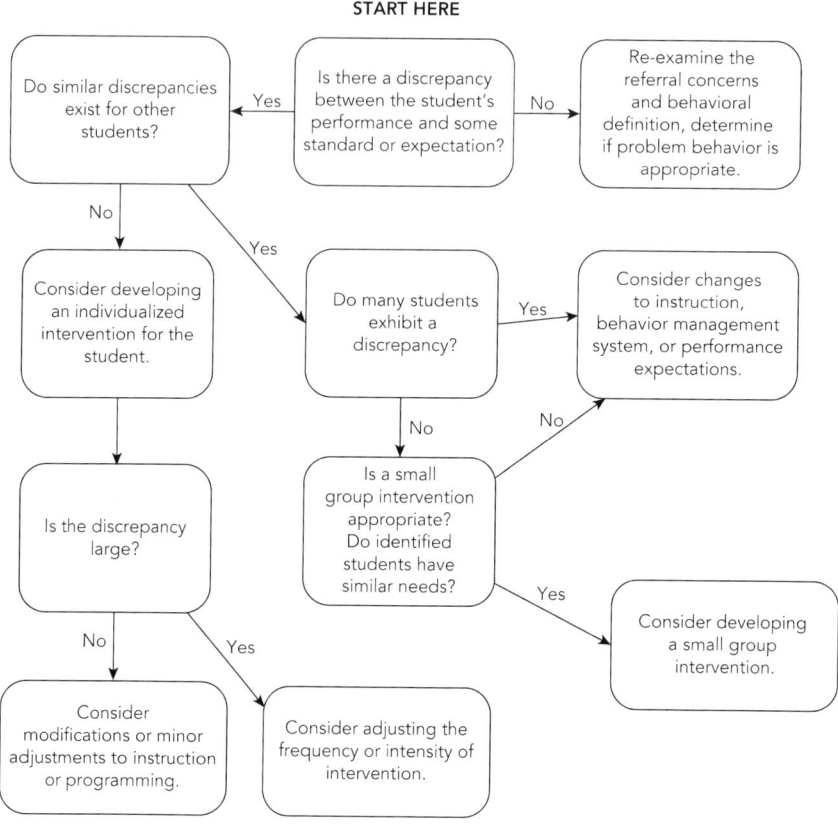

Figure 6.1   Problem Verification Flowchart

(see Upah, 2008). From this point, intervention development and implementation becomes the focus. When developing an intervention, school psychologists and other school professionals must be aware of the acceptability of their recommended course of action. In fact, change agents' (e.g., teachers, parents, students) acceptability of an intervention might be viewed as equally important as the literature's reported effectiveness of the intervention. An intervention's failure to enact change might have more to do with its acceptability among teachers, paraprofessionals, and parents than its reported effectiveness in the literature. Interventions that are not acceptable are likely to be met with resistance. Conversely, interventions that have moderate to low empirical support but are highly acceptable to educators or parents might produce positive effects for students.

Several authors have suggested various definitions and models of intervention acceptability. Not surprisingly, there is much overlap indicating a degree of consensus regarding a general framework for the term. Wolf (1978) hinted that intervention acceptability be equated with the procedure's social appropriateness and Kazdin

(1981) stated an intervention's acceptability involves judgments of "whether treatment procedures are appropriate, fair, and reasonable for the problem or client" (p. 493). Reimers, Wacker, and Koeppl (1987) described intervention acceptability as interactions between the target behavior, proposed intervention, and individual implementing the intervention, and offered a model that emphasized the consultee's understanding of and compliance with an intervention's procedures as a first step to evaluating intervention acceptability. That is, teacher and parent acceptability might be initially measured in terms of understanding of the intervention and the degree or level of implementation. Finally, Roach, Lawton, and Elliott (2014) described acceptability as a consultee's receptivity to an intervention's procedures. For example, disagreement among school psychologists and consultees (e.g., teachers, parents) when selecting interventions is likely associated with implementation failure. Taken altogether, intervention acceptability is best conceptualized as dynamic process that joins a consultee's opinion of, understanding about, and openness to an intervention.

Research on intervention acceptability involves two distinct methodological approaches. Some researchers assess intervention acceptability within a larger study of the intervention's effectiveness. For example, Axelrod, Bellini, and Markoff (2014) evaluated the acceptability of a video self-modeling intervention for three adolescents exhibiting high levels of noncompliance in a psychiatric hospital. After the intervention, the researchers surveyed staff asking for feedback on whether they would use the intervention again or recommend the intervention to other professionals. Staff were also asked about the level of difficultly implementing the intervention's procedures and to rate the intervention's effectiveness. Other researchers have used analog procedures to investigate intervention acceptability by presenting interventions to consumers (e.g., teachers, parents) hypothetically and asking for their opinions. For example, teachers might be provided with descriptions and vignettes of an intervention designed to increase on-task behavior and then asked to rate acceptability.

Researchers have identified several important and relevant variables related to intervention acceptability. For example, interventions that require a great deal of time or effort, and that are intrusive or disruptive to a routine have low acceptability (Reimers et al., 1987). While the literature provides little guidance as to what constitutes a low, moderate, and high amount of time or level of intrusiveness, school psychologists are encouraged to collaborate with consultees around these issues to ensure acceptability. Furthermore, an intervention's procedural complexity, including the need for multiple resources (e.g., people, materials) impacts acceptability (see Roach et al., 2014). Interventions that require less resources are more likely to be acceptable to teachers and parents. Also, interventions are most often rated acceptable when the problem is described as severe (Elliott, 1988). In fact, the type of intervention might not be important to acceptability when a student's problem is significant. For example, interventions targeting dangerous physical aggression, extremes in noncompliance, or significant academic skill deficits are likely to be accepted regardless of what is being asked of the teacher or parent. Interventions employing positive (e.g., behavior-specific praise) rather than negative (e.g., loss of privileges) procedures are more likely to be acceptable. For example, consultants might favor initially recommending behavior-specific praise for desirable behavior over loss of privileges for undesirable behavior. Finally, intervention acceptability is influenced by the reported effectiveness of the intervention (e.g., highly versus not effective). Furthermore, acceptability appears associated with the actual effectiveness of the intervention following its implementation (see Axelrod et al., 2014). For example, teachers are likely to rate an intervention as acceptable following success with that intervention. Consequently, a teacher or parent history with an intervention is important to consider. However, the consultee's hypothesis regarding a procedure's effectiveness and previous experience with the intervention will likely affect acceptability prior to implementation (Elliott, 1988). Best practices dictates that school psychologists and other consultants consider asking consultees about their previous experience with an intervention and hypotheses regarding its outcome with a particular student.

Not surprising, teacher background variables are important when considering acceptability of interventions delivered in school settings. Level of training and education, years of experience, familiarity with an intervention, and motivation all influence acceptability (Roach et al., 2014). For example, research has found that positive attitudes toward ABA coincides with increased knowledge about basic behavioral principles and increased acceptability of interventions derived from those principles (see Elliott, 1988). Moreover, acceptability is enhanced when a teacher fully understands an intervention's procedures and has been given a rationale for its use for a specific problem (Reimers et al., 1987). Finally, teachers with more experience find interventions less acceptable, regardless of intervention type, than those with less experience (Elliott, 1988).

School psychologists and other school professionals implementing interventions via a consultative model are encouraged to consider factors that affect acceptability. For example, modifying an existing intervention protocol so that it is implemented in fewer steps or less time might enhance teacher motivation. Furthermore, research exists indicating that providing knowledge or education to teachers might positively impact acceptability (Reimers et al., 1987). Providing training or professional development on ABA principles and paying special attention to rationales (e.g., 'behavior-specific praise can serve as positive reinforcement for a behavior we want to encourage or see more of') might improve teachers' knowledge and acceptance of behavioral principles. Finally, school psychologists need to consider equally both an intervention's reported effectiveness (e.g., 'is it an EBP?') and acceptability. Strongly supported interventions might have poor acceptability. For example, token economies are supported by research but are time and resource intensive. Consequently, a teacher being asked to implement a token economy for one student might be resistant despite the intervention's strong evidence base.

Intervention Fidelity

Intervention fidelity (or intervention integrity, procedural reliability) is defined as the extent to which an intervention is implemented as designed or planned (Roach et al.,

2014). In addition to teacher adherence to the intervention's steps, the literature describes intervention fidelity as the quality of intervention delivery (e.g., educator skill, decision making, timing of steps), dosage (e.g., how much of the intervention a student receives), and intervention acceptability. Intervention fidelity is more complex than a dichotomous model that indicates that the intervention was implemented either correctly or incorrectly. Roach and colleagues argued that both "the content (how much) and the process (how well)" (p. 134) should be considered when conceptualizing and assessing for intervention fidelity.

The importance of intervention fidelity cannot be overstated. Educators should not assume that an intervention was effective or ineffective unless the intervention was implemented with a certain degree of fidelity. Statements about the impact of an intervention on some targeted behavior or skill become complicated when intervention fidelity is poor. In addition, a relationship exists between intervention fidelity and outcomes. Not surprisingly, interventions implemented with low intervention fidelity have poorer outcomes than those implemented with high fidelity (e.g., Gresham, Gansle, Noell, Cohen, & Rosenblum, 1993). Finally, factors that appear to influence intervention acceptability also affect fidelity. For example, the intervention's complexity, and the time and resources required for implementation can have a profound impact on fidelity (Gresham, MacMillian, Beebe-Frakenberger, & Bocian, 2000).

Assessing and Understanding Intervention Fidelity

Intervention fidelity is typically assessed using checklists that provide clear descriptions of the intervention's procedures. Figures 6.2 and 6.3 show procedural checklists for an academic (i.e., oral reading fluency) and behavioral (i.e., self-monitoring) intervention. Peterson, Homer, and Wonderlich (1982) suggested that assessing the reliability of the independent variable can be accomplished in much the same way one might assess the reliability of a dependent variable. For example, school psychologists might employ a procedural checklist to guide observations and assess for intervention fidelity in much the same way as they might evaluate for interobserver agreement (IOA). Clearly written procedural checklists, like those in Figures 6.2 and 6.3, allow school psychologists to measure fidelity variables such as number of intervention steps completed and quality of implementation. In addition, school psychologists might develop rubrics to aid in the assessment of fidelity (see Figure 6.4). These rubrics could include degree or level of implementation integrity in columns, intervention components in rows, and specific descriptions of the intervention's procedures within each of the table's cells.

Directly observing the implementation of an intervention is ideal but not always feasible. When direct observation is not possible, indirect methods involving self-report rating scales, completed by a teacher or parent for example, or inspection of permanent products related to the intervention are appropriate (see Roach et al., 2014). Rating scales might include specific components of the intervention's

☐ Place the Phonics activity in front of the student. Place your copy in the protected sleeve.

☐ Say, **'I want you to read the sounds and words on this page. Start here** (point to the first sound/word) **and read across the page. Keep reading until I tell you to stop. You may not know all the sounds or words and that's ok, just do your best. Begin.'**

☐ Start timing for <u>1</u> minute when the student reads the first sound/word.

☐ Correct errors as they are made. Tell the student the correct sound/word and ask him to repeat it.
   • Errors are incorrect letter sound, omissions, and sounds not read within 3 seconds
   • If a student hesitates for 3 seconds, mark that letter as an error.

☐ Mark all errors on the examiner copy using the marker. Use a bracket ( ]) to mark where the student ended after 1 minute.
   • If the student finishes before the minute is up, ask him to begin again at the top and continue reading.

☐ After reading the probe, review errors again. Point to the first error and say, **'Look at this sound/word. This sound/word is** (tell the sound/word). **What sound/word?'** Continue for each error making sure the student reads each sound/word correctly.

☐ Add up the number of sounds/words read correctly and errors in 1 minute.

☐ Tell the student his score, and <u>mark it on the graph</u> (or have the student mark it on the graph). Record corrects with a dot, and errors with an x.

☐ Praise student for working hard.

☐ Say, **'Let's read again.'**

☐ Repeat this process <u>three times each session</u>. Make sure to erase marks each time on your copy so you can easily record errors each time.

☐ Once the student is able to read an activity in 1 minute or less with zero errors, he earns a prize from the prize box. Move on to the next probe.

Figure 6.2   Example of Phonics Intervention Fidelity Checklist

procedures (e.g., 'the adult delivered behavior-specific praise each time the student complied with a request') followed by a Likert-type rating system that ranges from Strongly Agree to Strongly Disagree. Examples of permanent products include calendars indicating when an intervention was implemented, completed forms noting what rewards were earned, academic intervention worksheets, or audio or video recordings of a letter-sound intervention. School psychologists might also ask teachers or other implementation agents to complete and return checklists that include all components of the intervention. These permanent products can be compared to one another to determine fidelity such as checklists of the same intervention completed by two different individuals (e.g., teacher and paraprofessional,

Self-Monitoring Intervention Procedures

Student: Sarah W.   **Teacher:** Mrs. Murray

Date: 3/14/15   **Instructional Period:** Math   **Time:** 10:00 to 10:45

Target Behavior: On-task/off-task behavior

1. **Provide student with the following intervention materials:**
   - Behavior recording form
   - Pencil
   - Auditory cueing device
2. **Set auditory cueing device to** ___5-___ **minute intervals**
3. **Remind student how to use behavior recording form**
   - 'Remember how to use the recording form? Check either yes or no depending on whether you were on-task or off-task. Yes means you were on-task and no means you were off-task. You do this right after you hear the beep. When you hear the next beep, be sure to check yes or no in the next row. You will hear the beep about every ___5___ minutes. This will go on for about 40 minutes or until we are done with math. Do you have any questions?'
4. **Remind student of the target behavior and its definition**
   - 'Remember, on-task means paying attention to the lesson or working independently on the assignment. This means you should be listening to me or a student talk, reading or writing about the subject, or asking a question. Listening means your eyes are on the speaker and asking a question means you're asking something relevant to the lesson or topic. You may also be out of your seat but only with permission. If you are out of your seat, you should be doing what you have been asked to do. If you are asked to sharpen your pencil, then you should be sharpening your pencil not visiting with a friend. Off-task means you're not watching the speaker, out of your seat without permission, reading or writing about something not related to the subject, or asking an unrelated question. Does this all make sense?'
   - The teacher might ask the student clarifying questions to ensure understanding.
5. **Remind student of the reward for accurate recording**
   - 'Also remember that you can earn __5 mins extra recess time__ if your recordings match my recordings six out of the eight times. Do you understand?'
6. **The teacher should start the auditory cueing device.**
7. **Student begins recording yes (on-task) or no (off-task) on behavior recording form.**
8. **Teacher begins recording yes (student was on-task) or no (student was off-task) on separate recording form.**
9. **When the instructional period is over, collect the student's behavior recording form and calculate percentage of agreement.**
10. **Provide student with reward if percentage of agreement is 75% or better.**

Figure 6.3   Example of Self-Monitoring Intervention Procedure Form

	High Fidelity	Moderate Fidelity	Low Fidelity
Provided student with intervention materials	All materials were provided		Some of materials provided
Set auditory cueing device	Cueing device set to 5 minutes		Cueing device set to a time different than 5 minutes
Reminded student of how to use recording form	Teacher read the statement word-for-word or accurately paraphrased the statement	Teacher read or correctly paraphrased some of the statement	Teacher failed to read or paraphrase the statement
Reminded student of target behavior, definition	Teacher read the definition word-for-word or accurately paraphrased the definition	Teacher read or correctly paraphrased some of the definition	Student was not reminded of the target behavior or definition
Reminded student of reward for accurate recording	Student was reminded about accurate recording and earning a reward	Student was reminded about either accurate recording or earning a reward, but not both	Student was not reminded about accurate recording or earning a reward
Started the auditory cueing device	Teacher started the device		Teacher failed to start the device
Recorded YES/NO on the recording form	Teacher recorded YES/NO on the recording form following all cues	Teacher recorded YES/NO on the recording form following some cues	Teacher failed to record YES/NO on the recording form
Collected the student's form, calculated agreement	Teacher collected form and calculated agreement	Teacher collected form but failed to calculate agreement	Teacher failed to collect form and calculate agreement
Provided reward, if earned	Teacher provided reward, if earned		Teacher failed to provide the reward, if earned or the reward was provided when not earned

Figure 6.4   Example of Intervention Fidelity Rubric for Self-Monitoring Intervention Procedures

mother and father, student and peer). Finally, teacher interviews might be helpful in gauging fidelity when direct observation is not possible and permanent products are unavailable. In addition, students might be interviewed to determine the extent to which they observed receiving a planned intervention. For example, asking a student if he or she earned a reward for appropriate cafeteria behavior might provide insight regarding intervention fidelity.

School staff are encouraged to directly observe intervention implementation as time, resources, and the context dictate. Complex interventions implemented by novice teachers might require more frequent observations than easy to implement interventions conducted by staff familiar with an intervention's procedures. Likewise, student-directed interventions (e.g., self-monitoring, peer tutoring) are likely to require more frequent observations when initially introduced. However, the frequency of conducting observations might decrease over time as the students become more competent at implementing the intervention.

Evaluating fidelity should involve conducting both an intervention component and session assessment (Gresham et al., 1993). Component fidelity is determined by computing the percentage of observations sessions in which each step of an intervention is implemented correctly. Session fidelity is the percentage of components implemented correctly during each observation session. Computing both component and session fidelity produces important data when providing feedback to the interventionist. Furthermore, both fidelity values can provide insight into anomalies in outcome data. For example, a student not responding to an oral reading fluency intervention implemented across several days might not be receiving critical components of the intervention (e.g., multiple opportunities to practice, immediate corrective feedback) or several intervention sessions might have been missed.

Unfortunately, little guidance is provided on interpreting fidelity levels. Perepletchikova and Kazdin (2005), based on their review of the literature, suggested fidelity levels over 80% (e.g., 80% of the intervention's components implemented accurately) are high and levels below 50% are low. However, they admitted that these figures were arbitrary. Roach and colleagues (2014) provided slightly different guidelines for evaluating intervention fidelity. They included five levels of implementation fidelity: greater than 95% (highest level of fidelity), 81–95%, 75–80% (labels 'satisfactory'), 51–74%, and below 50% (lowest level of fidelity). School psychologists are encouraged to consider these criteria but also consider local standards for fidelity and contextual variables that might influence fidelity such as the teacher's skill level and the intervention's complexity.

School psychologists should also consider that not all intervention components are created equal. That is, there are some components of an intervention that are essential to its effectiveness and some that are not (Sanetti & Kratochwill, 2009). For example, frequent and immediate behavior-specific praise may be related more to the outcomes of a behavioral intervention than the sticker chart, or reading directions for a math computation intervention verbatim from the protocol may be less important than the intervention's modeling and practice components. Consequently, low fidelity does not necessarily indicate the intervention was weak. It simply means that some components of the intervention were not delivered as prescribed. In fact, McCurdy and Watson (1999) reported data indicating that three students demonstrated improvements in behavior despite the behavioral intervention being implemented with low fidelity. When fidelity is poor however, a causal relationship between the independent and dependent variable cannot be inferred. Consequently, those charged with interpreting intervention fidelity data should proceed with caution and consider implementation and fidelity complexities when making decisions about interventions and students.

Improving Intervention Fidelity

Several authors have noted that consultation enhances intervention fidelity (see Roach et al., 2014). Within a consultative framework, school psychologists can establish a positive and collaborative relationship with a teacher to improve the teacher's commitment to an intervention. Moreover, collaborating with a teacher on the selection of target behaviors, interventions, and outcome goals might positively impact fidelity. For example, targeting behaviors the teacher prioritizes might solicit a high degree of cooperation. Descriptions of the intervention should be clear, concise, unambiguous, and objectively written (Gresham et al., 1993). Furthermore, intervention procedure planning should include assuring responsibilities and roles are clearly identified, and all materials are developed or secured prior to implementation. Finally, the school psychologist must ensure that adequate training and practice opportunities are available to those charged with intervention implementation. Verbal descriptions of an intervention's procedures are not likely to be enough to support intervention fidelity. Rather, support for teachers should involve written procedural checklists, modeling the intervention by someone familiar with its procedures, repeated practice until mastery is achieved, and ongoing consultation. Recognizing that intervention fidelity is poor should be best conceptualized as an opportunity to provide feedback to intervention agents rather than used to assign blame for why an intervention is failing to produce positive outcomes.

Performance feedback should be made an explicit part of ongoing consultation. Research in this area confirms the importance of performance feedback in maintaining high levels of intervention fidelity (Cooper et al., 2007). For example, Witt, Noell, LaFleur, and Mortenson (1997) found that fidelity decreased significantly after only ten days when performance feedback in the form of structured meetings between the teacher and consultant was not provided. Performance feedback meetings should involve a review of intervention fidelity and student outcome data, behavior-specific praise when intervention components are implemented accurately, corrective feedback and support when components are not implemented accurately or missed altogether, and additional collaboration to discuss any teacher concerns that might have surfaced since the previous meeting (Roach et al., 2014). Meetings should be scheduled frequently until an acceptable level of fidelity is achieved and between meeting communication should be done via email or phone. In addition, follow up meetings should occur even after fidelity has met acceptable standards and student outcomes have improved.

Conclusion

Designing and implementing an effective intervention within a school setting is not as simple as conducting a literature review to find an EBP. Issues related to identifying and selecting a target behavior or skill, teacher (or parent or other intervention agent) acceptability of an intervention, and implementation fidelity clearly impact an intervention's outcome. In fact, the interaction among these variables might have more influence over an intervention's effects within an applied setting than the degree of empirical evidence for the intervention. Consequently, research relevant to these issues, presented in this chapter, might be important when school psychologists are consulting with teachers and parents. Furthermore, guidance from behavior analysis might serve as a framework for school psychologists employing the problem-solving model.

References

Alberto, P. A., & Troutman, A. C. (2013). *Applied behavior analysis for teachers* (9th ed.). Upper Saddle River, NJ: Pearson.

Axelrod, M. I., Bellini, S., Markoff, K. (2014). Video self-modeling: A promising strategy for noncompliant children. *Behavior Modification, 38,* 567–586.

Baer, D. M., Wolf, M. M., & Risley, T. R. (1968). Some current dimensions of applied behavior analysis. *Journal of Applied Behavior Analysis, 1,* 91–97.

Bijou, S. W. (1970). What psychology has to offer education—now. *Journal of Applied Behavior Analysis, 3,* 65–71.

Christ, T. J. (2008). Best practices in problem analysis. In A. Thomas & J. Grimes (Eds.), *Best practices in school psychology V: Volume 2* (pp. 159–176). Washington, DC: National Association of School Psychologists.

Cook, B. G., & Odom, S. L. (2013). Evidence-based practices and implementation science in special education. *Exceptional Children, 79,* 135–144.

Cooper, J., Heron, T., & Heward, W. (2007). *Applied behavior analysis* (2nd ed.). Upper Saddle River, NJ: Merrill/Pearson Education.

Elliott, S. N. (1988). Acceptability of behavioral treatments: Review of variables that influence treatment selection. *Professional Psychology: Research and Practice, 19,* 68–80.

Ennett, S. T., Ringwalt, C. L., Thorne, J., Rohrbach, L. A., Vincus, A., Simons-Rudolph, A., & Jones, S. (2003). A comparison of current practices in school-based substance use prevention programs with meta-analysis findings. *Prevention Science, 4,* 1–14.

Erchul, W. P., & Martens, B. K. (2002). *School consultation: Conceptual and empirical bases of practice.* New York: Springer.

Forman, S. G., Shapiro, E. S., Codding, R. S., Gonzales, J. E., Reddy, L. A., Rosenfield, S. A., Sanetti, L. M. H., & Stoiber, K. C. (2013). Implementation science and school psychology. *School Psychology Quarterly, 28,* 77–100.

Gresham, F. M., Gansle, K. A., Noell, G. H., Cohen, S., & Rosenblum, S. (1993). Treatment integrity of school-based behavioral intervention studies: 1980–1990. *School Psychology Review, 22,* 254–272.

Gresham, F. M., MacMillian, D. L., Beebe-Frakenberger, M. E., & Bocian, K. M. (2000). Treatment integrity in learning disabilities research: Do we really know how treatments are implemented? *Learning Disabilities Research and Practice, 15,* 198–205.

Harrison, P. L., & Thomas, A. (Eds.) (2014). *Best practices in school psychology: Data-based and collaborative decision making.* Bethesda, MD: National Association of School Psychologists.

Howell, K., & Nolet, V. (2000). *Curriculum-based evaluation: Teaching and decision making.* Belmont, CA: Wadsworth/Thomason Learning.

Kazdin, A. E. (1981). Acceptability of child treatment techniques: The influence of treatment efficacy and adverse side effects. *Behavior Therapy, 12,* 493–506.

McCurdy, M., & Watson, T. S. (1999, February). *Techniques to strengthen the practice of school-based consultation using direct behavioral consultation.* Paper presented at the annual meeting of the National Association of School Psychologists, Las Vegas, NV.

Newell, M. L., & Newell, T. S. (2011). Problem analysis: Examining the selection and evaluation of data during problem-solving consultation. *Psychology in the Schools, 48,* 943–957.

O'Neill, R., Horner, R., Albin, R., Sprague, J., Storey, K., & Newton, J. S. (1997). *Functional assessment and program development for problem behavior* (2nd ed.). Pacific Grove, CA: Brooks/Cole Publishing Co.

Perepletchikova, F. and Kazdin, A. E. (2005). Treatment integrity and therapeutic change: Issues and research recommendations. *Clinical Psychology: Science and Practice, 12,* 365–383.

Peterson, I., Homer, A. L., & Wonderlich, S. A. (1982). The integrity of independent variables in behavior analysis. *Journal of Applied Behavior Analysis, 15,* 477–492.

Reimers, T. M., Wacker, D. P., & Koeppl, G. (1987). Acceptability of behavioral interventions: A review of the literature. *School Psychology Review, 16,* 212–227.

Roach, A. T., Lawton, K., & Elliott, S. N. (2014). Best practices in facilitating and evaluating the integrity of school-based interventions. In P. L. Harrison & A. Thomas (Eds.), *Best practices in school psychology: Data-based and collaborative decision making* (pp. 133–146). Bethesda, MD: National Association of School Psychologists.

Sanetti, L. M. H., & Kratochwill, T. R. (2009). Toward developing a science of treatment integrity: Introduction to the special series. *School Psychology Review, 38,* 445–459.

Skinner, B. F. (1953). *Science and human behavior.* New York: Free Press.

Skinner, B. F. (1968). *The technology of teaching.* New York: Appleton-Century-Crofts.

Tilly, W. D., III, & Flugum, K. R. (1995). Best practices in ensuring quality interventions. In A. Thomas & J. Grimes (Eds.), *Best practices in school psychology III* (pp. 485–500). Washington, DC: National Association of School Psychologists.

Upah, K. R. F. (2008). Best practices in designing, implementing, and evaluating quality interventions. In A. Thomas & J. Grimes (Eds.), *Best practices in school psychology V: Volume 2* (pp. 209–224). Washington, DC: National Association of School Psychologists.

Witt, J. C., Noell, G. H., LaFleur, L. H., & Mortenson, B. P. (1977). Teacher use of interventions in general education settings: Measurement and analysis of the independent variable. *Journal of Applied Behavior Analysis, 30,* 693–696.

Wolf, M. M. (1978). Social validity: The case for subjective measurement of how applied behavior analysis is finding its heart. *Journal of Applied Behavior Analysis, 11,* 203–214.

Changing Behavior Using Antecedent Strategies

7

Historically, ABA has emphasized manipulating consequences to change behavior. The systematic arrangement of consequential events can increase (i.e., reinforce) desirable and decrease (i.e., punish) undesirable behavior. However, seminal papers by Michael (1982) on motivating operations (environmental events that affect behavior, reinforcement, and punishment) and Iwata and colleagues (1982/1994) on functional analysis of SIB 'converged' to provide a framework for considering the role antecedent strategies, or interventions that address what occurs before a behavior, might play in changing behavior (Cooper, Heron, & Heward, 2007).

Educators have long known the value of organizing antecedents to improve behavior and decrease problems in the classroom. Teachers often arrange classroom seating so that two disruptive students are not near one another. Unlike consequent strategies that focus on events immediately following problem behavior, proactive interventions can teach prosocial behavior without the problem behavior needing to occur, which also decreases the possibility of students escalating their behavior (Axelrod & Zank, 2012). Moreover, proactive or antecedent strategies have the effect of quickly preventing or reducing problem behavior and are thought to promote generalization or maintenance of learned behaviors or skills (Kern & Clemens, 2007). Finally, proactive interventions might have higher social acceptability with consumers, especially when compared to reactive strategies. Teachers and parents are more likely to rate proactive interventions involving reinforcement as acceptable compared to reactive interventions that rely on punishment. Taken altogether, antecedent or proactive interventions might hold several advantages over consequent or reactive approaches when practitioners are looking to change problem behavior.

Chapter 7 presents several antecedent or proactive approaches to improve problem behavior or teach skills. Following a brief introduction to the topic, the chapter presents modeling, prompting, pre-teaching, issuing effective instructions, behavioral momentum, response effort, and function-based antecedent strategies. These approaches are categorized as contingency-dependent or function-based. Contingency-dependent strategies use antecedents to set the stage for a behavior or skill to be displayed and consequences to strengthen the behavior or skill. Function-based approaches capitalize on the relationship between a response and its function to improve behavior.

Understanding and Conceptualizing Antecedent Interventions

The chapter has already presented the terms *antecedent, motivating operation,* and *proactive* and, while these terms describe events or conditions that occur prior to a behavior, they should not be used interchangeably. The term antecedent, used in the three-term contingency (A-B-C), generally describes environmental events or stimuli occurring before a behavior (Cooper et al., 2007). Motivating operations are environmental events that either change the reinforcing or punishing effects of a stimulus or the occurrence of behavior that has been previously reinforced or punished by that stimulus. Motivating operations that increase a consequence's value are establishing operations. An abolishing operation is a motivating operation that decreases a consequence's value. For example, while hunger increases the reinforcing qualities of food (motivating operation, deprivation), having a full stomach might reduce its reinforcing qualities (abolishing operation, satiation). Proactive interventions are interventions that are delivered without the target behavior needing to be displayed. Proactive strategies that target motivating operations or setting events can be effective behavior change approaches in applied settings. For example, a teacher might make it easier for a student to complete independent seatwork by decreasing the length of the assignment, enhancing the student's access to instructional materials, or providing a peer tutor for support. These strategies decrease the student's response effort, which, in turn, increases the possibility that the student will complete the assignment. This approach addresses problem behavior proactively, while lessening the probability that the student will misbehave or escalate his or her behavior.

Many authors (e.g., Alberto & Troutman, 2013; Smith, 2011; Vargas, 2013) have included stimulus control in their descriptions of antecedents. Stimulus control (discussed in Chapter 2) describes a functional relationship occurring over time between a stimulus, usually something that occurs immediately before a behavior, and a behavior when that behavior has been reinforced only when following the stimulus. Prompting a student using pre-teaching (i.e., 'Kelly, we are about to transition from math to art class, which means we have to stop what we're doing now, put away our materials, and listen for instructions to line up at the door') plus behavior-specific praise for when the student engages in the appropriate behavior is an example of an effective stimulus control intervention.

Contingency-Dependent Strategies

Contingency-dependent strategies, such as stimulus control, rely on consequences to strengthen the stimulus-response relationship (Cooper et al., 2007). A classroom of students will quiet down when the teacher turns off the lights, not because the lights were turned off, but because their quieting down behavior was likely previously reinforced by the teacher when the lights were turned off. Chapter 2 describes stimulus control in more detail but one important point is that stimulus control does not happen unless the behavior that follows the stimulus is reinforced.

The following section focuses on stimulus control approaches that might improve behavior or be used to teach skills. However, remember that reinforcement is a requisite component of these approaches. Moreover, these strategies are only effective when students engage in the appropriate targeted behavior or exhibit the appropriate skill. For example, modeling alone will not likely improve behavior or enhance a skill. The student must correctly perform or approximately perform the behavior or skill so that it might be reinforced. Stimulus control or learning happens when a behavior or skill is modeled or pre-taught, practiced, and reinforced or corrected often over many repetitions resulting in correct responding.

Prompting

Prompts are antecedent stimuli that increase the probability of a behavior occurring (Cooper et al., 2007). Prompts are typically paired with differential reinforcement to strengthen the effect of the stimulus on the behavior. For example, a teacher wanting to have her class quiet down might consider prompting students nonverbally by turning off the classroom's lights and differentially reinforcing silence, or a school psychologist wanting to teach hand raising to an impulsive student might prompt the student by asking a question and then reinforcing hand raising behavior. Over many, or at least some, repetitions, the prompt becomes a discriminative stimulus. Not surprising, prompting has been shown to be an effective teaching tool for a wide variety of academic, behavioral, communication, and social skills (Noell, Call, & Ardoin, 2011). For example, Markey and Miller (2015) used a verbal prompting procedure to teach five students with ASD to use information-seeking skills in the context of a school library. However, prompts can also be visual, nonverbal, or physical.

Research supports taking a least-to-most approach (or most-to-least, the research on which is more effective is mixed) when prompting (e.g., Horner & Keilitz, 1975; Wilder & Atwell, 2006). 'Least' and 'most' refer to the level of restrictiveness, degree of adult involvement, or level of intensiveness of the prompting. Figure 7.1 provides a visual example of least-to-most prompting strategies beginning with using cues that naturally occur in the environment and ending with physical guidance (i.e., hand-over-hand assistance). Many least-to-most procedures utilize multiple prompts (MacDuff, Krantz, & McClannahan, 2001), such as saying, 'sit down,' while

Least Restrictive	**Naturally Occurring Cue**: Stimuli occurring in the environment that naturally cue behavior (e.g., bell ringing, other students putting away materials)
	Pausing: Teacher provides student time to respond, engage in a behavior, or exhibit a skill
	Indirect Verbal Prompt: Open-ended question to cue response or behavior (e.g., 'what do you do next?')
	Nonverbal Prompt: Nonverbal gesture to cue behavior (e.g., teacher points to door where student should line up)
	Partial Verbal Prompt: Provide student with some language that might prompt response, behavior, or skill (e.g., 'where should you line up?')
	Verbal Prompt: Provide student with verbal expectation of response, behavior, or skill (e.g., 'You should line up at the door.')
	Model: Teacher or other model (e.g., peer) demonstrates response, behavior, or skill
Most Restrictive	**Physical Assistance**: Teacher physically guides student, uses hand-over-hand assistance

Figure 7.1   Prompt Type and Level of Restrictiveness

simultaneously pointing to the chair. Using prompts to teach skills or establish stimulus control is made more effective when the following are considered:

- **Prompts should be as natural to the environment as possible**: Interventions that are minimally intrusive tend to be favored over those that require a high degree of adult involvement, many resources, and substantial changes to the environment. Regarding prompts, practitioners are encouraged to use cues already occurring in a classroom, such as verbal hesitations by the teacher to give students time to respond. Other examples include social interactions, nonverbal gestures such as pointing, and posted schedules.
- **Fade prompts as soon as possible**: Several researchers have recommended fading prompts quickly to promote independence and generalization (see Noell et al., 2011). Fading a prompt requires the gradual removal of the prompt so that student responses can become under control of more naturally occurring stimuli. Fading stimulus response prompts entails transferring stimulus control to a stimulus that is less intrusive and requires minimal adult involvement. Using a paradigm such as the least-to-most approach often accomplishes this transfer. Another fading strategy is stimulus shaping or initially teaching students to discriminate between two obvious stimuli and then gradually decreasing the difference between the two stimuli such that students can begin making subtle discriminations. For example, teaching a student appropriate hallway walking behavior might begin by introducing the student to walking and running. The student would then be exposed to less clear discriminations (e.g., walking with hands to the side versus hands waving around) once the initial discrimination has reliably been made.
- **Take care not to fade the prompt too quickly**: Be sure students demonstrate the behavior or skill multiple times before fading or eliminating prompts altogether.

- **Pair the prompt with differential reinforcement**: As mentioned earlier, prompting is more effective when combined with differential reinforcement. Reinforcement strengthens the stimulus-response association and potentially decreases the necessary number of learning trials.
- **Vary the prompts**: Teaching students to engage in the behavior or demonstrate the skill when different stimuli are presented varies the prompts, which might facilitate generalization.

Modeling

Modeling is a prompting procedure involving the demonstration of a behavior or skill (Cooper et al., 2007). This demonstration can be done just prior to the student engaging in the desired behavior or skill (referred to as *in vivo*), or represented through video or pictures presented at a neutral time (e.g., during a teaching session; Noell et al., 2011). Research on modeling suggests it is effective at teaching academic (e.g., Swain, Leader-Janssen, & Conley, 2013), behavioral (e.g., Axelrod, Bellini, & Markoff, 2014), and social skills (e.g., Matson, Matson, & Rivet, 2007). Moreover, modeling has been used to teach food acceptance to preschoolers (Hendy & Raudenbush, 2000), prepare children for surgery (Pinto & Hollandsworth, 1989), and increase verbalizations of children with selective mutism (Kehle, Madaus, Baratta, & Bray, 1998).

Modeling, as a procedure, is quite simple. The model engages in the behavior or skill while the student watches. Listening Passage Preview (LPP), a common oral reading fluency intervention, illustrates how modeling might be used to teach an academic skill. In LPP, the teacher or model reads a passage to the student while the student follows along. The student then reads the passage by himself while receiving corrective feedback from the model. Modeling compliance with adult instructions might involve having the student first issue an instruction to the model (e.g., 'please pick up the piece of trash and throw it in the trashcan'). The model might then say, 'okay,' pick up the trash, and throw it away. The student is then asked to follow the instruction after several successful repetitions of the model engaging in the behavior. However, modeling is most effective when students are required to immediately imitate the behavior or skill. Waiting too long between when the modeling occurs and when students are required to display the skill is likely to result in incorrect responding.

School psychologists might consider several factors when developing and implementing modeling-based interventions. First, the model should have the prerequisite behaviors or skills necessary to successfully engage in the target behavior or skills. For example, a peer with oral language deficits might not be an appropriate model when conversation skills are targeted for a student beginning to learn English. Second, the student must have imitation skills. That is, the student must be able to copy, exactly, the model's academic, motoric, social, or verbal behavior. Third, the student must be able to attend to the model or remain on-task for extended periods. Appropriate on-task behavior might be reinforced for students who struggle attending. Fourth, the student and the model should be as similar as possible (e.g., same age and sex). Furthermore, the environment where the modeling occurs should closely resemble the setting in which the student is required to engage in the behavior or skill. However, modeling might initially occur in an environment that limits distractions and maximizes success (e.g., counselor's office, resource room), and gradually move to the more natural setting. Finally, reinforcement should always follow the display of the targeted behavior or skill.

Pre-Teaching

Pre-teaching involves prompting a student by having a teacher or other adult describe to the student the context, the appropriate behaviors or skills expected during the ensuing period (e.g., a timeframe, academic task, transition from one activity to another), and the array of inappropriate behaviors the student could exhibit. Pre-teaching might include providing the student with a rationale for the appropriate behaviors or skills, checking for understanding, and reminding the student of the forthcoming situation. In addition, the student might be expected to practice the skill or demonstrate the ability to perform the behavior. Teachers and other adults are reminded to provide the student with behavior-specific praise or corrective feedback during the interaction. Teachers might also use preventative prompts (e.g., 'Do you remember what we do when getting ready for our spelling test?') when a student has already been exposed to numerous pre-teaching interactions. The following dialogue provides an example of a pre-teaching occurring between a student and her teacher:

TEACHER: Jenny, we are about to transition from free reading to lining up for art class. Remember, when the class lines up, I ask everyone to first put away their books. Do you remember what I then do?

STUDENT: You line us up by rows.

TEACHER: Great job, Jenny. Yes, I line the class up by rows. When your row is called, remember to walk over to the door, keep your hands down to your sides, and stay quiet. Do you remember why I want all of the students to stay quiet?

STUDENT: Yes, so that other kids can hear you call their row.

TEACHER: Well done, Jenny. You are getting very good at lining up. When everyone is in line, I'll open up the door and we'll begin walking down the hallway as a class. What are the hallway expectations?

STUDENT: Walk, don't run. Keep your hands down by your sides. Stay quiet or raise your hand if you need to say something to the teacher.

TEACHER: Anything else? How do you walk in line?

STUDENT: Oh yeah, you walk behind the person in front of you but always keep an arm's length between you and them.

TEACHER: Great job, Jenny. Because you remembered all the steps of lining up and walking in the hallway, I'll call your row first.

Research on the use of pre-teaching suggests it can be effective at improving behavior and enhancing skill development. LeGray, Dufrene, Mercer, Olmi, and Sterling (2013) demonstrated teachers could use pre-teaching plus differential reinforcement of alternative behavior (DRA) to decrease inappropriate, and increase appropriate, vocalizations for typically developing students in a classroom setting. The intervention involved the teachers reviewing behavioral expectations with students, reminding them to abstain from inappropriate vocalizations, checking understanding, and differentially reinforcing appropriate vocalizations and ignoring inappropriate vocalizations. Results indicated that the pre-teaching plus DRA was more effective than DRA alone for all participants. According to LeGray and colleagues, the pre-teaching procedure included additional learning trials for the skill and incorporated a unique discriminative stimulus in the pre-teaching interaction. Remember, however, pre-teaching by itself will not teach a behavior or skill. The student must still engage in the behavior or skill and the behavior or skill must be reinforced.

Issuing Effective Instructions

Student noncompliance is one of the most problematic and disruptive behaviors exhibited in schools and classrooms. Many teachers take a reactive stance to managing classroom noncompliance by addressing the problem from the consequent side of the three-term contingency. By addressing noncompliance on the antecedent side, a teacher can increase the probability a student complies with the request and decrease the probability a student escalates his or her behavior (Axelrod & Zank, 2012). For teachers, this means being thoughtful about how instructions are delivered.

Teacher verbal behavior is of paramount importance when issuing instructions. Teacher instructions should be brief, clear, and specific (see Chilcoat & Stahl, 1986). For example, 'please sit down' is favored over 'could you please take a seat so that I may finish speaking to the class about tomorrow's field trip?' Several scholars have re-commended enhancing compliance via the language used when issuing instructions (see Blum, Williams, Friman, & Christopherson, 1995; Walker, Ramsey, & Gresham, 2004). An example of this is by using 'start' versus 'stop' instructions (e.g., 'walk' versus 'stop running') and 'do' versus 'don't' instructions (e.g., 'voices silent' versus 'stop talking'), as verbal instructions are better for initiating an appropriate behavior than stopping an inappropriate behavior. Other examples include delivering one instruction at a time for tasks with multiple steps (e.g., issuing one instruction for each step), espe-cially for those students more likely to engage in noncompliant behavior or with atten-tion, developmental, or language impairments, and avoiding asking a student to do something (e.g., 'could you pick up the toy?'); rather, telling them what you want done (e.g., 'pick up the toy'). And finally, limiting verbiage to as few words as possible.

Contextual variables, such as the length of time or required materials needed to complete the task, should also be considered (Chilcoat & Stahl, 1986). Teachers should consider issuing only as many instructions as needed, as compliance decreases with increases in the number of instructions, and avoid repeating instructions to

---

Issuing Effective Instructions to Students

1. Get the student's attention before issuing the instruction.
2. Use a firm but nonthreatening voice.
3. Issue instruction using clear, specific, and simple language.
4. Give behaviorally specific instructions. Avoid using abstractions (e.g., 'be respectful') that might have different meanings to different students.
5. Do not give too many instructions at once or instructions with too many steps.
6. Do not phrase the instruction in the form of a question (e.g., 'can you pick up those books?') or use 'let's...' directions.
7. Combine the verbal instruction with physical prompts or guidance (e.g., pointing).
8. Use 'do' rather than 'don't' instructions.
9. Do not follow an instruction with reasoning or too much language.
10. Reinforce compliance immediately.

Figure 7.2   Issuing Effective and Avoiding Ineffective Instructions

students (Walker et al., 2004). Students should be disciplined appropriately when failing to comply with an instruction the first time asked. Teachers should also deliver instructions close in proximity to the student and use a neutral or unemotional tone. Finally, delivery variables, such as pace (e.g., speed that is matched to students' attention span and listening comprehension skills), fluency (e.g., use of short complete sentences), and pauses, allow for students to fully understand the instruction (Chilcoat & Stahl, 1986).

Behavioral Momentum

Behavioral momentum (BM) or the use of high probability command sequences can be an effective antecedent strategy for improving students' compliance (see Knowles, Meng, & Machalicek, 2015). These high probability command sequences involve a set of simple instructions with which the student is likely to comply immediately before the delivery of an instruction that has a lower probability of compliance (e.g., High-p, High-p, High-p, Low-p). For example, a teacher might ask a student to maintain eye contact, slide the chair closer to the table, and pick up the pencil just prior to asking the student to begin completing a worksheet independently (a task less likely to be complied with). Positive reinforcement (e.g., praise) is provided following each instance of compliance with special attention being paid to the low probability instruction.

BM could be used for most instructions a student is not likely to follow. For example, Axelrod and Zank (2012), in evaluating the efficacy of BM in a general education setting with students with emotional and behavioral disorders, empirically identified instructions that were antecedents to noncompliance. These instructions were assessed prior to the intervention and included typical instructions issued in a classroom (e.g., continue working on or begin completing an academic assignment, go back to your desk, stop talking, and put toys away). High probability instructions generally involved low effort behavior (e.g., put down or pick up pencil, give teacher high five).

There are several explanations for why BM might be effective. First, task interspersal strategies have been found to be effective for improving behavior. Horner, Day, Sprague, O'Brien, and Heathfield (1991) found interspersing difficult tasks with easy to complete tasks decreased rates of SIB and aggression. BM scatters low probability instructions within many high probability instructions. Second, increased compliance with low probability instructions might be a result of the momentum established from the preceding high probability instructions. Several brief request-response-reinforcement (RRR) trials is thought to serve as an antecedent that increases the probability students will comply with the low probability instruction (Oliver & Skinner, 2002). Third, the high probability instructional sequence leads to increases in reinforcement associated with compliance as a response class regardless of the type of request (Axelrod & Zank, 2012). Consequently, the student is more likely to comply with the low probability instructions. Finally, exposure to multiple RRR trials might establish a learning history that increases the probability the student will comply with future instructions.

Increasing Response Effort

Basic and applied research has found that making a behavior more effortful decreases the probability the behavior is exhibited, while making a behavior less effortful increases the probability the behavior is exhibited (Friman & Poling, 1995). Said differently, we engage more in behaviors or tasks we find easy to complete. Manipulating response effort as a strategy to increase desirable behavior and decrease undesirable behavior can be quite effective. Horner, Sprague, O'Brien, and Heathfield (1990) taught a 14-year-old boy with Intellectual Disability two methods of seeking teacher assistance using a communication device: typing 'help please' (high effort) and hitting one key (low effort). Not surprising, the student engaged in significantly less aggressive behavior when required to ask for help using the one key method.

Manipulating response effort can be easily achieved in a classroom setting by creative teachers. Increasing response effort to decrease behavior might involve requiring students to complete argument worksheets when wanting to argue about an adult decision or engage in switching tasks (e.g., brief academic tasks) when wanting to move impulsively from one activity to another (see Jacobsen, Bushell, & Risley, 1969). Decreasing response effort to increase behavior might involve making it easier for students to access instructional or academic materials, providing students with organizational supports (e.g., scaffolding notes), or allowing easy access to academic supports (e.g., peer tutors, calculators, web-based dictionaries).

Function-Based Strategies

School psychologists can work to align the intervention with a function when the behavior's function is known. For example, increasing the teacher's use of behavior-specific praise might be appropriate for a student engaging in problem behavior reinforced by teacher attention. However, developing interventions becomes more complicated when the function of the problem behavior is avoidance or escape. This section will focus on two function-based strategies: noncontingent reinforcement when attention is the function, and eliminating or fading in aversive stimuli and altering aversive stimuli or content when avoidance or escape is the function.

Noncontingent Reinforcement

Noncontingent reinforcement (NCR) involves delivering reinforcement independent of the individual's response (Smith, 2011). According to Cooper and colleagues (2007), NCR "may effectively diminish problem behaviors because the reinforcers that maintain the problem behavior are available freely and frequently" (p. 489). The underlying principle of NCR is that by flooding the individual's environment with a consequence that has historically followed the problem behavior, the problem behavior is no longer needed to elicit the reinforcer. For example, a student engaging in problem behavior that accesses teacher attention might be provided with teacher attention noncontingently using a fixed- or variable-interval schedule.

NCR is often equated with positive reinforcement. However, negative reinforcement can also be delivered noncontingently. Noncontingent negative reinforcement is most often used to allow escape when the behavior is dangerous (e.g., SIB). Most authors categorize NCR functionally; NCR with positive reinforcement is best used when the function of a problem behavior is attention or access to tangible items, and negative reinforcement is appropriate when the function involves avoidance or escape of an aversive stimulus (see Cooper et al., 2007; Smith, 2011). NCR is most frequently used with individuals with ASD or significant development or intellectual disabilities. Smith's discussion of NCR focused solely on using the procedure with individuals with ASD. However, NCR can be used to improve behavior of typically developing students when systematically applied. Practitioners considering NCR should pay attention to the schedule in which the NCR is delivered. Younger students or students with more severe behavior problems might require a very dense schedule of NCR that is then gradually thinned. For students exhibiting less severe problem behavior, the initial NCR schedule might be 15 minutes and either made dense if the behavior continues or worsens, or thinned if the behavior improves.

Eliminating or Fading in Aversive Stimuli

Avoidance or escape of an aversive task often follows student noncompliance (e.g., not following an instruction). The literature provides many examples where undesirable behaviors occur in the presence of some task demand and are absent when the demand is lifted (Smith, 2011). However, while the function might appear obvious, a solution is often difficult to find. Is the teacher expected to let the student out of the assignment by removing the demand (i.e., aversive stimuli)? If the teacher does, the problem behavior will likely go away. However, the student continues to avoid the task, which is problematic especially when the task involves academics. Moreover, the student quickly learns the problem behavior will likely result in the removal of the task demand.

However, removing the aversive stimulus might make sense in some cases. For example, removing the task demand on a temporary basis might be appropriate when the student's behavior is extreme or unsafe. Schools can begin reintroducing the aversive stimulus back into the environment once plans are made on how best to address the problem behavior. Researchers have also recommended the elimination of the aversive stimulus when the student has a medical (e.g., allergies, gastrointestinal upset) or another condition (e.g., sleep deprivation) that may be related to negatively reinforced behavior (Smith, 2011). Again, schools can reintroduce the stimuli once the conditions have been treated appropriately.

Gradually fading in the aversive stimulus is another method for managing behavior maintained by avoidance or escape. Fading in involves measured and systematic reintroduction of the aversive stimulus into the student's environment (Smith, 2011). Most often, the fading in of an aversive stimulus follows its elimination and is paired with extinction procedures. For example, a teacher might initially eliminate all task demands and then gradually and systematically fade in tasks on some predetermined schedule (e.g., fixed- or variable-interval), while, at the same time, ignoring the inappropriate behavior. The gradual fading in of the aversive stimuli appears to reduce the averseness of the stimuli, although the mechanisms underlying the procedure are not well understood (Smith, 2011). Research on fading in aversive stimuli is positive (e.g., Zarcone et al., 1993) but inconclusive when not paired with extinction (see Smith, 2011). Moreover, fading in task demands is not likely to be effective without reinforcing compliance with task demands.

However, the gradual fading in of the aversive stimulus when not paired with extinction might be useful in some academic contexts when the problem behavior is being maintained by avoidance or escape. For example, a student refusing to complete a math worksheet might simply be asked to complete one problem. The aversive task (i.e., math problems) is substantially changed, potentially making the task less aversive. After the student completes a one problem worksheet for, say, a week, the teacher would then introduce a math worksheet with only two or three problems. This process would continue until the student is compliant with completing the entire worksheet. In this example, compliance with the task, albeit reduced considerably from the initial request, is reinforced via the student's permitted escape from the remaining math problems. The procedure might also be paired with an incentive. For example, the student's compliance with completing one problem might be rewarded with some preferred activity such as playing a game.

Practitioners are encouraged to consider the elimination and then gradual fading in of aversive stimuli only when the problem behavior is not managed by other strategies or is sufficiently dangerous or unsafe. Academic task demands where the student has refused to complete even one problem over several days, might be substantially reduced initially with a plan to gradually and systematically fade in additional problems.

Although perhaps initially unacceptable to a teacher, having the student complete even just one math problem when previously completing zero math problems amounts to a 100% increase in problems completed and might represent a small step forward.

Modifying Aversive Stimuli

Again, students frequently engage in problem behavior leading to avoidance or escape of an aversive stimulus, typically a task demand such as an academic assignment. Eliminating and then gradually fading in the assignment or eliminating the assignment altogether might not be feasible or acceptable to the teacher. However, it might be possible to change or modify the aversive stimuli or its content. School psychologists and teachers can work together within a problem-solving paradigm to identify and alter stimuli students find aversive.

Researchers have found that changing or modifying aversive stimuli can have a positive effect on students' problem behavior. Ervin, DuPaul, Kern, and Friman (1998) modified a student's writing assignments by having him type on a computer rather than write by hand after conducting a functional assessment that suggested the student's behavior was maintained by avoiding or escaping writing tasks. The researchers found the student's on-task behavior improved dramatically when allowed to use the computer to complete the assignment. The aversive nature of the writing tasks appeared to decrease when the stimulus was changed from writing to typing on a computer.

Ervin and colleagues' (1998) study is an example of how practitioners might manipulate the aversive stimulus itself. However, it might not be feasible to modify the context so that the student is able to avoid the aversive stimulus. Furthermore, simply changing the aversive stimulus to something presumably less aversive might not always lead to improvements in behavior. In such cases, school psychologists might consider modifying features of the environment that decrease the aversive properties of the stimuli. For example, the student might be provided with a choice when the stimuli are aversive and evoke escape-maintained problem behavior.

There is an abundant literature which suggests providing opportunities for choice decreases students' problem behavior. Much of the literature investigates task order (e.g., how does the student want to order the assigned tasks) or either/or choices (e.g., which of these two tasks does the student want to complete) as the intervention. Research supports using choice as an intervention for problem behavior. A meta-analysis of single case design studies by Shogren, Faggella-Luby, Bae, and Wehmeyer (2004) found that providing children with choice resulted in noteworthy decreases in problem behavior in almost 75% of cases and reductions to near zero levels in almost half of cases. Furthermore, the researchers found that the type of choice (e.g., task order or either/or) had little effect on the results, suggesting both procedures were efficacious. Finally, choice interventions implemented following a functional assessment or analysis were more effective when escape was determined to be the consequence of the problem behavior. Interestingly, Vaughn and Horner

(1997) found that offering a choice of only less-preferred tasks that evoked escape-maintained behavior might be equally effective for some students when compared to a choice of highly-preferred tasks. Said differently, reinforcing desirable behavior using either highly-preferred tasks or less-preferred tasks that allow for escape of aversive stimuli might be equally effective at increasing desirable behavior for some students.

Conclusion

Proactive strategies hold several advantages over reactive approaches for managing problem behavior and teaching skills. In addition to not needing the problem behavior to occur in order to teach skills, proactive strategies prevent problems from starting or escalating, might promote generalization, and could be more socially acceptable to teachers and parent than reactive strategies. Furthermore, proactive strategies, including those that rely on contingencies to shape behavior, have strong support in the EBP literature. Finally, proactive strategies are easily combined with one another (e.g., pre-teaching and BM) or specific consequent strategies such as positive and negative reinforcement. School psychologists might consider initially recommending proactive strategies for behavior change, skill enhancement, and learning. Effective and socially acceptable to consultees, the antecedent strategies presented in this chapter have the likelihood of bringing about positive change in the school environment.

References

Alberto, P. A., & Troutman, A. C. (2013). *Applied behavior analysis for teachers* (9th ed.). Upper Saddle River, NJ: Pearson.

Axelrod, M. I., Bellini, S., & Markoff, K. (2014). Video self-modeling: A promising strategy for noncompliant children. *Behavior Modification, 38*, 567–586.

Axelrod, M. I., & Zank, A. J. (2012). Increasing classroom compliance: Using a high-probability command sequence with noncompliant students. *Journal of Behavioral Education, 21*, 119–133.

Blum, N. J., Williams, G. E., Friman, P. C., Christopherson, E. R. (1995). Disciplining young children: The role of verbal instructions and reasoning. *Pediatrics, 96*, 336–341.

Chilcoat, G. W., & Stahl, R. J. (1986). A framework for giving clear directions: Effective teacher verbal behavior. *The Clearing House, 60*, 107–109.

Cooper, J., Heron, T., & Heward, W. (2007). *Applied behavior analysis* (2nd ed.). Upper Saddle River, NJ: Merrill/Pearson Education.

Ervin, R. A., DuPaul, G. J., Kern, L., & Friman, P. C. (1998). Classroom-based functional and adjunctive assessments: Proactive approaches to intervention selection for adolescents with attention deficit hyperactivity disorder. *Journal of Applied Behavior Analysis, 37*, 65–78.

Friman, P. C., & Poling, A. (1995). Making life easier with effort: Basic findings and applied research on response effort. *Journal of Applied Behavior Analysis, 28*, 583–590.

Hendy, H. M., & Raudenbush, B. (2000). Effectiveness of teacher modeling to encourage food acceptance in preschool children. *Appetite, 34*, 61–76.

Horner, R., Day, H., Sprague, J., O'Brien, M., & Heathfield, L. (1991). Interspersed requests: A nonaversive procedure for reducing aggression and self-injury during instructions. *Journal of Applied Behavior Analysis, 24,* 265–278.

Horner, R. D., & Keilitz, I. (1975). Training mentally retarded adolescents to brush their teeth. *Journal of Applied Behavior Analysis, 8,* 301–309.

Horner, R. H., Sprague, J. R., O'Brien, M., & Heathfield, L. T. (1990). The role of response efficiency in the reduction of problem behaviors through functional equivalence training: A case study. *Journal of the Association for Persons with Severe Handicaps, 15,* 91–97.

Iwata, B. A., Dorsey, M. F., Slifer, K. J., Bauman, K. E., & Richman, G. S. (1982/1994). Toward a functional analysis of self-injury. *Journal of Applied Behavior Analysis, 27,* 197–209. (Reprinted from *Analysis and Intervention in Developmental Disabilities, 2,* 3–20, 1982.)

Jacobsen, J. M., Bushell, D., & Risley, T. (1969). Switching requirements in a Head Start classroom. *Journal of Applied Behavior Analysis, 2,* 43–47.

Kehle, T. J., Madaus, M. R., Baratta, V. S., & Bray, M. A. (1998). Augmented self-modeling as a treatment for children with selective mutism. *Journal of School Psychology, 36,* 247–260.

Kern, L., & Clemens, N. H. (2007). Antecedent strategies to promote appropriate classroom behavior. *Psychology in the Schools, 44,* 65–75.

Knowles, C., Meng, P., & Machalicek, W. (2015). Task sequencing for students with emotional and behavioral disorders: A systematic review. *Behavior Modification, 39,* 136–166.

LeGray, M. W., Dufrene, B. A., Mercer, S., Olmi, D. J., & Sterling, H. (2013). Differential reinforcement of alternative behavior in center-based classrooms: Evaluation of pre-teaching the alternative behavior. *Journal of Behavioral Education, 22,* 85–102.

MacDuff, G. S., Krantz, P. J., & McClannahan, L. E. (2001). Prompts and prompt-fading strategies for people with autism. In C. Maurice, G. Green, & R. M. Foxx (Eds.), *Making a difference: Behavioral intervention for autism* (pp. 37–50). Austin, TX: Pro-ed.

Markey, P. T., & Miller, M. L. (2015). Introducing an information-seeking skill in a school library to student with autism spectrum disorders: Using video modeling and least-to-most prompts. *School Library Research, 18,* 1–30.

Matson, J. L., Matson, M. L., & Rivet, T. T. (2007). Social-skills treatments for children with autism spectrum disorders: An overview. *Behavior Modification, 31,* 682–707.

Michael, J. (1982). Distinguishing between discriminative and motivational functions of stimuli. *Journal of the Experimental Analysis of Behavior, 37,* 149–155.

Noell, G. H., Call, N. A., & Ardoin, S. P. (2011). Building complex repertoires from discrete behaviors by establishing stimulus control, behavioral chains, and strategic behavior. In W. W. Fisher, C. C. Piazza, & H. S. Roane (Eds.), *Handbook of applied behavior analysis* (pp. 250–269). New York: Guilford.

Oliver, R., & Skinner, C. H. (2002). Applying behavioral momentum theory to increase compliance: Why Mrs. H. RRRevved up the elementary students with the hokey-pokey. *Journal of Applied School Psychology, 19,* 75–94.

Pinto, R. P., & Hollandsworth, J. G. (1989). Using videotape modeling to prepare children psychologically for surgery: Influence of parents and costs versus benefits of providing preparation services. *Health Psychology, 8,* 79–95.

Shogren, K. A., Faggella-Luby, M. N., Bae, S. J., & Wehmeyer, M. L. (2004). The effect of choice-making as an intervention for problem behavior: A meta-analysis. *Journal of Positive Behavioral Interventions, 6,* 228–237.

Smith, R. G. (2011). Developing antecedent interventions for problem behavior. Schedules of reinforcement. In W. W. Fisher, C. C. Piazza, & H. S. Roane (Eds.), *Handbook of applied behavior analysis* (pp. 297–316). New York: Guilford.

Swain, K., Leader-Janssen, E., & Conley, P. (2013). Effects of repeated reading and listening passage preview on oral reading fluency. *Reading Improvement, 50,* 12–18.

Vargas, J. S. (2013). *Behavior analysis for effective teaching*. New York: Routledge.

Vaughn, B. J., & Horner, R. H. (1997). Identifying instructional tasks that occasion problem behaviors and assessing the effects of student versus teacher choice among these tasks. *Journal of Applied Behavior Analysis, 30,* 299–312.

Walker, H. M., Ramsey, E., & Gresham, F. M. (2004). *Antisocial behavior in schools: Evidence-based practices* (2nd ed.). Belmont, CA: Wadsworth/Thompson Learning.

Wilder, D. A., & Atwell, J. (2006). Evaluation of a guided compliance procedure to reduce noncompliance among preschool children. *Behavioral Interventions, 21,* 265–272.

Zarcone, J. R., Iwata, B. A., Vollmer, T. R., Jagtiani, S., Smith, R. G., & Mazaleski, J. L. (1993). Extinction of serious self-injurious escape behavior with and without instructional fading. *Journal of Applied Behavior Analysis, 26,* 353–360.

Changing Behavior Using Consequent Strategies

8

What immediately follows a behavior influences the frequency of that behavior. For example, earning praise for assisting a peer increases the probability the student will assist the peer in the future. The systematic delivery, manipulation, and arrangement of consequential events drive many of the evidence-based interventions that are employed in schools. This chapter presents consequent strategies that may serve to change behavior or teach skills. The strategies are conceptually divided between those approaches that aim to increase desirable behavior and those that target decreasing undesirable behavior.

Organizing Consequences to Increase Desirable Behavior

Using Positive Reinforcement to Improve Behavior

Interventions derived from positive reinforcement have a longstanding history of use in schools. As a classroom behavior management strategy, positive reinforcement holds several advantages over other approaches including ease of use, acceptability with teachers and parents, and its demonstrated effectiveness with all populations of students. Furthermore, positive reinforcement, as a principle and procedure, is essential to learning. Positively reinforcing correct responding leads to correct responding in the future. However, practitioners are reminded that a positive reinforcer only positively reinforces behavior when the individual displays the behavior more often in the future. A teacher might be conceptually incorrect in saying that positive reinforcement does not work for a student but accurate in saying that a particular consequential event had no effect on that student's behavior. Understanding this point is critical, as school psychologists can work collaboratively with teachers to develop interventions that capitalize on arranging consequential events or selecting positive reinforcers that have the capacity to impact student behavior and learning.

Positive reinforcers should only be delivered contingent on or subject to the display or occurrence of the desired or required behavior or skill. Inadvertently positively reinforcing inappropriate behavior with teacher attention or access to a preferred activity or item will increase the likelihood of the inappropriate behavior occurring in the future. For example, those that promote sensory integration interventions for aberrant behavior assume the aberrant behavior is a result of some sensory processing deficiency. Within the sensory integration model, students exhibiting aberrant behavior are immediately whisked off to a sensory room where they are able to sit on bouncy balls, play games, and have their arms brushed. Admittedly, the problem behavior is eliminated at that moment but an analysis of the contingencies operating in the environment tell a different story. Aberrant behavior ceases when the student is taken to the sensory room but, over time, the aberrant behavior might increase in frequency. Why? Access to preferred activities are consequential events of undesirable behavior. Compounding the problem, undesirable behavior might also be negatively reinforced by the removal of some aversive task demand. It is for this reason teachers and other educators must be aware of the consequences that follow inappropriate behavior. Again, teachers must only positively reinforce appropriate behavior.

Other features of positive reinforcement include delivery timing and satiation. Regarding the former, positive reinforcement is best delivered immediately following the display or occurrence of the desired or required behavior or skill. Immediacy ensures that the behavior a teacher wants to reinforce is actually the behavior being reinforced. Regarding the latter, positive reinforcers can lose their reinforcing qualities as students satiate on attention, activities, or tangible items. Recognizing the role motivating operations play in creating reinforcer value is important when wanting to increase desirable behavior through reinforcement.

SELECTING POSITIVE REINFORCERS

Observing the student or asking someone with experience with the student (e.g., teacher, caregiver) about preferred items (e.g., toys, foods) or activities (e.g., recess) is the most straightforward method for identifying effective positive reinforcers. While simple and possibly an appropriate first step, these methods are not always dependable (see Hanley & Tiger, 2011). For example, observation of a student in the natural environment is subject to contextual effects including abolishing and establishing operations. Candy, used as a reinforcer the day after Halloween, is not likely to be an effective reinforcer. Using direct assessment methods that rely on observation are more reliable but also more time and resource intensive. The following three positive reinforcer assessment strategies are most common in the literature (see Cooper, Heron, & Heward, 2007 or Ivancic, 2000 for comprehensive reviews):

1. **Single-item or -stimulus presentation**: Items are presented one at a time. Frequency data (i.e., the number of times an item was selected) are recorded to determine if an item is preferred. Simplicity is the primary advantage of this approach.
2. **Multiple-item or -stimulus presentation**: All items are presented at once. Items are removed once selected. This approach assesses the student's preference when all potential positive reinforcers are present.
3. **Paired-item or choice presentation**: Items are presented in pairs or groups. The purpose is to identify the comparative preference of the item against other items. The advantage of this approach is that preferences can be ranked from high to low.

Many authors have provided guidance regarding the selection of positive reinforcers for students (e.g., Hall & Hall, 1980; Hanley & Tiger, 2011; Rhode, Jenson, & Reavis, 1992). Recommendations typically begin with a consideration of the student's chronological and developmental age, sex, interests, and preferences. An adolescent's behavior is not likely to be positively reinforced by a sticker. However, access to friends or free time is likely to reinforce a teenager's behavior. The value of the positive reinforcer should equate to the behavior or skill being positively reinforced. It would be inappropriate to positively reinforce compliance with a simple request using a day off from school. Teachers might consider Premack's principle of using preferred activities as reinforcement for low probability, high effort behavior (e.g., compliance with academic task demands). Teachers might also use different or novel positive reinforcers, ask students what they might prefer for a positive reinforcer, and consider developing positive reinforcer menus, as choice and variation are frequently recommended in the literature. Positive reinforcers should be practical (e.g., able to be provided) and cost-efficient. In addition, teachers should operationally define the behavior for the student when delivering positive reinforcement (e.g., behavior-specific praise), act enthusiastically, and attempt to pair positive reinforcers together (e.g., praise plus tangible reward). Finally, teachers should consider the student's history with the positive reinforcer. Students can easily satiate on a positive reinforcer that is overused. Conversely, decreasing or limiting access to a positive reinforcer potentially increases the positive reinforcer's value to the student.

Positive reinforcement should be delivered as frequently as possible. For example, the appropriate behavior of students with disabilities (e.g., ADHD, ASD) or students who exhibit frequent and/or intense behavior problems should be positively reinforced every few minutes or following every few appropriate responses. Dense reinforcement schedules are especially important when initially targeting a behavior or teaching a new skill. Positively reinforcing appropriate behavior frequently provides the student with not just the reinforcer but also feedback on behavior and can serve as a prompt for ongoing appropriate behavior. In addition, thinning the schedule of positive reinforcement as the student engages in more appropriate behavior or learns a skill might be important for generalization and maintenance. For example, reinforcement for compliance might be delivered on a continuous schedule but thinned, over time, to a VR4: range 2–6 (i.e., an average of four responses required for reinforcement).

Teachers and other adults should attempt to maintain a 4:1 positive to negative interaction ratio when working with students. That is, teachers should positively interact (e.g., praise, acknowledge, reinforce) with students four times for every negative interaction (e.g., redirection, verbal reprimand, disciplinary interaction). Research shows that students, especially those with disabilities, rarely receive positive reinforcement for desirable behavior and that increasing the positive to negative ratio can profoundly impact student behavior via increases in appropriate and decreases in inappropriate behavior (Latham, 1997). Moreover, boosting the ratio of positive to negative interactions has high social validity (e.g., easy to apply, appropriate for different settings, uncomplicated procedures) with teachers and parents. The matching law partially explains the effectiveness of high positive to negative interaction ratios. The relative rates of responding match the relative rates of reinforcement. Injecting the student's environment with high rates of positive reinforcement for desirable behavior will be matched by increases in desirable behavior. For students displaying exceptionally low rates of desired behavior, increasing the ratio to 10:1 might be considered.

TYPES OF POSITIVE REINFORCERS

Technically speaking, a positive reinforcer is anything that positively reinforces a behavior, so the types of reinforcers are almost endless. However, Alberto and Troutman (2013) categorized reinforcers by differentiating between primary (e.g., edible, sensory) and secondary (e.g., tangible, activity, social). There are also generalized reinforcers, such as points or tokens, which are reinforcing because of their relationship to primary or secondary reinforcers. Table 8.1 provides examples of positive reinforcers within each category. Figure 8.1 provides details about acknowledgment as a positive reinforcer. The term *acknowledgment* is favored over *praise* when consulting with teachers and parents about problem behavior. In practice, teachers and parents often respond to recommendations involving 'more praise' by saying either 'praise doesn't work for him' or 'I praise him enough already.' Rather than problem-solve through these responses, the consultant is advised to use language less provoking like acknowledgment.

Using Negative Reinforcement to Improve Behavior

Student misbehavior is often reinforced through avoidance or escape of some aversive stimulus. In most cases those aversive stimuli involve task demands, unfavorable decisions, unwanted social attention, or classroom activities. However, students can

Table 8.1   Examples of Positive Reinforcers by Category

Primary (Edible or Sensory)	Secondary	Generalized
• Food snacks • Drinks • Music • Preferred scents	• Praise or acknowledgment • Phone call or note home to parents praising behavior • Special time with preferred adult or peer • Extra recess time • Play a game • Extra screen time • Posters • Stickers • Toys	• Points or tokens traded in for primary or secondary reinforcer

Types of Acknowledgment	1. **Verbal**	'I really appreciate that you lined up properly' 'Outstanding job getting that assignment done on time'	Good for students who like attention
	2. **Nonverbal**	High-five, wave, fist-pound, smile, thumbs up	Best when teacher does not want to cause disruption
	3. **Tangible item, extra time**	See Table 8.1	Appropriate for students who are not motivated by social attention; sometimes students just need a reward

How Often Should the Student Be Acknowledged?

- Every three to five minutes for students who exhibit frequent and/or intense misbehavior (think almost a continuous schedule)
- Consider the 4:1 (or higher) Positive to Negative Ratio
  - If a student is redirected, reprimanded, or disciplined five times during the day, the teacher should acknowledge that student at least 20 times that day
  - Increase the ratio (e.g., 10:1) for students with significant behavior problems
- Teachers can thin the schedule of acknowledgment so that the student is not acknowledged so often; consider increasing frequency of acknowledgment should the student's behavior become more problematic

Figure 8.1   Acknowledgment

be taught to engage in appropriate behavior or exhibit appropriate skills that are functionally equivalent (Alberto & Troutman, 2013). That is, they can be taught to engage in appropriate behavior by providing escape contingent on an appropriate behavior. For example, Carr and Durand (1985) taught students engaging in high intensity behaviors (e.g., tantrums, physical aggression) to use help-seeking language (e.g., 'Help me, I don't understand') that provided escape from an academic task demand. The frequency of students' challenging behavior decreased as they increased their use of the taught phrases. In another study, Marcus and Vollmer (1995) used negative reinforcement contingently to decrease the disruptive behavior of a five-year-old girl with a history of challenging behavior. Their procedure involved providing the student with a brief break from work contingent on com-pliance with an instruction. The researchers compared this procedure with one that allowed for a brief break contingent on the use of appropriate communication skills (e.g., 'finished') and found that both were effective at decreasing disruptive behavior but only the compliance contingent break was effective at increasing overall compliance.

Negative reinforcement strategies can be divided into several categories. Carr and Durand's (1985) study is an example of teaching the student an alternative replacement behavior (i.e., verbal communication) for an undesirable behavior (i.e., tantrum) without removing the function of the undesirable behavior. Another negative reinforcement category involves adding an aversive, such as using reprimands, providing physical guidance, or increasing instructional time either by removing instructional materials for a brief period or adding academic task demands in response to student misbehavior or task demand errors (see Iwata, 1987). Appropriate student behavior is then negatively reinforced via avoidance or escape of these possibly aversive stimuli. For example, a teacher might add additional math problems to an independent seatwork assignment for a student's off-task behavior. The strategy takes advantage of negative reinforcement if an increase in on-task behavior is observed. The student is then said to engage in on-task behavior in order to avoid the consequential event of additional math problems. Marcus and Vollmer (1995) illustrated how educators might use negative reinforcement contingent on the display of appropriate student behavior. Allowing a student to 'earn out of' an academic task demand he or she finds aversive, contingent on completion of some of the required work, can be an effective strategy that increases compliance and academic productivity. According to Alberto and Troutman (2013), it might be best for the teacher to set the conditions in which avoidance or escape occur rather than have avoidance or escape be "a reaction to the student's inappropriate behavior" (p. 253).

Consider the following points when using negative reinforcement to increase desirable behavior. First, understanding the function of a student's undesirable behavior is paramount, particularly for interventions that teach functionally equivalent alternative or replacement behaviors (Iwata, 1987). Second, a student's behavior might escalate quickly when aversive stimuli are presented (Alberto & Troutman, 2013). It is not uncommon for a student with a severe emotional or behavioral disorder to engage in high intensity behavior (e.g., aggression, elopement) when pressed to complete an aversive task. Finally, the use of negative reinforcement to increase desirable behavior should be considered in the context of a larger, more comprehensive behavior plan that includes positively reinforcing appropriate behavior and other evidence-based strategies (e.g., behavioral momentum).

Organizing Consequences to Decrease Undesirable Behavior

While positive, proactive approaches to behavior change and skill development are preferred, consequences aimed at decreasing behavior are sometimes necessary. The term punishment describes consequential events that decrease the probability undesirable behavior occurs in the future. Punishment can either involve the delivery of something aversive (e.g., extra work) or removal of something reinforcing (e.g., losing recess). Punishment should be contingent on inappropriate behavior and delivered as immediately as possible. Punishment can be a naturally occurring feature of the environment (e.g., student is ignored by peers when teasing others) but should be used cautiously with students when part of an intervention plan. Finally, consequences designed to decrease behavior are more likely to be effective when paired with reinforcement-based interventions. For example, a behavior plan that combines acknowledgment of appropriate behavior with punishment for inappropriate behavior might be more effective than either approach by itself. Furthermore, teaching skills or replacement behaviors, and positively reinforcing appropriate behavior, should be considered before punishment-based procedures when designing an intervention plan.

School psychologists should attend to the following points when considering recommending punishment as a behavior reduction strategy. First, students' prior learning histories might influence "a behavior's sensitivity to punishment" (Lerman & Vorndran, 2002, p. 435). Teachers, principals, and parents often find it difficult to identify effective punishers for students with chronic behavior problems. Behaviors that are frequently punished are susceptible to habituation or the principle that aversive consequences lose their aversive qualities when an individual experiences those consequences over multiple repetitions. When the aversive consequence fails to reduce undesirable behavior, attempts are made to identify more punishing consequences for students' misbehavior, unreasonable consequences are used (e.g., student loses recess for three months), or highly punitive punishers with little empirical support are employed (e.g., suspension). Second, consequences that aim to decrease undesirable behavior are more efficacious when the function of the undesirable behavior is identified. Withdrawing a teacher's social attention when the misbehavior is maintained by escape from teacher attention is contraindicated. Similarly, removing a student from the classroom for misbehavior when clearly the inappropriate behavior is maintained by escape from task demands may actually increase the behavior's frequency or intensity. As a result, thinking about organizing consequences to decrease problem behavior requires careful planning with the problem behavior's function in mind. Finally, increases in aggression and emotional over-reactivity have been observed in applied settings where punishment has been used with students prone to behavioral escalations (see Lerman & Vorndran, 2002). Again, school psychologists should be mindful of the possible pitfalls associated with punishment and either begin with reinforcement-based tactics or pair punishment with reinforcement.

Selecting Punishment Strategies

The literature provides little guidance on the selection of punishment procedures. However, ethical guidelines clearly state that nonpunitive and least restrictive strategies should be initially considered (Cooper et al., 2007). Furthermore, data-based decisions should be made when considering moving from a nonpunitive to a punitive strategy. For example, Alberto and Troutman (2013) recommend collecting intervention outcome data as part of the process of moving from least to more restrictive strategies. However, the literature is replete with examples of effective strategies that are consider highly punitive. For example, water mist and the introduction of other aversive stimuli (e.g., exercise) contingent on inappropriate or dangerous behavior have been shown to be effective (see Lerman & Toole, 2011). However, these approaches were only considered when other procedures failed and targeted behavior involved injury to self or others (e.g., head banging, aggression). Moreover, conducting a functional behavior analysis and developing a functionally-driven intervention is preferred over punitive punishment procedures.

Verbal Reprimands

Verbal reprimands involve a teacher expressing disapproval of a student's inappropriate behavior (Beaman & Wheldall, 2000). Teachers often use reprimands as either a consequence for inappropriate behavior or to redirect misbehavior. Not surprising, research on teacher use of reprimands indicates that this classroom behavior management strategy is used more often than praise (e.g., Yildiz & Pinar, 2014). Regarding effectiveness, the literature is mixed when comparing reprimands to praise or encouragement (see Cooper et al., 2007). However, the literature provides some guidance on variables that may impact the effectiveness of reprimands. For example, reprimands are more effective when paired with eye contact and delivered in close proximity to the student (Lerman & Toole, 2011). Cooper and colleagues recommended that reprimands be delivered in a verbally forceful manner (e.g., 'SIT DOWN'), although teachers are encouraged to use appropriate volume. Students, especially at the middle and high school levels, typically respond better to private reprimands. Reprimanding students in front of their peers might serve as an antecedent for additional behavior problems.

School psychologists consulting with teachers about the use of reprimands should consider whether the verbal attention the student receives is positively reinforcing the misbehavior. It is not unusual for teachers, principals, and parents to wonder why their reprimands fail to decrease student misbehavior and, in response to continued student misbehavior, either increase the frequency of reprimands or the volume of their voice when delivering reprimands. In such cases, the failure to reduce student misbehavior via reprimands is likely related to the consequential event (i.e., verbal attention), which might be positively reinforcing the misbehavior. This is particularly true in cases where the student is not receiving much attention from the teacher (i.e., in a deprived attention state). Consequently, reprimands are contraindicated in such cases. Taken altogether, the school psychologist should consider the misbehavior's function when consulting with teachers about the use of reprimands.

Extinction

Extinction is when a previously reinforced behavior is no longer reinforced resulting in a decrease or elimination of the behavior. Most often, interventions based on extinction take the form of ignoring student misbehavior. Accordingly, people use the terms extinction and ignoring interchangeably. However, ignoring is not extinction. Rather, ignoring is a consequential event that might result in the extinction of a behavior. Why is this important? Extinction procedures can take two primary forms: extinction of behavior reinforced by positive reinforcement and extinction of behavior reinforced by negative reinforcement. Ignoring is only an example of the former.

EXTINCTION OF POSITIVELY REINFORCED BEHAVIOR

Extinction of behavior reinforced by attention most often takes the form of ignoring. Removing attention serves to decrease the behavior over time. If the attention is teacher attention, the school psychologist can collaborate on ways to effectively ignore student misbehavior. If the attention is peer attention, the teacher can reinforce peers with teacher attention, extra recess time, or removal of an assignment when they ignore the target student's misbehavior. As with other behavioral procedures, acknowledging or positively reinforcing desirable behavior should be used in combination with ignoring undesirable behavior.

EXTINCTION OF NEGATIVELY REINFORCED BEHAVIOR

Extinction of behavior reinforced by avoidance or escape is more complicated. The literature on escape extinction typically targets serious problems (e.g., food refusal, SIB) and involves physical guidance or force (see Cooper et al., 2007). The interventions rely on procedures that do not allow the individual to escape the demand or task. In the context of a classroom or school, this might translate into requiring the student to complete the task or assignment before moving on with the day (i.e., nothing happens for the student, except bathroom or lunch breaks, until the task is complete). This approach might pose some problems. For example, a student might continue to refuse to complete an academic task demand over many days resulting in the school needing to reallocate resources for supervision and space. In addition, acknowledgment for appropriate behavior might be reduced by staff trying to create an environment that limits available positive reinforcement. Overall reductions in positive reinforcement and positive adult interactions are likely to reduce the student's appropriate behavior and cooperation.

FEATURES OF EXTINCTION

There are several features of extinction that influence its effect on student behavior. First, the effects of extinction are often delayed. In fact, ignoring a behavior rarely results in an immediate change to the behavior. Moreover, there is often a burst or increased rate, duration, and intensity of the behavior. These two issues pose problems for school psychologists recommending interventions based on extinction. Teachers are most often interested in strategies that produce rapid improvements and it is exceptionally difficult to ignore student misbehavior, especially when that behavior is annoying, disruptive to others, or dangerous. Consequently, school psychologists should work collaboratively with teachers to problem-solve around these issues. Perhaps ignoring is not a viable intervention for some students, behaviors, or settings. Second, previously extinguished behavior can reemerge. In such cases, teachers are encouraged to ignore the misbehavior. Third, extinction used in one context (e.g., general education classroom) might not generalize to other contexts (e.g., music classroom, recess, hallway). Finally, extinction procedures should be paired with positive reinforcement for appropriate behavior (i.e., differential reinforcement). For example, a teacher might differentially reinforce alternative behaviors and, at the same time, ignore misbehavior. This combination of approaches is potentially powerful and might reduce the possibility of an extinction burst, result in more immediate results, and address concerns related to difficulties ignoring misbehavior. Figure 8.2 offers questions that might help determine the appropriateness of extinction in a classroom.

---

1. Can the behavior be tolerated (topography, frequency, rate)?
2. Can an increase in, or worsening of, the behavior be tolerated?
3. Is the behavior disruptive to the learning environment?
4. Is the behavior disruptive to peers? Do peers mimic the behavior?
5. Is the behavior reinforced positively (e.g., attention) or negatively (e.g., escape task demand)?
6. Can reinforcement be removed from the setting?
7. Can an appropriate behavior (e.g., incompatible, alternative) be reinforced?

Figure 8.2 Questions to Ask when Considering Interventions that Utilize Extinction

Removal of Reinforcing Stimuli

Removing reinforcing stimuli, such as attention or tangible items, is a common consequential behavior reduction strategy. Response cost and timeout from positive reinforcement are the two most commonly used approaches in this category. The former involves the removal of a reinforcing activity or item. The latter involves the removal of all positive reinforcement including attention. Both have been shown to be effective and can be easily implemented in a classroom or school setting.

RESPONSE COST PROCEDURES

Response cost as a behavior reduction strategy simply involves taking away a reinforcer contingent on inappropriate behavior (Sulzer-Azaroff & Mayer, 1991). Common school-based examples of response cost include loss of recess or free time and taking away preferred items. Response cost is frequently combined with token economies (see Chapter 9), where the student loses tokens or points contingent on inappropriate behavior. Such a strategy has probably been used by teachers and parents since the beginning of classrooms and schools, and for good reason. The literature suggests that interventions based on response cost are effective at reducing problem behavior. For example, Rapport, Murphy, and Baily (1982) found that a simple response cost intervention consisting of loss of free time contingent on off-task behavior was more effective at increasing on-task behavior and decreasing off-task behavior than medication for two boys diagnosed with ADHD. In another study, Carlson, Mann, and Alexander (2000) found that response cost was more effective than an incentive system for improving academic task accuracy for 40 students with ADHD.

Response cost procedures can take many forms. For example, teachers might implement a system whereby the student is 'fined' one minute of recess time for each instance of calling out. Setting up this contingency (i.e., every call out equals one minute less of recess) requires the student to understand the behavioral expectation and the consequential events for misbehavior. Furthermore, the teacher must have an accurate and acceptable record-keeping procedure. Many teachers put checks or marks next to student names written on the board, which might single out or embarrass students. Like other consequences that aim to decrease misbehavior, response cost should be used in conjunction with positive reinforcement of appropriate behavior. Positively reinforcing appropriate responding (e.g., raising hand to answer question) with praise or extra recess time could be combined with response cost. In addition, behavior reduction procedures, such as response cost, that rely on punishment must be used consistently. Punishment that occurs on an intermittent schedule is not likely to be effective. Finally, teachers can use response cost procedures with a group. For example, the accumulated number of call outs might result in lost recess time for the entire class. Again, the teacher should also positively reinforce appropriate behavior and, in this example, might devise a game whereby students earn extra recess time for the class contingent on hand raising.

Many authors (e.g., Alberto & Troutman, 2013; Cooper et al., 2007) have outlined positive features of response cost interventions including ease of implementation (e.g., rule violations result in loss of recess), adaptability to multiple environments and settings (e.g., classrooms, playgrounds, home), and almost immediate effects resulting in a quick assessment of the intervention's effectiveness. Many of these same authors offer cautions when implementing response cost interventions. Like many punishment-based procedures, response cost might lead to increased aggression and unintended decreases in appropriate behavior. Consequently, response cost should not be overused with a student or group. Furthermore, the teacher's verbal and nonverbal attention when delivering the 'fine' might actually reinforce the misbehavior leading to increased misbehavior. Collaborating with teachers on how to issue response cost fines to students is important and school psychologists should be mindful of how teacher attention during these interactions might inadvertently reinforce undesirable behavior. Finally, a student losing recess for disruptive behavior during math, for example, might continue to misbehave or refuse to engage in academic tasks altogether because the anticipation of recess has now been lost. Not making access to a reinforcer an 'all or nothing' proposition and allowing students to earn back lost privileges contingent on desirable behavior is advised.

TIMEOUT FROM POSITIVE REINFORCEMENT

Timeout from positive reinforcement is a consequential event involving the removal of positively reinforcing stimuli contingent on the display of an inappropriate behavior. Practically, this might mean placing a student in a location with limited reinforcing stimuli (e.g., attention, access to tangible reinforcers) for a period of time (Webster, 1976). Conceptually, timeout is a condition in which all positive reinforcement is withdrawn for a period of time contingent on inappropriate behavior (Cooper et al., 2007). Positive reinforcement is introduced back into the student's environment contingent upon some predefined criteria (e.g., quiet for three minutes, completion of a task). As a strategy to decrease misbehavior, timeout is effective in a variety of applied settings (e.g., schools, home) with a variety of populations (e.g., toddlers, students with emotional or behavior disorders, adults with Intellectual Disability; see Shriver & Allen, 1996). However, timeout is often misunderstood and misused (Wolf, McLaughlin, & Williams, 2006). Consequently, timeout as a behavior reduction strategy can be ineffective.

Timeouts can be broadly categorized as inclusionary or exclusionary. Inclusion timeouts remove reinforcement from the student, while exclusion timeouts remove the student from reinforcement (Cooper et al., 2007). Inclusion timeouts are less restrictive, easier to implement, and less likely to violate guidelines regarding student discipline. Thinking about timeout further using a continuum from least-to-most restrictive is helpful for intervention planning (see Figure 8.3).

Inclusion timeouts include planned ignoring, withdrawal of materials, contingent observation, and the timeout ribbon. Planned ignoring involves the withdrawal of

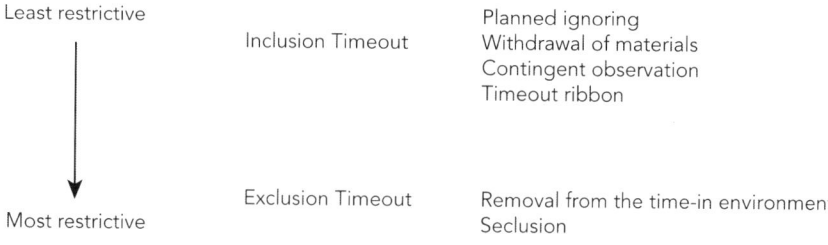

Figure 8.3 Continuum of Timeout Strategies

teacher attention contingent on misbehavior (see Extinction, p. 132). Teacher attention can simply be reintroduced when the student's behavior improves. A slightly more restrictive timeout is the withdrawal of tangible items or activities. This should sound similar to response cost but, unlike response cost, withdrawal of items or activities occurs only for a brief period of time, or until the student has calmed down and completed a task. Contingent observation involves moving the student to a location in the classroom that is away from peer and teacher attention, and materials, for a period of time. Advantages of contingent observation include the student might still benefit from instruction and peers might serve as models for how to behave appropriately. Research suggests contingent observation might be more effective than more restrictive forms of timeout like exclusion and seclusion (see Ryan, Sanders, Katsiyannis, & Yell, 2007). Finally, the timeout ribbon involves having a student or students wear a marker (e.g., bracelet around the wrist, button pinned to a sleeve) indicating reinforcement is available. The marker is removed contingent on misbehavior, signaling to the teacher and reminding the student that reinforcement is unavailable (e.g., cannot engage in a task or participate in an activity). In some instances, removal of the marker means the student must remain within arm's length of the teacher.

Exclusion timeout involves the removal of the student from the reinforcing environment. Typically, this timeout form removes the student from the classroom to an environment with limited reinforcing stimuli. Within a school setting, exclusionary timeouts most often occur in a different room or the hallway, or separating the student from peers within the classroom. Ryan and colleagues (2007) noted there is less research on exclusion timeouts when compared to inclusion timeouts. However, exclusion timeouts have been shown to decrease noncompliance and disruptive behavior in elementary school settings. Seclusion timeouts involve isolating the student in a timeout room contingent on serious misbehavior (e.g., aggression, destruction of property). Research on the effectiveness of this timeout procedure in school-based settings is limited and precautions should be taken to ensure the student's safety and avoid misuse or abuse of the timeout (Frampton, 2011). Consequently, seclusion timeouts should only be considered as a last resort or for behavior that is dangerous.

Removing a disruptive student from the classroom might seem attractive to practitioners looking for consequent strategies that target inappropriate behavior. Additionally, exclusion timeouts hold several advantages over inclusion timeouts including the quick removal of a student from the classroom and reduced risk of the target student or classmates being hurt because of escalating behavior. However, exclusion timeouts can be problematic for several reasons. First, special resources (e.g., staff, space) are needed to fully implement an exclusion timeout. Second, removal from the classroom can serve as an antecedent to escalations in behavior (e.g., aggression) and inadvertently reinforce behavior by providing access to staff attention or escape of aversive stimuli (e.g., academic task demands). Finally, exclusion timeouts limit the student's opportunity to benefit from instruction or peer models.

Using inclusion or exclusion timeouts effectively involves considering several factors. First, timeout is only as effective as time-in. That is, the time-in environment must be reinforcing for the student. Furthermore, appropriate behaviors and skills should be reinforced on a dense schedule (e.g., every five minutes) with a positive to negative interaction ratio of at least 4:1. Failure to provide a reinforcing environment or infrequent reinforcement of appropriate behavior will negate the effects of the timeout. Second, school staff should clearly define behaviors that lead to timeout by providing examples and nonexamples. Related, school psychologists should consult with teachers on developing a misbehavior hierarchy that identifies behaviors that should always be addressed, targeted when contextually possible, or ignored (see Table 8.2). This might help teachers avoid overusing timeout. Third, exit criteria should be clearly defined. In most cases, the student should be calm and quiet for at least one minute, acknowledge a readiness to exit timeout, comply with between one and two simple, one-step instructions, and make retribution for what earned him the timeout (e.g., comply with request, apologize to peer). Students might also be required to remain in timeout for more than a few minutes, especially when there is a history of re-escalating problem behavior, or engage in a post-timeout interview with staff to discuss the misbehavior. However, leaving students in timeout for too long might lead to escalation in problem behavior and too much attention immediately following a timeout might reinforce the behavior that resulted in the timeout. Fourth, students should be fully aware of the timeout guidelines including where timeouts will be taken and what is required to exit the timeout. Fifth, timeout

Table 8.2   Example of a Misbehavior Hierarchy Developed by a School Psychologist and Teacher during Consultation

Dangerous or Unsafe Behavior	Behavior Targeted for Intervention	Behavior that Might Be Ignored
• Physical aggression toward peers • Bullying behavior • Elopement • Running with sharp objects (scissors, pencils) • Standing on furniture	• Noncompliance • Inappropriate language • Arguing with adults • Playing with toys during instruction or independent seatwork time	• Leaving seat without permission • Making comments under breath • Talking with peers appropriately but at inappropriate times

YES/NO	Question
	Is the timeout location away from reinforcement or distractions?
	Did you place the student in timeout within 30 seconds of the misbehavior?
	Did you briefly state the rule violation before placing the student in timeout?
	Did you avoid showing anger (e.g., yelling) when placing the student in timeout?
	Did you use the correct amount of time (30 seconds to 5 minutes)?
	Did the timeout begin when the student was compliant with the timeout?
	Did you avoid talking to the student when he was in timeout?
	Did you go to the timeout location and state to the student, 'you have been quiet and compliant during the timeout, now you must...'?
	Did you require the student to complete an appropriate exit behavior (e.g., comply with request)?
	Does the student know and understand the behaviors that will result in timeout?
	Does the student know the steps involved in completing a timeout (e.g., quiet, exit criteria)?

Figure 8.4   Timeout Checklist

is generally contraindicated when the target behavior is reinforced by avoidance or escape of task demands (see Alberto & Troutman, 2013; Lerman & Toole, 2011). For example, a student not wanting to complete math worksheets might continue to misbehave when the consequence is always removal from math class. However, the procedure can be effective when the student is not allowed to avoid or escape the task demand. In such cases, focusing on exit criteria that involves completion of the avoided task is recommended. Finally, timeout should be delivered consistently. Like all punishment-based procedures, a continuous schedule is recommended so that students can predict the teacher's response to misbehavior. Figure 8.4 provides a timeout checklist to help assess implementation integrity.

Overcorrection

Overcorrection is a consequential event whereby students engage in a corrected version of the behavior or skill contingent on misbehavior. Overcorrection is differentiated from simple error correction by the exaggeration of the correction (Alberto & Troutman, 2013). Simple error correction requires the student to correctly engage in the behavior or skill once. Overcorrection requires the student to engage in a related and effortful behavior with some amplification (e.g., demonstrating appropriate hallway behavior over several repetitions). Research on the use of overcorrection indicates it is effective for a variety of problem behaviors and with all populations (see Miltenberger & Fuqua, 1981).

The literature divides overcorrection interventions based on the specific consequence of the misbehavior or the type of correction that is required of the student. Restitution overcorrection involves the student correcting the misbehavior by correcting the environment in which the misbehavior occurred. This form of overcorrection will mostly likely take the form of fixing any damage to the environment or apologizing for an inappropriate social interaction (e.g., teasing). However, the student must make amends by going beyond what was done. For example, the class might be expected to pick up all the papers thrown on the floor and clean the floor of a neighboring classroom, a student might apologize to the person he or she teased and all the peers who witnessed the teasing, or a group of students might have to remain quiet for 15 minutes following disruptive cafeteria behavior. Positive practice overcorrection requires the student to repeatedly engage in a positive version of the behavior or skill following the display of the misbehavior (see Figure 8.5). Requiring a class to walk down the hall appropriately several times after most students ran or having a student write a spelling word correctly five times following a misspelling are examples of positive practice. This version of overcorrection can include modeling and feedback to encourage engaging in the correct behavior or enhance skill development.

School psychologists should consider several contextual variables before recommending overcorrection. First, overcorrection procedures demand a teacher's full attention. The teacher must be ready to provide corrective feedback, deliver the overcorrection instruction, and ensure students comply with the procedure. Second, the teacher must have the time to follow through on the entire overcorrection procedure. Brief or shortened versions of overcorrection tend to be less effective (see Alberto & Troutman, 2013). This also means the teacher must be willing to follow through with additional consequences (e.g., response cost) should the student refuse to comply

Step	Example
1. Get the student's attention.	'Mark, I need for you to listen to me right now.'
2. Tell the student he is engaging in inappropriate behavior.	'Mark, right now you're running in the hallway.'
3. Tell the student the appropriate behavior and provide a brief rationale.	'Mark, you need to walk in the hallway because it's safer for you and others.'
4. Provide details regarding the appropriate behavior.	'Mark, walking in the hallway means walking slowly, keeping our hands by our sides, and we should be quiet or use inside voices if given permission.'
5. Model the appropriate behavior, if needed.	'Mark, watch me walk in the hallway. Am I doing all the steps correctly?'
6. Require the student to practice the appropriate behavior.	'Mark, now it's your turn to walk appropriately in the hallway. I would like for you to walk down to Mrs. Pollard's door and back three times.'
7. Observe student and provide feedback.	'Nice job, Mark. You've shown me how you walk in the hallway.'
8. Prompt student to continue with activity or task.	'Mark, now you may walk to the cafeteria.'

Figure 8.5   Positive Practice Intervention Protocol

with the request. For noncompliant students, Azrin and Besalel-Azrin (1999) recommended reminding the student of additional consequences, pre-teaching the behavior or skill, and making error correction a standard practice. Third, the teacher should provide detailed verbal instructions and monitor the student as she engages in the behavior or skill. Fourth, be careful not to inadvertently reinforce the inappropriate behavior by providing the student with too much attention or allowing him a 'break' from an aversive task or activity during the overcorrection. Finally, overcorrection should be balanced with positive reinforcement in the form of acknowledgment or incentives should be provided for appropriate displays of the behavior or skill.

Conclusion

Effective behavior management plans combine antecedent and consequent strategies. For example, combining behavior momentum with differential reinforcement is preferred over implementing each intervention by itself. Likewise, addressing behavior problems by joining consequent strategies that increase appropriate and decrease inappropriate behavior is encouraged. When consulting with school staff or parents on the use of consequent strategies, school psychologists should initially consider organizing consequences that increase desirable behavior. Strengthening appropriate behavior through positive reinforcement is more effective than weakening inappropriate behavior through punishment (Bijou, 1988). Furthermore, school psychologists should consider the misbehavior's function when selecting an intervention. Verbal reprimands and overcorrection might be contraindicated for misbehavior reinforced by attention, and timeout might be contraindicated for misbehavior reinforced by escape (Lerman & Toole, 2011). Consequently, behavior plans that emphasize positive reinforcement strategies and rely on understanding functions of misbehavior are most likely to be effective.

References

Alberto, P. A., & Troutman, A. C. (2013). *Applied behavior analysis for teachers* (9th ed.). Upper Saddle River, NJ: Pearson.

Azrin, N. H., & Besalel-Azrin, V. A. (1999). *How to use positive practice, self-correction, and overcorrection* (2nd ed.). Austin, TX: Pro-Ed.

Beaman, R., & Wheldall, K. (2000). Teachers' use of approval and disapproval in the classroom. *Educational Psychology, 20*, 431–446.

Bijou, S. W. (1988). Behaviorism: History and educational implications. In T. Husen & T. N. Postlethwaite (Eds.), *The international encyclopedia of education* (pp. 444–451). New York: Pergamon Press.

Carlson, C. L., Mann, M., & Alexander, D. K. (2000). Effects of reward and response cost on the performance and motivation of children with ADHD. *Cognitive Therapy and Research, 24*, 87–98.

Carr, E., & Durand, M. (1985). Reducing problem behavior through functional communication training. *Journal of Applied Behavior Analysis, 18*, 111–126.

Cooper, J., Heron, T., & Heward, W. (2007). *Applied behavior analysis* (2nd ed.). Upper Saddle River, NJ: Merrill/Pearson Education.

Frampton, K. T. R. (2011). The effectiveness of isolation timeouts for students with severe emotional disabilities attending a therapeutic day school (Unpublished doctoral dissertation). Loyola University, Chicago.

Hall, R. V., & Hall, M. C. (1980). *How to select reinforcers*. Lawrence, KS: H&H Enterprises.

Hanley, G. P., & Tiger, J. H. (2011). Differential reinforcement procedures. In W. W. Fisher, C. C. Piazza, & H. S. Roane (Eds.), *Handbook of applied behavior analysis* (pp. 229–249). New York: Guilford.

Ivancic, M. T. (2000). Stimulus preference and reinforcer assessment applications. In J. Austen & J. E. Carr (Eds.), *Handbook of applied behavior analysis* (pp. 19–38). Reno, NV: Context Press.

Iwata, B. A. (1987). Negative reinforcement in applied behavior analysis: An emerging technology. *Journal of Applied Behavior Analysis, 20*, 361–378.

Latham, G. (1997). *Behind the schoolhouse door: Eight skills every teacher should have*. Logan, UT: Utah State University.

Lerman, D. C., & Toole, L. M. (2011). Developing function-based punishment procedures for problem behavior. In W. W. Fisher, C. C. Piazza, & H. S. Roane (Eds.), *Handbook of applied behavior analysis* (pp. 348–369). New York: Guilford.

Lerman, D. C., & Vorndran, C. M. (2002). On the status of knowledge for using punishment: Implications for treating behavior disorders. *Journal of Applied Behavior Analysis, 35*, 431–464.

Marcus, B. A., & Vollmer, T. R. (1995). Effects of differential negative reinforcement on disruption and compliance. *Journal of Applied Behavior Analysis, 28*, 229–230.

Miltenberger, R. G., & Fuqua, R. W. (1981). Overcorrection: A review and critical analysis. *The Behavior Analyst, 4*, 123–141.

Rapport, M. D., Murphy, H. A., & Bailey, J. S. (1982). Ritalin vs. response cost in the control of hyperactive children: A within-subject comparison. *Journal of Applied Behavior Analysis, 15*, 206–216.

Rhode, G., Jenson, W. R., & Reavis, H. K. (1992). *The tough kid book: Practical classroom management strategies*. Longmont, CO: Sopris West.

Ryan, J. B., Sanders, S., Katsiyannis, A., & Yell, M. L. (2007). Using time-out effectively in the classroom. *Teaching Exceptional Children, 39*, 60–67.

Shriver, M. D., & Allen, K. D. (1996). The time-out grid: A guide to effective discipline. *School Psychology Quarterly, 11*, 67–74.

Sulzer-Azaroff, B., & Mayer, R. (1991). *Behavior analysis for lasting change*. Fort Worth, TX: Holt, Reinhart & Winston, Inc.

Webster, R. E. (1976). A time-out procedure in a public school setting. *Psychology in the Schools, 13*, 72–76.

Wolf, T. L., McLaughlin, T. F., & Williams, R. L. (2006). Time-out interventions and strategies: A brief review and recommendations. *International Journal of Special Education, 21*, 22–29.

Yildiz, N. G., & Pinar, E. S. (2014). Examining approval and disapproval behaviors of teachers working in inclusive classrooms. *International Journal of Instruction, 7*, 35–46.

Changing Behavior Using Contingency Management Strategies

9

Contingencies describe dependent relationships between responses or behaviors and their consequences. Many evidence-based interventions apply contingencies to increase desirable behavior, decrease undesirable behavior, and teach new behaviors or skills. This chapter describes several EBPs that use contingencies to change behavior: the token economy (TE), contingency contracting, the Mystery Motivator and Response Cost Raffle, and group contingencies. These interventions are well supported in the literature, can be easily combined with other approaches, and have the flexibility to target individuals or groups (Cooper, Heron, & Heward, 2007). Furthermore, these approaches can be used to increase desirable and decrease undesirable behavior, and enhance skill development (Alberto & Troutman, 2013).

Token Economy

The TE is a contingency management strategy that strengthens behavior via positive reinforcement. However, the reinforcers are generalized reinforcers, such as tokens, chips, or points, which are later exchanged for primary or secondary reinforcers called backup reinforcers. The cycle of a TE is as follows: (1) the child has no tokens and limited access to something desirable, (2) the child engages in a target behavior, (3) the child earns a token for engaging in the behavior, and (4) the child trades the token or tokens for something desirable (Alberto & Troutman, 2013; Cooper et al., 2007).

Research supports using TEs in applied settings. Ayllon and Azrin (1965) were among the first applied researchers to demonstrate the effectiveness of a token economy for aberrant behavior. Kazdin and Bootzin (1972), in their review of the early literature, found that TEs showed promise as a behavior change strategy. More recently, Boerke and Reitman (2011) described research demonstrating the effectiveness of TEs in school settings targeting common academic (e.g., reading) and behavior (e.g., peer relations, on-task behavior) problems, and Cooper and colleagues (2007) provided several examples of how interventions utilizing a TE were effective at improving students' academic, behavioral, and social functioning. TEs can also be paired with other interventions when targeting problems that are difficult to treat. For example, Zlomke and Zlomke (2003) demonstrated how a TE could decrease a 13-year-old boy's disruptive behavior at home and school. However, these researchers added a self-monitoring component that decreased problem behavior at school to near zero levels. Methodological weaknesses do pose some problems when evaluating the TE literature. Maggin, Chafouleas, Goddard, and Johnson (2011) found that three of four meta-analytic techniques yielded high effect size estimates but cautioned interpreting the results as positive. They noted poor methodological rigor, including limited reporting of intervention fidelity and interobserver agreement, plagued many of the studies included. Taken altogether, school-based TEs have the potential to be effective with a variety of student populations presenting with a variety of concerns.

As a classroom management strategy, TE holds several advantages over other behavior management approaches. First, tokens provide students with tangible feedback about their behavior. Second, delivering tokens can be done immediately. Moreover, delivering tokens might be less disruptive to students when compared with verbal praise. Third, the economy can be adjusted to reflect changes in behavior or skills. For example, a student might earn a token every time his or her hand is raised. After several weeks of success, the student might instead earn a token every three times his or her hand is raised. Fourth, students can learn to delay gratification by having to wait until accessing the primary or secondary reinforcer. Fifth, a token can serve to mark a behavior or skill. Students with attention problems, or developmental or intellectual disabilities might find the token a more salient indicator of appropriate behavior than teacher verbalizations. Finally, TEs aid in generalization, as the intervention might be used across settings (e.g., different classrooms, recess) and with different adults (e.g., teachers, cafeteria supervisors, parents). Furthermore, students can earn tokens for different behaviors concurrently, making the TE a flexible intervention option.

Designing a Token Economy

Table 9.1 presents a general outline for developing TEs. However, several additional steps might be required. First, deciding where (e.g., classroom, playground) and when (e.g., morning, reading and math periods) the TE will be implemented is likely to be necessary. A thorough evaluation of student behavior in multiple settings during different times and with different adults should identify contextual variables that require attention. Second, designing the TE means designing an economy that is easy to understand and implement. In its simplest form, one token would equal one backup reinforcer. However, the economy can be more complex. Higher valued backup reinforcers might be worth more tokens or tokens could be exchanged for time (e.g., one token = one minute of iPad time). Inflation might raise backup reinforcer prices when the student's behavior begins to improve (i.e., the cost of backup reinforcers increases) or deflation might lower backup reinforcer prices should the student find it difficult to earn tokens and become discouraged. Third, the school psychologist or teacher should develop a detailed write-up of the TE's procedures as outlined in Table 9.1. Additional information might include how to respond verbally to the student when a token or backup reinforcer is or is not earned. Pairing positive social attention with the earning of a token or backup reinforcer is always recommended. For example, teachers might join behavior-specific praise with the delivery of tokens and backup reinforcers (e.g., 'great job staying in your seat during reading time, you've earned one token and you can earn another token if you stay seated during current events'). Regarding negative interactions, Cooper and colleagues (2007) suggested having a matter-of-fact approach such as saying, 'sorry you didn't earn a chip' or 'maybe you'll earn more chips tomorrow.' The write-up should also include how to manage a student who fails to comply with the TE (e.g., student says he or she does not want to be a part of the token economy). Here, Cooper and colleagues recommended proactively allowing the student to participate in the setup of the TE (e.g., select and establish the price of backup reinforcers) or be involved in helping manage a backup reinforcer 'store' associated with the TE.

RESPONSE COST

TEs may include a response cost component involving the loss of tokens contingent on misbehavior. Like establishing the system for earning tokens, setting up clear expectations regarding the conditions in which tokens might be lost (e.g., what behaviors are deemed inappropriate enough to lose tokens, how many tokens are lost for each misbehavior) would be an initial step. In addition, the procedures should state what happens when a student loses all tokens (although it is not recommended that students go into debt) and how to manage student upset when tokens are lost. This point is particularly important for students engaging in high rates of misbehavior and low rates of appropriate behavior. These students are likely to quickly lose tokens with little opportunity to earn them back, contraindicating the use of response cost procedures within a TE. Finally, Boerke and Reitman (2011) recommended initially assessing whether a response cost added to the TE is necessary. A TE, by itself, might be all that is needed to improve behavior.

Response cost within a TE system holds several advantages over other behavior reduction strategies (e.g., timeout). First, combining positive reinforcement from the TE with punishment from a response cost creates greater consequential contrast between appropriate and inappropriate behavior, thus potentially accelerating the effects of the intervention. Second, adding a TE to the response cost intervention allows students contingent access to reinforcement despite the possibility of losing some privileges (e.g., extra recess). This minimizes the potential for escalation of problem behavior or noncompliance with the intervention.

Table 9.1 Designing a Token Economy

Step	Comments
Operationally define the target behavior	Staff working with the student should be able to recognize the behavior
	Behavior should be socially important to those implementing the intervention
Develop token system	Identify tokens (e.g., chips, macaroni, monopoly money)
	Identify array of available backup reinforcers or reinforcer menu
Define the economy	Indicate how many tokens it takes to buy backup reinforcers
Define schedule for token delivery	Specify how frequently tokens will be delivered to student
	Consider schedules of reinforcement (see Chapter 2)— continuous schedule for new target behaviors, intermittent schedule for behaviors already exhibited
Decide when backup reinforcers may be 'purchased'	Indicate when the student is able to exchange tokens for backup reinforcers
Determine where tokens are stored	Specify where the tokens will be kept by the student (e.g., envelope for monopoly money, a plastic cup for dry macaroni)
Training	Ensure that all staff working with the students are trained in implementation
	Model implementation for staff, allow for practice, and provide ongoing feedback
Develop outcome measures	Determine how the student's behavior will be assessed, using accumulated tokens as an outcome measure might be problematic
Develop intervention fidelity measures	Determine how fidelity of the token economy will be assessed
	Direct observation and permanent products are recommended

Research comparing TEs with and without response cost components is limited. Fiksdal (2014) found that a TE alone and in combination with response cost were equally effective at increasing the academic engagement and decreasing the disruptive behavior of first grade students in two classrooms. Other research has compared token reinforcement by itself to a response cost only intervention whereby students begin with tokens or points which are lost contingent on misbehavior. Interestingly, both Iwata and Bailey (1974) and McGoey and DuPaul (2000) found the variations (i.e., token economy vs. response cost) to be equally effective in school-based settings. However, Iwata and Bailey (1974) also found that the teacher was more negative with the students when employing the response cost in the classroom. Again, a TE might be effective by itself. Ongoing collection of intervention outcome data will help school psychologists and others make decisions about how best to proceed.

Other Variants of the Token Economy

Several authors describe level or point systems as a variation on the TE (see Cooper et al., 2007). Level systems provide a structure for students to access backup reinforcers or privileges contingent on appropriate behavior. However, level systems tend to be more involved and, thus, more complicated. The levels define the available reinforcers—the more advanced the level, the better the available reinforcers. For example, moving up levels might lead to an extra recess, the student moving his or her desk to a preferred location in the classroom, or the freedom to sit anywhere in the cafeteria. Collecting points contingent on appropriate behavior or display of skills allows students to move up levels. That is, students move up levels after earning a predetermined number of points. Some level systems incorporate response cost procedures whereby students lose points for misbehavior, which has the effect of then potentially dropping levels. Level systems are meant to gradually thin the schedule of token reinforcement to approximate a more natural setting (Cooper et al., 2007). Furthermore, students are expected to display more appropriate behavior and exhibit more independence while earning more valuable privileges (Cooper et al., 2007). Level systems are often combined with other interventions such as self-monitoring and can be modified based on contextual variables (e.g., student's developmental level, setting).

In lottery systems, tokens represent chances to win backup reinforcers. Students earn tokens, typically slips of paper containing the student's name or some special identification, which are collected during the exchange period. The teacher holds a drawing with backup reinforcers going to only those students whose names were selected. Students with more tokens have a better chance of winning. While this modification to the TE allows for the teaching of disappointment to students and requires fewer backup reinforcers, the lottery system might not be appropriate for students who have difficulty managing their behavior when disappointed or understanding the relationship between appropriate behavior and reinforcement (e.g., younger students, students with significant behavior problems who are just learning basic compliance skills, students with intellectual or developmental disabilities).

TEs can be implemented with both individuals and groups (e.g., whole class). In fact, some variants on the TE are more suited for group-based interventions (e.g., lottery system). Moreover, implementing a TE within a classroom makes sense especially when several students are exhibiting high frequency, low intensity problem behavior. The literature is replete with examples of classwide TEs that demonstrate decreases in undesirable behavior and increases in desirable behavior for multiple students in one classroom (see Doll, McLaughlin, & Barretto, 2013). However, school psychologists should consider the time and additional effort often required when implementation occurs at the group level before making any recommendations (Filcheck & McNeil, 2014).

Final Considerations

Cooper and colleagues (2007) suggested that students participating in the TE intervention receive initial and ongoing education about the TE. Initial training could simply involve instructions, examples, and modeling of how students earn and exchange tokens. Students should also be shown the available backup reinforcers and told how many tokens each reinforcer is worth. TE 'stores' might be set up providing students with a visual reminder of the available backup reinforcers and corresponding prices. Ongoing training is likely to involve reorienting students to the intervention's procedures and reminding students of target behaviors, available backup reinforcers, and the value of each backup reinforcer. It might also be important to draw students' attention to changes in the value of backup reinforcers and the economy in general.

Goal setting with students is another important component of the TE. School psychologists and teachers might work with students to set outcome goals involving increases in desirable behavior or skills and decreases in undesirable behavior. No longer needing the TE as a support is a primary goal for all students. Consequently, planning for the fading out of the token economy will become necessary. Table 9.2 provides several steps to help with intervention withdrawal. Ideally, fading the TE would involve a thinning of the reinforcement schedule and inflating the value of backup reinforcers.

Research on the social acceptability of TEs is mixed. Following the implementation of several variations of the TE, Fiksdal (2014) found that two first grade teachers preferred the TE with response cost over the response cost alone. However, other research has found teacher acceptability of TEs to be more variable (e.g., Reitman, Murphy, Hupp, & O'Callaghan, 2004). Low social acceptability is not surprising given the time and effort required by teachers to fully implement the procedures. School psychologists are encouraged to simplify the intervention when possible and support teachers through regular communication and follow-up. Teachers might also have philosophical concerns with using TE (see Filcheck & McNeil, 2014). While clearly unsubstantiated by research, there are opinions that rewarding students undermines motivation and creativity. Consequently, school psychologists might consider

Table 9.2   Fading the Token Economy

Step	Example
Pair token reinforcer with a secondary reinforcer	Use social praise when delivering tokens
Change expectations required to earn tokens	Increase the number of appropriate behaviors or decrease the number of inappropriate behaviors needed to earn tokens
Change when the token economy is in effect	Implement the token economy during the morning or independent seatwork periods
Change backup reinforcers to only items or privileges found in natural setting	Backup reinforcers become extra recess or iPad time. Remove tangible or edible reinforcers that are not available in the classroom
Change the economy	More valuable items cost more tokens
Change the tokens	Replace physical tokens with points on an index card. Eventually fade to teacher recording tally marks that student cannot review during class

reframing the TE by using language less divisive to teachers. For example, using the term incentive rather than reward might reduce teacher resistance.

Contingency Contracting

Contingency or behavioral contracts describe a contingency between a behavior and positive reinforcer. Specifically, contingency contracts are written agreements between two parties describing the contingency between the behavior or task and the consequence or reward. For example, a teacher might write a contingency contract with a student stipulating that the student will earn an extra recess on Friday if math homework is completed each night of the week (see Figure 9.1). Also, the contract includes details of the student's expected behavior or task (e.g., accuracy of the assignment, at what time the assignment is to be turned in), specific parameters of the reward (e.g., length of the extra recess), and a specified method of tracking the behavior. Note that the contract is a written, not verbal, agreement. According to Cooper and colleagues (2007), a written agreement's highly detailed description and evaluation is more than what might be expected of a verbal agreement. Furthermore, they noted that the actual signing and posting of the document represents something more than simply verbally stating the agreement.

Contingency contracts are effective for a variety of populations and problems (see Cooper et al., 2007). For example, Kelly and Stokes (1982) demonstrated how

---

School Contract Between Mr. McQuade and Roger

When signed, this contract represents an agreement between Mr. McQuade, 4th grade teacher, and Roger, 4th grade student. This contract begins Monday October 1st and ends Friday October 5th.

The contract states:

Roger will:
- Turn in all math homework assignments during the week
- Turn in assignments by 8:25am each morning
- Attempt all assigned problems
- Complete all assignments with 90% accuracy

Mr. McQuade will:
- Record, on this contract, all completed assignments turned in on time and with 90% accuracy
- Reward Roger with 30 minutes of extra recess time Friday at 2:00pm if all boxes below are checked
- Allow Roger to choose two friends to join him in the extra recess time

Signatures

Roger: Date:

Mr. McQuade: Date:

Record of completed assignments:

Day	Monday	Tuesday	Wednesday	Thursday	Friday
Assignment completed					

Figure 9.1   Contingency Contract

contingency contracting increased the academic productivity (i.e., number of problems completed, percent accuracy) of 13 adolescents enrolled in a vocational training program. The literature also provides some guidance to practitioners using contingency contracts. Individualizing contracts for students is important and can be done by identifying specific behaviors that the teacher wants to see more of, using individualized reinforcers, and clearly stating expectations (i.e., the contingency). Following the successful application of contingency contracts with two students with ASD, Mruzek, Cohen, and Smith (2007) noted the importance of fading procedures and increasing students' self-management. They increased the expectations required for the reward and decreased teacher support. They also recommended reducing the physical size of the contract.

Alberto and Troutman (2013) noted that contingency contracts hold several advantages over other reinforcement-based interventions. First, contracts serve as a permanent product for target behaviors and consequences (i.e., rewards) discussed between students and teachers. Second, students are actively involved in selecting target behaviors and rewards, and can learn important negotiation skills (e.g., communication, compromise). Third, written contracts are individualized programs that describe expected goals and outcomes, and can be easily inserted into a student's Individualized Education Plan.

Developing Contracts

Many authors have offered steps for developing contingency contracts with students beginning by meeting with everyone involved (e.g., student, teacher, parent) to describe the details of the intervention and discuss responsibilities. The student and teacher (or parent) might also separately list potential behaviors or skills that could be targeted. Finally, a list of possible reinforcers should be generated by the student, teacher, and parent. Involving everyone in the process is likely to enhance participation and follow through (see Cooper et al., 2007).

Setting up the contract is a rather straightforward process. Figure 9.2 presents a task list like that used by Mruzek and colleagues (2007). They stressed initially identifying alternative behaviors or coping skills (e.g., 'When peers tease me, I can walk away and talk with a teacher') that could replace problem behavior. They also recommended keeping documents (e.g., contracts, data collection forms) organized in a dedicated binder or folder. Finally, having clear start and end dates in the contract, and displaying the contract for the student to regularly see are recommended (Alberto and Troutman, 2013).

1. Select alternative behaviors and coping strategies
2. Select target behaviors or skills
    a. Develop student, teacher, parent list
    b. Collaborate with teacher on identifying socially important or keystone behaviors
3. Select possible rewards
    a. Develop student, teacher, and parent list
    b. Conduct reinforcer assessment, if necessary
    c. Emphasize practical rewards
4. Write contract. Include:
    a. Student and teacher names
    b. Student and teacher responsibilities
    c. List alternative behaviors or coping strategies
    d. Contingency (e.g., if...then)
    e. Signature and date lines
    f. Behavior or skill tracking mechanism
5. Review contract with student and teacher
    a. Model for student appropriate behaviors or skills
    b. Emphasize student expectations and contingent reward
    c. Review procedures with teacher
        i. Provide rationale for intervention
        ii. Discuss expectations
        iii. Discuss reward details
        iv. Review tracking procedures
6. Sign and implement contingency contract

Figure 9.2 Steps for Implementing a Contingency Contract

Considerations

Contracts should be fair for the student and complied with by the teacher (Cooper et al., 2007). Specifically, the student should be able to meet the expectation or goal and earn the reward if expectations are met. Frustration, upset, discouragement, and noncompliance with future contracts are likely to follow frequent failure to earn the reward. Cooper and colleagues also recommended selecting behaviors or skills that result in some achievement (e.g., completed assignment) or happen in the company of the teacher (e.g., teacher observes student remaining seated during independent seatwork time), including several reward levels (e.g., bonus reward for accuracy or improvements over previous week), and renegotiating with the student when necessary. Finally, contracts might be written for small approximations of a target behavior or skill (Homme, Csanyi, Gonzales, & Rechs, 1970). This is particularly important when targeting behavior not in the student's repertoire or skills the student has not previously displayed or mastered. Related, target behaviors or skills must be in the student's repertoire.

Other Contingency Management Interventions

The literature provides many examples of innovative interventions derived from a contingency management perspective. The Mystery Motivator rewards students for appropriate behavior but with the uncertainty of what reward will be earned (see Rhode, Jensen, & Reavis, 1992). Figure 9.3 offers an example of how the Mystery Motivator might be used. Randomizing reinforcers address the limitation that some rewards might not be reinforcing for a student or could be punishing (Kelshaw-Levering, Sterling-Turner, Henry, & Skinner, 2000). Conceptually like the lottery system within a TE, the Response Cost Raffle allows students to trade raffle tickets for rewards (see Witt & Elliott, 1982). Students are provided a predetermined number of tickets at the beginning of the day or class period. The teacher takes tickets away for targeted misbehaviors (e.g., calling out, noncompliance). Students can purchase rewards with the remaining tickets. A variant of the Response Cost Raffle involves students earning raffle tickets for desirable behavior. When the raffle is conducted, students with more raffle tickets stand a better chance of winning.

Group Contingencies

Many of the interventions already discussed can be applied to both individual students and groups (e.g., class- and school-wide). Furthermore, these interventions can target problems in multiple settings (e.g., classroom, hallway, playground, bus). For example, either the Mystery Motivator or the Response Cost Raffle can easily be adapted to target whole classes in settings where problems are most frequent. Group

Development

1. **Determine when the intervention will occur**. The Mystery Motivator (MM) should be implemented when student behavior is most problematic and limited to a 30–40-min session.
2. **Define target behavior or skills**. Target problems or skills that are observable, measureable, and socially important. Identify replacement behaviors (e.g., target problem is calling out, replacement behavior is raising hand).
3. **Develop a system to record behavior or skills**. System should be easy to use and displayed for the class to see. Posters and dedicated smartboard space are effective at communicating expectations and progress.
4. **Identify rewards**. Consider group preferences such as extra recess time, removal of an assignment or task (e.g.,'no math homework tonight'), or a movie party. Be sure to have a continuum of rewards (i.e., highly to less preferred).
5. **Define expectations**. Identify the performance level required to earn the reward.
6. **Develop the MM**. Many teachers write the reward on an index card and then place the card in a large envelope. Students, especially at the elementary level, enjoy coloring over a reward written in invisible ink.

Implementation

1. **Teacher announces to students the MM is in effect**. Be sure to indicate start and stop times, and remind students of contingency (i.e., performance standards, reward).
2. **Teacher records behavior**. Again, this should be visible to students.
3. **If students meet expectations, reward is revealed and provided**.
4. **If students fail to meet expectations, teacher encourages students to try again during next MM session, reviews expectations**.

Other Considerations

1. **Initially select performance standards that are achievable**. Students are more likely to be motivated if they are able to meet expectations.
2. **Change performance standards**. Increase or decrease expectations for success depending on student performance.
3. **Add 'No Reward' to the intervention**. As students become more successful, include an option that no reward is earned. This teaches students to accept disappointment and limits their reliance on rewards.
4. **Be sure to pair social praise with earned tally marks or points**.

Figure 9.3 Classwide Mystery Motivator Intervention Protocol

contingencies involve a common consequence (e.g., reward, punishment) contingent on the behavior of the group, part of the group, or one student in the group (Cooper et al., 2007). Group contingencies are usually identified as independent, dependent, and interdependent (see Table 9.3). When properly implemented, group contingency interventions can be effective and efficient behavior change strategies for groups of students (see Alberto & Troutman, 2013). They can also save time and be applied to situations where several individual contingency-based interventions are required but impractical. Finally, group contingencies can be used to encourage positive peer interactions within a group by making the reward contingent on the appropriate social behavior of the group.

Table 9.3   Group Contingencies

Type	Antecedent	Consequence	Example	Considerations
Independent	Criterion presented to all students	Reinforcer delivered to only those students meeting criterion	Only those students that complete 4 of 5 worksheets before 2PM earn extra afternoon time	Can be combined with TE and contingency contract
Dependent	Criterion presented to one student or small group of students	Reinforcer delivered to all students if selected student meets criterion	Student name selected from jar in morning; class earns extra afternoon recess if selected student completes 4 of 5 worksheets before 2PM	Facilitates positive interactions among students such as encouragement and support
Interdependent	Criterion presented to all students	Reinforcer delivered to all students only if all students meet criterion	Class earns extra afternoon recess if all students complete 4 of 5 worksheets before 2PM	Encourages students to work for a common goal, theoretically uses positive peer pressure

The steps for designing and implementing a group contingency generally mirror those of individual contingency interventions. The first step is to identify the behaviors and rewards that will determine the contingency (e.g., inside voices = extra recess time). The second step involves setting the contingency's expectations by selecting the performance level required to earn the reward. Hamblin, Hathaway, and Wodarski (1971) recommended considering the group's high-, average-, and low-performance levels. For example, everyone might be required to achieve 90% correct on a test (high-performance) or the total number of disruptions during a class period might be set at ten (low-performance). However, Hamblin and colleagues found student performance was poor when group standards were set too high. Consequently, practitioners should consider setting expectations low at first with the goal of increasing them systematically as student performance improves. The third step involves matching the intervention's goal with group contingency type (i.e., independent, dependent, interdependent).

Independent group contingencies are most appropriate when a teacher wants to reinforce students independent of the behavior or performance of other group members. Dependent and interdependent group contingencies are used when teachers want to facilitate or promote positive social interactions and cooperation among the group. Finally, it is important for teachers to evaluate individual and group performance. Group performance might improve but not the performance of some students in the group (Cooper et al., 2007). In addition, some students might sabotage the intervention, making it difficult for the group to earn the reward. In these cases, individual contingency-based interventions are recommended.

School-based group contingencies are effective behavior change strategies and, in some contexts, more effective for increasing desirable behavior than most other interventions (Maggin, Johnson, Chafouleas, Ruberto, & Berggren, 2012; Stage & Quiroz, 1997). There are numerous examples in the literature of applications of group contingency interventions that target student behavior. For example, Thorne and Kamps (2008) demonstrated how a group contingency intervention decreased problem behavior and increased academic engagement in four elementary classrooms. Likewise, Kelshaw-Levering and colleagues (2000) implemented an interdependent group contingency in a second grade classroom using a randomized reward (i.e., Mystery Motivator) then an interdependent group contingency where all components (e.g., reward, behavior, criteria for reward, individual or group) were randomized. They found both group contingency interventions were effective at decreasing problem behavior and concluded that randomizing contingencies (i.e., behaviors, criteria, rewards) might address limitations associated with the intervention's procedures (e.g., students escalating their behavior after knowing the criteria cannot be met, students engaging in appropriate behavior across several target areas). Finally, Ennis, Blair, and George (2016) found that four different group contingency types (independent, dependent, interdependent, randomized) reduced classroom disruptive behavior and increased appropriate behavior for three elementary classrooms. Perhaps equally important, high teacher intervention acceptability was reported across all three studies.

Conclusion

Contingency management approaches hold promise for school psychologists looking for effective interventions that increase desirable behavior, decrease undesirable behavior, and improve skills. Strategies presented in this chapter offer school psychologists and teachers much flexibility in implementation. For example, TEs can be implemented with an entire class, contingency contracts can target multiple behavior, and group contingencies can include randomized components. Consequently, these interventions are appealing to school psychologists looking for classroom management strategies or interventions for students exhibiting challenging behavior.

References

Alberto, P. A., & Troutman, A. C. (2013). *Applied behavior analysis for teachers* (9th ed.). Upper Saddle River, NJ: Pearson.

Ayllon, T., & Azrin, N. H. (1965). The measurement and reinforcement of behavior of psychotics. *Journal of the Experimental Analysis of Behavior, 8,* 357–383.

Boerke, K. W., & Reitman, D. (2011). Token economies. In W. W. Fisher, C. C. Piazza, & H. S. Roane (Eds.), *Handbook of applied behavior analysis* (pp. 370–382). New York: Guilford.

Cooper, J., Heron, T., & Heward, W. (2007). *Applied behavior analysis* (2nd ed.). Upper Saddle River, NJ: Merrill/Pearson Education.

Doll, C., McLaughlin, T. F., & Barretto, A. (2013). The token economy: A recent review and evaluation. *International Journal of Basic and Applied Science, 2,* 131–149.

Ennis, C. R., Blair, K. S. C., & George, H. P. (2016). An evaluation of group contingency interventions: The role of teacher preference. *Journal of Positive Behavior Interventions, 18,* 17–28.

Fiksdal, B. L. (2014). *A comparison of the effectiveness of a token economy system, a response cost condition, and a combination condition in reducing problem behaviors and increasing student academic engagement and performance in two first grade classrooms* (Doctoral dissertation). Retrieved from Theses, Dissertations, and Other Capstone Projects (Paper 343).

Filcheck, H. A., & McNeil, C. B. (2014). The use of token economies in preschool classrooms: Practical and philosophical concerns. *Journal of Early and Intensive Behavior Intervention, 1,* 94–103.

Hamblin, R. L., Hathaway, C., & Wodarski, J. S. (1971). Group contingencies, peer tutoring and accelerating academic achievement. In E. A. Ramp & B. L. Hopkins (Eds.), *A new direction for education: Behavior analysis Volume 1* (pp. 41–53). Lawrence, KS: The University of Kansas.

Homme, L., Csanyi, A., Gonzales, M., & Rechs, J. (1970). *How to use contingency contracting in the classroom.* Champaign, IL: Research Press.

Iwata, B. A., & Bailey, J. S. (1974). Reward versus cost token system: An analysis of the effects on students and teacher. *Journal of Applied Behavior Analysis, 7,* 567–576.

Kazdin, A. E., & Bootzin, R. R. (1972). The token economy: An evaluative review. *Journal of Applied Behavior Analysis, 5,* 343–372.

Kelly, M. L., & Stokes, T. F. (1982). Contingency contracting with disadvantaged youths: Improving classroom performance. *Journal of Applied Behavior Analysis, 15,* 447–454.

Kelshaw-Levering, K., Sterling-Turner, H. E., Henry, J. R., & Skinner, C. H. (2000). Randomized interdependent group contingencies: Group reinforcement with a twist. *Psychology in the Schools, 37,* 523–533.

Maggin, D. M., Chafouleas, S. M., Goddard, K. M., & Johnson, A. H. (2011). A systematic evaluation of token economies as a classroom management tool for students with challenging behavior. *Journal of School Psychology, 49,* 529–554.

Maggin, D. M., Johnson, A. H., Chafouleas, S. M., Ruberto, L. M., & Berggren, M. (2012). A systematic review of school-based group contingency interventions for students with challenging behavior. *Journal of School Psychology, 50,* 625–654.

McGoey, K. E., & DuPaul, G. J. (2000). Token reinforcement and response cost procedures: Reducing the disruptive behavior of preschool children with attention deficit/hyperactivity disorder. *School Psychology Quarterly, 15,* 330–343.

Mruzek, D. W., Cohen, C., & Smith, T. (2007). Contingency contracting with students with autism spectrum disorders in a public school setting. *Journal of Developmental and Physical Disabilities, 19,* 103–114.

Reitman, D., Murphy, M. M., Hupp, S. D. A., & O'Callaghan, P. M. (2004). Behavior change and perceptions of change: Evaluating the effectiveness of a token economy. *Child and Family Behavior Therapy, 26,* 17–36.

Rhode, G., Jensen, W. R., & Reavis, H. K. (1992). *The tough kid book: Practical classroom management strategies.* Longmont, CO: Sopris West.

Stage, S. A., & Quiroz, D. R. (1997). A meta-analysis of interventions to decrease disruptive classroom behavior in public education settings. *School Psychology Review, 26,* 333–368.

Thorne, S., & Kamps, D. (2008). The effects of a group contingency intervention on academic engagement and problem behavior of at-risk students. *Behavior Analyst in Practice, 1,* 12–18.

Witt, J. C., & Elliott, S. N. (1982). The response cost lottery: A time efficient and effective classroom intervention. *Journal of School Psychology, 20,* 155–161.

Zlomke, K., & Zlomke, L. (2003). Token economy plus self-monitoring to reduce disruptive classroom behaviors. *The Behavior Analyst Today, 4,* 177–182.

Interventions for Teaching Behavioral and Social Skills

10

Conceptually, the distinction between skill acquisition and performance deficits is a fundamental feature of teaching academic, behavior, and social skills to students (Bellini, 2016). Skill acquisition deficits involve the absence of a skill because either the skill has not yet been learned (i.e., the student does not have knowledge about how to execute the skill) or has been acquired but is not exhibited in appropriate contexts. Performance deficits describe skills that have been learned but are not consistently or appropriately displayed or exhibited. Skill acquisition deficits are characterized as 'can't do,' while performance deficits are characterized as 'won't do.' The antecedent and consequent strategies, including contingency management approaches, already discussed, generally focus on 'won't do' deficits. However, interventions relying on positive reinforcement, for example, might be ineffective for students unable to perform a skill because the skill has yet to be acquired or is rarely or never displayed. Consequently, there is no correct response to reinforce.

Teaching replacement behaviors is another important conceptual feature of teaching skills to students. Replacement behaviors are behaviors exhibited instead of a problem behavior but that serve the same function as the problem or behavior (Gresham, Van, & Cook, 2006). For example, work completion might be an acceptable replacement behavior for disruptive behavior when both behaviors are functionally related to teacher attention. Teaching students to engage in prosocial behaviors that are functionally equivalent to the undesirable behavior addresses many of the problems cited in the skill training literature including poor generalization and maintenance (Maag, 2005).

This chapter outlines three interventions that address skill acquisition deficits by teaching prosocial alternative or replacement behaviors: (1) behavioral skills training, (2) video modeling, and (3) self-management. While antecedent and consequent strategies (e.g., positive reinforcement) are necessary for learning to occur, the primary focus of the interventions presented in this chapter involves teaching students to consistently and fluently engage in behaviors or skills that can, in turn, be positively reinforced. Specifically, these interventions rely on the student learning skills via the process of teaching, modeling, practice, and feedback. In some cases, the modeling will be self-modeling and the feedback will be delivered through self-observation and self-reinforcement. However, such approaches allow for students to become more independent while enhancing skill and behavior generalization.

Behavioral Skills Training

Behavioral skills training (BST) is a comprehensive teaching model that incorporates instruction and education, modeling, practice, praise, and corrective feedback (Miles & Wilder, 2009). BST, in various forms, has been used to teach behavioral (e.g., compliance with adult instructions), safety (e.g., avoidance of strangers, fire drill safety, gun play), and social skills to children (see Hanley & Tiger, 2011). In addition, BST has been successfully used in caregiver and teacher training of guided compliance procedures (i.e., adult use of prompts, reinforcement, and error correction to teach skills to children), and other behavior management and teaching procedures (e.g., Wilder & Atwell, 2006). Finally, common instructional approaches that teach

Table 10.1 Behavioral Skills Training

Step	Description	Examples
Explicit Instruction	1. Describe the skill or behavior	• 'To follow instructions you look at the person, listen to the instruction, ask questions if you don't understand what you are being asked to do, say "okay," complete the task, and check back with the teacher so teacher can check your work'
	2. Provide examples and non-examples	• 'Asking the teacher questions about the instruction, saying "okay," completing the task, and checking back with the teacher are all part of following instructions—ignoring the teacher's instruction, laughing, saying "no," and doing something other than the task are all examples of not following instructions'
	3. Check for understanding	• 'Is saying "okay" a part of following instructions?'; 'what should you do if you are unsure of the teacher's instruction?'; 'what do you do after you complete the teacher's instruction?'

Step	Description	Examples
Modeling	Demonstration of the skill or behavior	• School psychologist demonstrates how to follow instructions using a script • School psychologist shows a brief video depicting a student following the teacher's instructions • School psychologist and student role play following instructions with the school psychologist playing the part of the student
Practice	Rehearsal or role play with feedback	• Student demonstrates the step of following instructions • School psychologist and student role play following instructions with the school psychologist playing the part of the teacher • Student practices following instructions with teacher in the school psychologist's office • Student practices following instructions in the classroom
Feedback	• Behavior-specific praise for appropriate displays of the target skill or behavior • Corrective feedback for failure to appropriate display the skill or behavior	• 'Wonderful job following that instruction. You gave me eye contact, asked a question, said "okay," completed the task immediately, and checked back. You're getting very good at this.' • 'Nice try. You gave me eye contact and said "okay." However, you didn't check to make sure you understood the instruction and didn't get started immediately. Let's try this again. What are the steps for following instructions?'

academic skills include BST components (Martens, Daly, Begeny, & VanDerHeyden, 2011). For example, evidence-based instructional approaches rely on an 'I do, we do, you do' paradigm, where the teacher first models the skill by herself, then completes the skill together with the student, and finishes with the student demonstrating the skill alone, all in rapid succession.

Implementing BST is a simple process. First, the teacher provides the student with explicit instruction on the target behavior or skill, as well as situations and settings in which the behavior might be appropriate or necessary. Explicit instruction typically takes the form of the teacher or instructor describing the behavior or skill using developmentally appropriate language, providing examples and non-examples, and checking for understanding by eliciting frequent responses from students through questions (Archer & Hughes, 2011). Second, the teacher or another model (e.g., peer) demonstrates the behavior or skill for the student. This is best done in the context or situation in which the skill or behavior is most likely appropriate or necessary (e.g., modeling appropriate hallway behavior in the hallway where problems occur), although the modeling might first happen in another location. Moreover, modeling should include a range of situations the student is likely to encounter. For example, using different models or modeling several different responses to a social interaction demonstrates different responses or stimuli to students, which aids in generalization. Confederates (i.e., individuals playing a role in the modeling scenario) might also be important during modeling. For example, recruiting several peers to line up with the student during practice sessions might be helpful when attempting to recreate the context in which lining up behavior is needed. Third, the student practices, rehearses, or role-plays the behavior or skill while receiving feedback (i.e., praise, correction). Like modeling, practice is best done using a range of related contextual or situational factors (e.g., practice complying with different instructions in different settings). Feedback is delivered immediately (or as immediately as possible) following a correct or incorrect response. Feedback should be detailed and specific (e.g., 'Well done, James. You walked down the hallway quietly, with your hands and arms to your sides, and at just the right distance from the peer in front of you'). Ideally, practice sessions are conducted over time until the behavior or skill has been mastered (e.g., displayed correctly and automatically). Behavior-specific praise and corrective feedback are delivered throughout BST including when the student engages or fails to engage in the behavior or skill outside the training setting. Teachers and other school staff should be alerted to the behaviors or skills being taught to students so that they might increase their efforts at providing feedback.

Students failing to respond to BST might require additional instruction, modeling, and practice. Many students need multiple repetitions to learn a behavior or skill and allowing for many instruction, modeling and practice sequences might be necessary. Moreover, modeling and practice sessions might begin far removed from real-life situations but resemble closer approximations of real-life as students become more proficient and successful. Axelrod, Butler, and Handwerk (2004) found that gradually increasing the realistic nature of a response cost for misbehavior (e.g., loss of recess) during practice sessions greatly improved high school students' skills to appropriately accept discipline without becoming angry or upset. The researchers began by exposing students to outrageous practice scenarios (e.g., 'you've lost recess because your shoe is untied') but slowly increased the scenario's realism. The researchers also initially pre-taught skills to the students and warned them when a consequence might occur (e.g., 'you should be ready to accept a consequence, no matter how outrageous').

While clearly an exemplary instructional framework, BST is not without its limitations. Miltenberger and Gross (2011), after reviewing the literature on BST to teach safety skills to children, provided several important points to consider. First, although research shows that BST works for skill acquisition deficits, generalization and long-term maintenance of effects have been limited. These findings confirm what many claim to be a significant limitation of social skills training programs and only underscore the need to systematically program for generalization and maintenance (Bellini, 2016; Gresham et al., 2006; Maag, 2005). For example, instruction might focus on the many settings in which a behavior is needed, and modeling and practice could be done in those settings. Second, BST might be best suited for individual students. While working with groups of students might be more resource friendly, the research on group skills training (e.g., safety or social skills) is not positive. Individualizing the training might be necessary, as contextual factors that contribute to problem behavior are often student and setting specific. Furthermore, group BST might not afford individual students the amount of practice required to master a behavior or skill. Third, group settings might limit the frequency and immediacy of feedback provided to an individual student. Fourth, BST might not be effective when practice occurs in non-natural settings (e.g., school psychologist's office). Miltenberger and Gross (2011) found in some studies that BST was more effective when naturalistic practice settings were introduced. Again, these findings confirm the need to devise practice scenarios that replicate specific situations that require the behavior or skill. Finally, BST is more effective than strategies that include education without modeling and practice components. This finding is not surprising as modeling provides a demonstration of the target behavior or skill and practice allows for feedback (e.g., reinforcement, correction) leading to mastery. Finally, Miltenberger and Gross noted that BST is time- and resource-intensive, especially when generalization and maintenance are primary objectives.

School psychologists are encouraged to consider these limitations. However, BST can be highly effective at addressing a range of behaviors and skills, and research on teaching behaviors or skills to individuals highlights the importance of explicit instruction, modeling, practice, and feedback. Moreover, BST often features in a comprehensive intervention package. For example, video modeling and self-management interventions incorporate BST elements in their procedures.

Video Modeling

Modeling is clearly an important component of teaching and learning as it acts as a response prompt that evokes a similar behavior. Modeling is based, in part, on Bandura's (1977) work on social learning theory. Planned models are planned antecedent stimuli that demonstrate for students precisely how to perform a skill (Cooper, Heron, & Heward, 2007). Modeling, planned or unplanned, can also improve behavior including compliance, and academic behavior such as reading fluency (see Axelrod, Bellini, & Markoff, 2014a; Schounard, Sutton, & Axelrod, 2012). Coupled with other strategies (e.g., practice, reinforcement), modeling can be a potent intervention for behavioral or skill deficits.

Modeling has been creatively applied to teaching skills and behaviors to a range of populations and a myriad of problems. For example, researchers over the past

20 years have demonstrated that modeling via video can be employed to teach social and behavioral skills to, and improve disruptive behavior of, students with ADHD, ASD, behavior disorders, communication disorders, and disruptive behavior disorders (Axelrod et al., 2014a). Meta-analytic research has found video modeling and video self-modeling (VSM) to be an EBP for students with ASD who have significant social skill deficits (see Bellini & Akullian, 2007). Furthermore, VSM frequently produces immediate and robust results with very little required of students or adults (Bellini & Akullian, 2007). In fact, Bellini (2016) indicated that, based on his clinical experience and research, "video modeling is without a doubt the most effective social skills intervention strategy" (p. 109) used with students with ASD. Video modeling and VSM incorporate visual learning, focus student attention on the modeled skill or behavior, can be reinforcing (i.e., watching videos can be a highly preferred activity), and assist in the development of self-awareness.

Video modeling simply involves viewing a video demonstration of a skill or successful behavior and then imitating the behavior or skill. Adults or peers serve as the model or, in the case of VSM, the target student serves as the model. In recent years, much of the video modeling literature has focused on VSM. Dowrick (1999) separated VSM interventions into two categories, positive self-review (PSR) and video feedforward (VFF). PSR involves students viewing themselves successfully engaging in a behavior or skill currently in their behavioral repertoire, but emitted at a low frequency. For example, if a student complies with teacher instructions, but at a very low frequency, then the intervention would consist of capturing the student's compliant behavior on video and editing out all instances of noncompliance. The student would then be shown a brief video depicting only instances of compliance. VFF is another category of VSM interventions where students observe themselves successfully engaging in behaviors or skills that are never or almost never performed autonomously. A VFF intervention may involve the use of hidden supports. For example, prompting or cueing might be provided behind the scenes to encourage the student to engage in compliant behavior. The prompting is then edited out of the video. Another example of VFF involves splicing together separate footage of the teacher giving an instruction and the student completing the task. Using VFF in this way is fitting for students who refuse to comply with adult instructions despite prompting, cueing, or reinforcement. Video footage of the students sitting down in a chair or picking up a pencil is spliced together with footage, recorded at a separate time, of the teacher issuing an instruction to 'sit down' or to 'pick up the pencil.' The student then views the edited video clip depicting himself seemingly complying with the request to sit down or pick up the pencil.

There are several benefits to employing video modeling or VSM for students with skill acquisition deficits or who have failed to master important behavioral milestones (e.g., compliance with teacher instructions). First, video modeling can be a component of a larger BST intervention that includes instruction, practice, and feedback. Second, video modeling allows practitioners to target replacement behaviors or skills that are critical to a student's academic, behavioral, or social success. Said differently, video modeling is an intervention that lends itself nicely to individualization and is ideal for students with specific behavior problems or skill acquisition deficits. Third, the replacements behaviors or skills do not necessarily need to be in the student's repertoire. Peers who possess the skills or have mastered the behaviors can be used as models. Prompts or cues and video splicing technology can also be employed to create video clips depicting the target student engaging in the target behaviors or skills. Finally, research on the social validity of video modeling interventions is positive (Bellini, 2016). For example, Axelrod and colleagues (2014a), employing VSM with noncompliant students, found that teachers and other staff reported the intervention procedures were easy to implement and beneficial for all participants.

Below is a summary of guidelines for developing and implementing a video modeling or VSM intervention.

1. **Selecting a skill or behavior**. There are several recommendations presented elsewhere in this book for selecting target behaviors or skills (e.g., select a target behavior that is observable and measureable). However, selecting a behavior or skill within the context of a video modeling intervention requires some additional considerations. First, select only one or, at the most, two behaviors or skills. Teachers and other school professionals often want to include all a student's behavior problems or skill deficits in an intervention. Starting small enhances the probability of success. Second, the behavior or skill should be captured within a brief (i.e., two to three-minute) video clip. Selecting behaviors or skills that play out over ten minutes or more are difficult to stage and capture on video. Moreover, students are less likely to maintain attention and the specific behaviors or skills targeted might be missed by students while watching lengthy videos. However, using video modeling to target more complex behaviors or skills might be effective if considered within a shaping framework in which successive approximations of the more complex behavior or skill is modeled and reinforced.

2. **Selecting a model or models**. Again, the model may be a peer, an adult, or the student involved. When considering the student as the model, first ask if the student can engage in the behavior or skill with no or minimal prompting or cueing. Also, consider if the student will be appropriate when filmed, as some students shy away from the camera, while others might clown around or become disruptive when the camera is on. Finally, multiple models might enhance the emphasis placed on a behavior or skill. For example, using two peer models to demonstrate an appropriate conversation highlights multiple conversational skills and the nonverbal social behavior that occurs during conversations.

3. **Identifying other actors**. There might be other parts to play in the video. For example, social interactions between two students require more than just the model. Including people that are part of the naturally occurring environment in the video enhances contextual validity. Bellini (2016) recommended using peers when targeting social skills, and relevant teachers and other school staff should be included when appropriate. Keep in mind that schools and school districts might require parental permission to record students.

4. **Selecting the setting**. Similarly, decisions need to be made as to where the videos will be filmed. Bellini (2016) recommended considering either the natural environment or role-play productions. Recording in the natural environment (e.g., classroom, playground) enhances contextual validity but might pose problems for students who rarely or never engage in the behavior or skill. Moreover, recording in a natural setting requires cooperation from other students, which might be enhanced with pre-teaching and reinforcement or contingency contracts. Finally, identifying how to best capture the topography of the behavior or skill is important. For role-play scenarios, Bellini suggested developing story boards, writing scripts, and rehearsing with students.

5. **Identifying supports**. Filming the student engaging in the appropriate behavior or skill is, of course, critical. Consequently, practitioners should consider cuing or prompting the behavior or skill followed by reinforcement. In addition, pre-teaching and using contingencies might encourage students to engage in the behavior or skill.

6. **Preparing to film**. Before filming ensure that the lighting and sound quality is adequate, the actors are prepared, and the cameraperson is familiar with the hardware. Consider using additional lighting, wireless microphones, and reviewing recordings between 'takes.' Keep in mind that several hours of raw footage might be necessary to create 20 minutes of usable video, especially for students with more significant behavior problems or skill acquisition deficits.

7. **Editing**. Editing and splicing together footage following filming might be necessary to adequately depict the student displaying the behavior or skill. Fortunately, the process of editing video has become less complicated with the widespread use of digital cameras. However, editing might remain the most difficult and time-intensive component of the intervention. Solicit support from technology experts or develop your own expertise by learning to use editing software. Do not worry about subpar editing such as abrupt cuts and keep the length of the videos short (e.g., two to three-minute clips).

8. **Showing the video clips to the student**. Determine where, when, and for how long to show the video clips. Videos can be shown at school or home. Bellini (2016) recommended showing the video clip shortly before the behavior or skill is required. For example, the student might view a video of himself engaging in appropriate playground behavior ten minutes before recess. If not feasible, videos may be shown in the morning before class begins, after lunch, or during a visit with the school counselor. This flexibility adds to the intervention's simplicity. Regarding how long to show the video clips for, Axelrod and colleagues (2014a) showed students four one-minute videos in the morning and again in the afternoon of themselves complying with adult instructions. Students could choose which video clips were viewed from a list of 12. When discussing the intervention with the student (at either the outset of filming or while viewing the video), teachers and staff should be brief (e.g., 'we are making/ showing these videos to help/teach/encourage you to . . .'). Furthermore, behavior-specific praise should be provided to students compliant during

the video viewing sessions. Distracted or noncompliant students should initially be redirected using verbal and nonverbal prompts. Response cost and contingency-based strategies might be considered should problems persist.

Self-Management Interventions

Independence is an important educational outcome and functioning independently requires students to be proficient at self-managing their behavior (Alberto & Troutman, 2013). By conceptualizing self-management as a skill rather than some internal mechanism, students with and without disabilities can be taught to manage and regulate their own behavior. As a testament to how important educators view these skills, teaching self-management and self-regulation skills is a part of many schools' social and emotional learning curricula. For students with disabilities, self-management of academic and social behavior is a common Individualized Education Program goal.

Conceptualizing Self-Management Interventions

Self-management is a complex process comprised of goal setting, monitoring and evaluating behavior, and reinforcing positive behavior change (Alberto & Troutman, 2013; Mace, Belfiore, & Hutchinson, 2001). Goal setting involves identifying behaviors requiring change and establishing contingencies for behavior change. Monitoring and evaluating one's own behavior typically includes self-awareness (e.g., knowing when you engage in a target behavior), self-observation (e.g., observing when you engage in a target behavior), self-recording (e.g., noting instances when you engage in a target behavior), and self-assessment (e.g., comparing current behavior to goals or standards). Self-reinforcement, which occurs following the desired behavior, involves the individual him- or herself reinforcing positive behavior change.

The literature describes several self-management interventions, although variations among the different approaches are subtle and, perhaps, not important for practice. Conceptually, self-management interventions should include teaching students to be more self-aware and accurate in evaluating their own behavior. In fact, many studies investigating self-management interventions include discrimination of the occurrence and nonoccurrence of the target behavior or skill, self-recording, and assessment of accuracy (Alberto & Troutman, 2013; Mace et al., 2001; Reid, Trout, & Schartz, 2005). Moreover, students should be a part of the goal-setting and reinforcement process. In some intervention protocols, each of these are provided by someone other than the student (e.g., teacher, parent; see Axelrod, Zhe, Haugen, & Klein, 2009). However, fading adult involvement by increasing the student's responsibility for goal setting and reinforcement is simple and might contribute to generalization and maintenance. However, an initial assessment of the student's ability to set their own goals and self-reinforce appropriate behavior is likely needed.

Finally, self-management interventions might be used to supplement existing evidence-based interventions that rely on contingency management and principles of learning and behavior (e.g., positive reinforcement). For example, adding a self-management intervention to a token economy might help facilitate stimulus and response generalization, and maintenance (Davies, Jones, & Rafoth, 2010).

Teaching Students to Self-Manage Their Own Behavior

GOAL SETTING

Teaching students to negotiate goals for success is important for independence. Furthermore, involving students in the goal-setting process can enhance compliance with an intervention. The first step in developing goals with students is a discussion with the student about targeting behaviors or skills for change. School psychologists or other educators might ask the student to select from a pre-developed list of behaviors interfering with the student's performance or skills that are necessary for success. Next, the adult and student negotiate outcomes or expectations that are specific, measurable, attainable, and realistic. For example, a student struggling to turn in homework might negotiate the following goal with the teacher: at the beginning of class, turn in 60% of all homework assignments during the week. The teacher might have wanted 90% (unrealistic) and the student might have wanted 30% (too easy), so a compromise is struck. Finally, the adult and student collaborate on the specific behavior necessary to be successful meeting the goal. Ideally, these behaviors are within the student's current repertoire and represent replacement behaviors for undesirable behavior or behaviors that are part of a more complex skill. For instance, reading a chapter on colonial expansionism in the Americas and writing three main ideas might be a first step toward the goal of completing a full social studies assignment.

Goal setting as a part of a larger self-management intervention is supported in the research literature. For example, Gureasko-Moore, DuPaul, and White (2006) supplemented self-recording and self-assessment with goal setting for 12-year-old students with ADHD. The students were provided with a list of six class preparation behaviors (e.g., obtain all materials before class begins) and asked to select which behaviors each wanted to target during the week. The researchers found the procedures to be successful at improving the targeted behaviors and results were maintained even when the intervention was faded out.

SELF-MONITORING

Self-monitoring involves the multistep process of observing and then recording one's own behavior (Epstein, Mooney, Reid, Ryan, & Uhing, 2005; Mace et al., 2001). Self-monitoring interventions typically involve the student being prompted by a cue (aural, tactile, verbal, or visual) to self-record the presence or absence of a predetermined skill or behavior. In some cases, students are rewarded for accurate

Student Name: THOMAS **Today's Date:** APRIL 10 **Time:** 10:00 to 11:00

Target Behavior: ON-TASK DURING INDEPENDENT SEATWORK TIME—COMPLETING

ASSIGNMENT, WRITING, READING, RAISING HAND, ASKING QUESTIONS ABOUT

LESSON OR ASSIGNMENT, LISTENING TO SPEAKER, STAYING SEATED

OFF-TASK—TALKING TO OTHERS WITHOUT PERMISSION, BEING OUT OF SEAT, PLAYING

WITH TOYS, LOOKING OUT WINDOW OR INTO HALLWAY

Interval	On-Task	Off-Task	Accuracy Check
1	×		Match
2	×		Match
3	×		Match
4		×	Match
5	×		No Match
6	×		Match
7	×		Match
8		×	Match
9		×	Match
10		×	Match
11	×		No Match
12	×		No Match
13	×		Match
14		×	Match
15		×	Match
16		×	Match
17	×		No Match
18	×		Match
19	×		Match
20	×		Match
Totals	13	7	80% Match

Match Goal (completed by teacher): 80%

On-Task Goal (completed by teacher and student): 15/20 INTERVALS

Figure 10.1 Self-Monitoring Form for On-Task Behavior

recording to encourage truthfulness in their self-evaluations (see Axelrod et al., 2009). The process involves the following steps:

1. **Select and operationally define a target behavior or skill**. Practitioners should ensure target behaviors or skills are specific, operationally defined, and socially important. The student might also need to be taught the behavior or skill using a BST format.
2. **Identify a recording system and develop a form for student use**. Recording systems and forms should mirror the observational recording methods described in Chapter 3 (e.g., frequency counting, interval recording, momentary time

Sarah's Behavior Form

How was Sarah's behavior today?

Date: March 12, 2016

Rating Your Behavior:
A = 3 or more problems
B = 1 or 2 problems
C = 0 problems

Class/Activity	Sarah's Rating	Teacher's Rating	Match?
Playground/Line Up/ Cubby Time	C	C	Yes
Circle/Sharing	C	C	Yeah
Writing	B	A	Almost
Reading Lesson	B	B	Good
Snack/Recess	C	C	Way to go
Music	C	B	Close
Spring Time Project	C	C	Awesome
Lunch/Recess	C	C	Yeah
Quiet Time	C	C	Thumbs Up
Math Lesson	B	B	Way to Go
Math Practice	C	C	Yes
Partner Work	A	A	Good Match
Listening Time	C	A	Pay attention to your behavior
Pack-Up Time	C	C	Great job
Line Up & Get on the Bus	C	B	Close match

Number of Matches: 11   **Goal**: 10   **Reward**: 10 minutes of Arts & Crafts

Figure 10.2   Self-Evaluation Form

sampling, permanent products). Unfortunately, the empirical literature provides little guidance on appropriate time intervals when using discontinuous recording methods (e.g., momentary time sample). Axelrod and colleagues (2009) compared three-minute and ten-minute intervals within a self-monitoring intervention for students with ADHD and found that both conditions were equally effective at improving students' on-task behavior. However, no other empirical studies experimentally compare different intervals. In practice, begin with shorter intervals and gradually increase the time between self-observations and recordings as students' behaviors or skills improve.

3. **Identify a prompting system**. Frequency counting will require a simple start/ stop prompting system that cues the student to begin and end the observation and recording session. A teacher or other staff member can indiscreetly provide

these cues. Interval recording and momentary time sampling systems will need a more elaborate method to alert students that the interval has started or ended. Early self-monitoring intervention studies relied on audio recorded beeps or teacher prompting to signal the intervals. However, available options have expanded in recent years to include tactile prompting devices clipped to the student's belt and computer or tablet applications. Each of these technologies allow for the intervals (i.e., time between prompts) to be set by the adult.

4. **Teach the student to attend to the prompt and correctly self-record**. Explicit instruction, modeling, and practice with feedback are likely needed to ensure the student has mastered the intervention's procedures. Do not discount the importance of this step. The intervention is not likely to be successful without student understanding of the procedures.

5. **Determine the appropriateness of rewarding accurate recording**. Several researchers have preferred positively reinforcing students' accurate recording of the target behavior or skill. Because some students might be less proficient at assessing their own behavior or lie about their behavior to obtain reinforcement, emphasizing accuracy within a reinforcement system might be necessary. Most studies have identified a criterion that students are required to meet. For example, Axelrod and colleagues (2009) provided students small rewards (e.g., candy) if their self-recordings matched a staff member's observations with at least 80% accuracy.

6. **Implement the intervention**. Attend to the following to promote high treatment fidelity: (1) ensure the student has all the materials before each self-monitoring session begins, (2) remind the student of the target skill or behavior before each session begins, and (3) maintain regular contact with the teacher so that questions and concerns can be addressed. In addition, school psychologists should collect recording forms regularly or conduct observations to assess progress. Collaborating with teachers to determine necessary adjustments to the intervention's procedures (e.g., decrease time interval, reteach recording system) is also recommended.

Meta-analytic research and reviews of the literature provide support for the use of self-monitoring in educational settings to increase on-task behavior, improve academic accuracy and productivity, and decrease disruptive school behavior (Reid et al., 2005; Stage & Quiroz, 1997). Self-monitoring has also been used to improve on-task behavior and work completion during homework time and enhance newly acquired classroom preparation skills (Axelrod et al., 2009; Gureasko-Moore et al., 2006). In addition to school and classroom settings, self-monitoring intervention have been successfully implemented in homes, residential treatment settings, and after-school programs (e.g., Axelrod, Nierengarten, & Fontanini-Axelrod, 2014b). Finally, research on the social acceptability of self-monitoring intervention is positive. Axelrod and colleagues (2009, 2014b), in two separate studies, found that teachers and afterschool staff reported that self-monitoring interventions were beneficial for students engaging in high rates of off-task behavior and noted the procedures were easy to implement.

SELF-REINFORCEMENT

Self-reinforcement or allowing students to be a part of selecting contingencies is a common component of self-management interventions and can also be used by itself within a token economy. Within such a system, students choose reinforcers or the cost of reinforcers (i.e., what is required for reinforcement to occur, such as the number of tokens earned for completing an assignment). Self-reinforcement can also be used more naturally in a classroom setting. When teacher attention is reinforcing, students could be taught to seek teacher attention in appropriate ways (e.g., asking for feedback on assignments) that could serve to positively reinforce both the asking for feedback but also completion of the assignment.

Similar to self-monitoring, self-reinforcement interventions are likely to require explicit instruction, modeling, practice, and feedback before implementation. The primary goal of self-reinforcement is for students to use the same logic employed by teacher-determined contingencies. Self-reinforcement strategies should only be used when a student has expressed understanding of teacher-determined contingencies and has the behavior or skill in his or her current repertoire.

Contingencies selected by students might be as effective as teacher-selected contingencies. For example, Frederiksen and Frederiksen (1975) found that self-determined token reinforcement was as effective as teacher-determined reinforcement for increasing middle school students' on-task behavior. However, other research has found self-determined reinforcement fails to increase performance of the target behavior but, rather, encourages students to inflate self-evaluations of behavior (e.g., Speidel & Tharp, 1980). Thus, practitioners should employ self-reinforcement only when students have demonstrated success in accurately self-evaluating behavior or teachers can evaluate student behavior concurrently with the student's own self-evaluation.

Conclusion

The three interventions presented in this chapter represent different EBPs that enhance skill acquisition deficits. However, each capitalizes on a model of learning that includes explicit instruction, modeling, practice, and positive or corrective feedback. Thus, the three interventions are likely to work seamlessly together to improve students' skill acquisition deficits. Video modeling or VSM naturally fits with BST and self-monitoring makes sense as a method of teaching students to be more independent at managing their behavior. Moreover, practitioners can fade or reintroduce VSM and self-monitoring easily within a BST framework. Doing so will likely enhance intervention outcomes and sustain behavior change over time.

References

Alberto, P. A., & Troutman, A. C. (2013). *Applied behavior analysis for teachers* (9th ed.). Upper Saddle River, NJ: Pearson.

Archer, A. L., & Hughes, C. A. (2011). *Explicit instruction: Effective and efficient teaching*. New York: Guilford.

Axelrod, M. I., Bellini, S., & Markoff, K. (2014a). Video self-modeling: A promising strategy for noncompliant children. *Behavior Modification, 38*, 567–586.

Axelrod, M. I., Butler, T., & Handwerk, M. L. (2004, May). Evaluating a clinical application of an in-vivo, exposure-based anger management intervention for adolescents in residential care. In C. E. Field (Chair), *New win for an old bottle: Innovative solutions for common clinical challenges*. Paper presented at the Annual Conference of the Association of Behavioral Analysis International, Boston, MA.

Axelrod, M. I., Nierengarten, B. L., & Fontanini-Axelrod, A. (2014b). Using self-monitoring to improve students' on-task homework behavior at an after-school program. *Journal of Education and Training, 1*, 58–71.

Axelrod, M. I., Zhe, E. J., Haugen, K. A., & Klein, J. A. (2009). Self-management of on-task homework behavior: A promising strategy for adolescents with attention and behavior problems. *School Psychology Review, 38*, 325–333.

Bandura, A. (1977). *Social learning theory*. Englewood Cliffs, NJ: Prentice-Hall.

Bellini, S. (2016). *Building social relationships—2: A systematic approach to teaching social interaction skills to children and adolescents with autism spectrum disorders and other social difficulties*. Shawnee Mission, KS: Autism Asperger Publishing.

Bellini, S., & Akullian, J. (2007). A meta-analysis of video self-modeling interventions for children and adolescents with autism spectrum disorders. *Exceptional Children, 73*, 264–287.

Cooper, J., Heron, T., & Heward, W. (2007). *Applied behavior analysis* (2nd ed.). Upper Saddle River, NJ: Merrill/Pearson Education.

Davies, S. C., Jones, K. M., & Rafoth, M. A. (2010). Effects of a self-monitoring intervention on children with traumatic brain injury. *Journal of Applied School Psychology, 26*, 308–326.

Dowrick, P. W. (1999). A review of self-modeling and related interventions. *Applied and preventative psychology, 8*, 23–39.

Epstein, M. H., Mooney, P., Reid, R., Ryan, J. B., & Uhing, B. M. (2005). A review of self-management interventions targeting academic outcomes for students with emotional and behavioral disorders. *Journal of Behavioral Education, 14*, 203–221.

Frederiksen, L. W., & Frederiksen, C. B. (1975). Teacher-determined and self-determined token reinforcement in a special education classroom. *Behavior Therapy, 6*, 310–314.

Gresham, F. M., Van, M. B., & Cook, C. R. (2006). Social skills training for teaching replacement behaviors: Remediating acquisition deficits in at-risk students. *Behavioral Disorders, 31*, 363–377.

Gureasko-Moore, S., DuPaul, G. J., & White, G. P. (2006). The effects of self-management in general education classrooms on the organizational skills of adolescents with ADHD. *Behavior Modification, 30*, 159–183.

Hanley, G. P., & Tiger, J. H. (2011). Differential reinforcement procedures. In W. W. Fisher, C. C. Piazza, & H. S. Roane (Eds.), *Handbook of applied behavior analysis* (pp. 229–249). New York: Guilford.

Maag, J. W. (2005). Social skills training for youth with emotional and behavioral disorders and learning disabilities: Problems, conclusions, and solutions. *Exceptionality, 13*, 155–172.

Mace, F. C., Belfiore, P. J., & Hutchinson, J. M. (2001). Operant theory and research on self-regulation. In B. Zimmerman & D. Schunk (Eds.), *Learning and academic achievement: Theoretical perspectives* (pp. 39–65). Mahwah, NJ: Lawrence Erlbaum.

Martens, B. K., Daly, E. J., Begeny, J. C., & VanDerHeyden, A. (2011). Behavioral approaches to education. In W. W. Fisher, C. C. Piazza, & H. S. Roane (Eds.), *Handbook of applied behavior analysis* (pp. 385–401). New York: Guilford.

Miles, N. I., & Wilder, D. A. (2009). The effects of behavioral skills training on caregiver implementation of guided compliance. *Journal of Applied Behavior Analysis, 42*, 405–410.

Miltenberger, R. G., & Gross, A. C. (2011). Teaching safety skills to children. In W. W. Fisher, C. C. Piazza, & H. S. Roane (Eds.), *Handbook of applied behavior analysis* (pp. 417–432). New York: Guilford.

Reid, R., Trout, A. L., & Schartz, M. (2005). Self-regulation interventions for children with attention deficit/hyperactivity disorder. *Exceptional Children, 71*, 361–377.

Schounard, C. A., Sutton, M. J., & Axelrod, M. I. (2012, May). *Investigating the consistency of results obtained from a brief experimental analysis of oral reading fluency.* Poster session presented at the meeting of the Association for Behavior Analysis International, Seattle, WA.

Speidel, G. E., & Tharp, R. G. (1980). What does self-reinforcement reinforce? An empirical analysis of the contingencies in self-determined reinforcement. *Child Behavior Therapy, 2*, 1–22.

Stage, S. A., & Quiroz, D. R. (1997). A meta-analysis of interventions to decrease disruptive classroom behavior in public education settings. *School Psychology Review, 26*, 333–368.

Wilder, D. A., & Atwell, J. (2006). Evaluation of a guided compliance procedure to reduce noncompliance among preschool children. *Behavioral Interventions, 21*, 265–272.

Promoting and Enhancing Academic Skills

11

This chapter presents a framework for designing instructional programs for students using principles derived from ABA. The chapter begins by introducing important evidence-based features of effective instruction. Next the chapter describes the instructional hierarchy as a model for considering the dynamic process of promoting and enhancing academic skills. The chapter concludes by highlighting two instructional programs, Direct Instruction and Precision Teaching, derived from behavioral principles of learning.

Fundamentals of Effective Instruction

Skinner (1953) viewed learning as a change in overt behavior that occurred as a function of an individual's response to changes in the environment. Consistent with Skinner's perspective, Greer (2002) stated that teaching involves the "identification and arrangement of optimal learning environments" (p. 9). Thus, a teacher's (broadly defined as anyone providing instruction to a student) role is to arrange instructional variables to enhance the learning environment. Many years of teacher effectiveness research indicates teachers' use of certain instructional approaches enhance learning outcomes (Rosenshine, 1995). Consequently, teachers have a great deal of influence over students' learning. Moreover, characterizing students' failure to learn as an internal defect, such as a learning disability or poor motivation, ignores the critical role the environment, instruction, and teachers play in the learning process. Given that teachers and their arrangement of instructional variables is so crucial to enhancing students' academic skills, identifying effective instructional practices seems important. This section highlights several features of instruction that have support in the literature. Specifically, the section will present readers with a model of instruction that includes developing learning objectives, introducing a lesson, providing instruction using the three-term contingency (A-B-C), and objectively measuring outcomes.

Learning Objectives

Identifying what students are expected to learn and formally writing learning objectives are logical first steps when designing an instructional plan (Fredrick and Hummel, 2004). This process typically begins by considering multiple variables (e.g., assessment data, curricular programming, individual learner needs, and larger classroom or school goals) that help guide an answer to the question 'what should students learn?' Developing and writing learning objectives becomes the next step once the teacher identifies what students should learn. Well written learning objectives contain an operational definition of the skill, including examples and nonexamples, essential instructional components and materials, current levels of performance and predetermined performance mastery criteria, and measurement strategies for formative and summative assessment. Tables 11.1 and 11.2 provide examples of learning objectives written for math fact fluency and reading sight words.

Table 11.1 Learning Objectives for Math Fact Fluency

Learning Objective Element	Example
Skill	Addition and Subtraction Fact Fluency; all known facts
Operational Definition	Addition Facts: 1-digit plus 1- and 2-digit w/ or w/o carrying Subtraction Facts: 1- or 2-digit minus 1-digit w/o borrowing Fluency: rate of correct responses
Example	Example: 6 13 10 3 8 16 14 5 4 19 +7 –2 +8 +8 –5 –4 +7 +6 –4 –7
Current Level of Performance	16 digits correct per min 1 incorrect problem per worksheet
Criteria for Mastery	32 digits correct per min 0 incorrect problems per worksheet
Time Frame	1 week Practice occurs each day
Assessment Strategies	Pre-/post-practice measure: Student completes 1-min probe w/teacher immediately before and after each practice session

Table 11.2   Learning Objectives for Reading Sight Words

Learning Objective Element	Example
Skill	Correctly reading sight words from list
Operational Definition	Read sight word correctly w/o teacher assistance within 3 secs
Words	*cat hat bat mat sat fat that vat rat pat*
Current Level of Performance	0 words read correctly
Criteria for Mastery	10 words read correctly
Time Frame	3 consecutive days, 20-min sessions
Assessment Strategies	Student reads list on day 4

Learning objectives are best written to target improving students' accuracy of responding or fluency with a skill. For example, increasing oral reading fluency by 30 words (read) correct per minute or recalling the six times table with 100% accuracy are preferred over simply stating that improvements in reading and math are expected. Those learning objectives that aim to improve students' understanding of a concept might be too ambiguous and, thus, difficult to objectively measure. Learning objectives that target accuracy or fluency lend themselves well to ongoing progress monitoring, a hallmark of the tiered model of service delivery (e.g., Response to Intervention). Frequent measurement of accuracy or fluency will help determine the degree to which students have achieved their learning objectives. Knowing the degree to which students have met or not met their learning objectives allows for data-based decision making regarding the appropriateness and effectiveness of instruction, and a need for more intensive academic supports exists.

Beginning a Lesson

Research has found that beginning instruction with a statement of the current lesson's goals and a brief review of relevant previously learned content characterize effective teaching practices (see Rosenshine, 1995). Archer and Hughes (2011) noted that students are more likely to benefit from instruction when understanding the lesson's purpose, expected outcomes, and how the skill will be presented or taught. Exposure to previously learned material provides students with additional opportunities to respond and offers teachers additional opportunities to assess for generalization and maintenance. Moreover, reviewing previously learned content or skills could aid in the presentation of new content or skills, especially when new content or skills build upon what was previously learned.

The Three-Term Contingency or Learning Trial

Conceptualizing instruction using the three-term contingency (i.e., A-B-C) can effectively organize the instructional session. In the context of promoting or enhancing academic skills, the three-term contingency, or learning trial, contains an antecedent stimulus, an academic response, and immediate reinforcement or corrective feedback (Cooper, Heron, & Heward, 2007). Albers and Greer (1991) suggested feedback contingent on the academic response is what differentiates a learning trial from academic responding (i.e., stimulus-response). A learning trial has occurred only after the consequence has been delivered.

The use of learning trials to teach academic content and skills is supported in the literature. Maccini and Hughes (1997), in their review of 20 math interventions for high school students with learning disabilities, found that learning trials were related to effective instruction and positive student outcomes, and Albers and Greer (1991) noted that increasing the number of learning trials increased rates of correct responding while keeping error rates low. The remainder of this section highlights effective instructional practices that consider features of the learning trial.

DEMONSTRATION AND EFFECTIVE MODELS

Academic content and skills are best learned when "correct responses are clearly distinguishable from incorrect responses" (Hendrickson & Gable, 1981, p. 26). Consequently, antecedent stimuli must aid students in differentiating correct and incorrect responses. In most cases, academic antecedent stimuli take the form of demonstrations. Demonstrations, or observations by the learner of someone else performing the skill, involve modeling with some explanation (see Allington & Cunningham, 2007). For example, a teacher might demonstrate decoding by

Teacher: We're going to read the word cat. What word are we going to read?
Students: Cat!
Teacher: Great job. We're going to read the word cat. The first letter is c. The c in cat makes the /k/ sound. /k/. What sound does the c make?
Students: /k/.
Teacher: Yes! Wonderful job class. The c makes the /k/ sound. We've already learned what sound the a and t make together. What sound do the a and t make together?
Students: /at/.
Teacher: Correct. Again, what sound do the a and t make together?
Students: /at/.
Teacher: Wonderful class. Now, I'm going to put the c together with the a and the t. /k/-/at/. /kat/. Now it's your turn to put the c together with the a and the t.
Students: /k/-/at/. /kat/.
Teacher: Great job everyone. /k/-/at/. Put them together and we read the word /kat/.

Figure 11.1 Modeling Decoding

Oral Presentation of Lesson	Visual Presentation of Lesson
Teacher: How do you divide a 3-digit number by a 2-digit number? For example, we want to split 312 students into 12 groups for the class field day. How many students will be in each group?	312 students 12 groups
Teacher: Let's first review the long division algorithm. We have 7 divided by 3. 3 times 2 equals 6. 7 minus 6 equals 1. The answer to 7 divided by 3 is 2 with a remainder of 1.	$$\begin{array}{r} 2r1 \\ 3\overline{)7} \\ -6 \\ \hline 1 \end{array}$$ $3 \times 2 = 6$
Teacher: Now back to our long division problem. We have 312 students and need to divide them into 12 groups. The equation looks like this. First, we ask if 3 can be divided by 12 groups. Manny, can 3 by divided by 12 groups? Manny: No. Teacher: Good, Manny, can 31 be divided by 12 groups? Manny: Yes, I think it can.	$12\overline{)312}$ = Can 3 be divided by 12? No Can 31 be divided by 12?
Teacher: Good job, Manny. 31 can be divided by 12. Sarah and Demetri, please come up to the board and show the class how to divide 31 by 12. Teacher: Good job! Our answer is 2 with a remainder of 7. So let's get back to the problem. 12 times 2 is 24. We put the 2 above 312 and substract 24 from 31. We now move the 2 from 312 down next to the 7. Our next step is to divide 72 by 12. This is a little tricky. Let's start with 10 times 12. Sarita, what's 10 times 12?	$$\begin{array}{r} 2r7 \\ 12\overline{)31} \\ -24 \\ \hline 7 \\ 2 \\ 12\overline{)312} \\ -24 \\ \hline 72 \end{array}$$
Sarita: 120. Teacher: Well done! 10 times 12 equals 120. Too high, maybe. Remember, we want to get as close to 72 as possible without going over. Let's try 8 times 12. We can use the distributive property to solve this multiplication problem. James, what's the distributive property? James: It's when you split up one of the numbers to make it easier to multiply. Teacher: Good, James. That's the first step. Remember a times b plus c equals a times b plus a times c. Watch me on the board. Now let's try it with 8 times 12. We can split 12 into 10 and 2. 8 times 10 plus 8 times 2 equals what, Sarah? Sarah: 80 plus 16, which equals 96. Teacher: So, 8 times 12 equals 96. Probably too high as well. Let's try 6 times 12. Ben, use the distributive property to calculate 6 times 12. Ben: Split 12 into 10 and 2. Multiply 10 and 6 and 2 and 6. 10 times 6 is 60 plus 2 times 6, which is 12, equals 72. Teacher: Good, Ben, well done! 6 times 12 equals 72, which is the number we're looking for. Let's go back to the problem. We put the 6 next to the 2, multiply 6 and 12 to get 72. Subtract 72 from 72 and get 0. So, the answer is 26. If we split the class into 12 groups, we'll have 26 students in each group. 312 divided by 12 equals 26, which means 12 groups times 26 students in each group should equal 312. Everyone, check our answer by calculating 12 times 26.	$10 \times 12 = 120$ $8 \times 12 = 96$ $6 \times 12 = 72$ $a(b + c) =$ $8 \times 12 =$ $(a \times b) +$ $8(10 + 2)$ $(a \times c)$ $(8 \times 10) +$ $(8 \times 2) =$ $80 + 16 =$ 96 $$\begin{array}{r} 26 \\ 12\overline{)312} \\ -24 \\ \hline 72 \\ -72 \\ \hline 0 \end{array}$$

Figure 11.2   Modeling Long Division

modeling each sound alone and then together, or long division by modeling each step on the board and providing commentary of what he or she is doing and why (see Figures 11.1 and 11.2). Explanations can also be nonverbal. Pointing, for example, might be all that is needed to explain a concept.

Demonstrations and, more specifically, modeling are common teaching practices because of their efficiency and effectiveness at enhancing academic skills (Hendrickson & Gable, 1981; Polk, 2006). Instruction that includes modeling can increase the frequency of correct responding and decrease the frequency of errors, thus maximizing instructional time (Fredrick & Hummel, 2004) and minimizing learner frustration. Furthermore, research on effective instructional practices has highlighted demonstration and modeling within an evidence-based teaching paradigm. Specifically, direct instructional approaches involving modeling are more effective at promoting academic skills and increasing academic knowledge than discovery-based learning, which has failed to establish itself as a research-supported teaching method (Kirschner, Sweller, & Clark, 2006). Evidence exists indicating modeling is an effective instructional approach for teaching math, spelling, reading, written language, and handwriting (Hendrickson & Gable, 1981).

Anyone (e.g., teacher, peer, parent) can model an academic skill and modeling can occur via many mediums (e.g., live demonstration, video, computer). Effective models demonstrate the skill by slowly performing each step in sequential order, complementing the demonstration with clear and concise explanations, and using an assortment of examples and non-examples (Archer & Hughes, 2011; Rosenshine & Stevens, 1986). Examples should sufficiently offer students cases or instances of how or where the skill should be applied. The purpose of non-examples is to decrease the possibility students will use or apply the skill inappropriately or incorrectly.

RESPONSE PROMPTS

Response prompts, broadly speaking, are antecedent stimuli that facilitate accurate responding. In the context of academic instruction, response prompts help students respond accurately to academic content to promote or enhance an academic skill. According to Vargas (2013), response prompts "may consist of highlighting or underlining, giving parts of an answer, physical guidance, or anything else that helps a student respond correctly" (p. 200). Teachers might also remind students of previous examples, provide clues to an answer, or offer the first steps of a procedure to prompt accurate responding. However, response prompts should be faded or withdrawn as students become more accurate in their responding or demonstrate fluency with a skill. Ideally, fading will systematically reduce the prompts provided beginning with those that model steps or skills students have mastered. Textbooks often demonstrate academic skills before presenting practice items to students and typically fade visual response prompts over two or more examples (see Figure 11.3).

Adding Fractions:

$$\frac{1}{3} + \frac{1}{2} = -$$

1. Find common denominator

$3 \times 2 = 6$

2. Make equivalent fractions with new denominators and numerators

$$\frac{1}{3} \times \frac{2}{2} = \frac{2}{6} \quad \frac{1}{2} \times \frac{3}{3} = \frac{3}{6}$$

3. Rewrite the equation using equivalent fractions

$$\frac{2}{6} + \frac{3}{6} =$$

4. Add the top numbers and put the answer over the same denominator

$$\frac{2}{6} + \frac{3}{6} = \frac{5}{6}$$

Now you try:

$$\frac{1}{4} + \frac{1}{3} = -$$

1. Find common denominator

$4 \times \square = 12$

2. Make equivalent fractions

$$\frac{1}{4} \times \frac{3}{3} = -$$

$$\frac{1}{3} \times \frac{}{4} = \frac{4}{12}$$

3. Rewrite the equation using equivalent fractions

$$\frac{}{12} + \frac{4}{12} =$$

4. Add the top numbers and put the answer over the same denominator

$$\frac{}{12} + \frac{4}{12} = \frac{}{12}$$

Figure 11.3   Fading Response Prompts when Demonstrating the Skill of Adding Fractions

PROVIDING OPPORTUNITIES TO RESPOND THROUGH GUIDED PRACTICE

The second term in the three-term contingency is the academic response. Not surprising, effective instruction provides students with multiple opportunities to respond. While viewing a demonstration and being provided with a response prompt is usually beneficial, affording students opportunities to respond allows for learning to unfold. Fredrick and Hummel (2004) provided two examples illustrating the necessity of responding during instruction. They suggested envisioning learning to write cursive or shoot a basketball by only watching others engage in the behavior. Developing mastery of a skill, especially a complex skill, requires more than simply observing demonstrations. Mastery requires practice, and effective instruction highlights repetition of learning trials to allow for multiple opportunities for students to respond.

Teacher effectiveness research emphasizes the importance of practice but only practice that is closely regulated and supported (Archer & Hughes, 2011). Leaving students to practice a new skill on their own can increase the frequency of errors and lead to students learning the skill incorrectly. Unsupported practice, or practice that does not allow students to ask questions or receive immediate feedback, is likely to be frustrating and discouraging for students. For example, independent seatwork is an excellent opportunity for students to practice a new skill. However, many students are likely to struggle when teachers are not available to provide support or feedback. Homework might also offer students an opportunity to practice newly learned skills but only when they have achieved near-mastery. Homework becomes frustrating and intolerable for both students and parents when the skills being practiced have not been adequately taught and practiced at school.

There are several features of practice worth noting. First, interspersing practice with the presentation and demonstration of material or skills is suggested. Rosenshine (1995) reported that least effective teachers presented entire lessons before allowing for students to respond or practice covered material. He recommended that academic material or skills be taught in small amounts with teacher-guided practice occurring often within an instructional session. Second, practice should allow for frequent opportunities for students to respond to academic prompts that are like those that have been modeled. However, including prompts that vary, but are similar enough to the type of responding that will be expected for the students to demonstrate mastery, is important when skill maintenance and generalizability are objectives. Consequently, practice designed to begin with already modeled responses, and transition to items that require responses to material not modeled, is recommended. Additionally, interspersing known items with unknown items aids in fluency building (Burns, 2005). That is, practice should mix content already mastered with new material. Third, opportunities to respond can take many forms. For example, students might be asked to respond verbally or in writing on a worksheet or on the board. Students can practice in groups and prompts can be questions posed by teachers or peers, paper worksheets, or computer-presented problems. Finally, increased opportunities for students to respond provide increased opportunities for teachers to monitor performance, check for understanding, and provide feedback (Fredrick & Hummel, 2004; Skinner, 1998). Doing this also allows teachers to adjust, modify, or repeat instruction.

REINFORCEMENT AND FEEDBACK

Reinforcement, the final term in the three-term contingency, is often described as feedback within the learning trial. Many authors writing on effective instructional practices speak about the importance of feedback for learning (see Archer & Hughes, 2011; Alberto & Troutman, 2013). For example, Rosenshine (1995) reported that the literature routinely describes systematic feedback, either positive or corrective, as a characteristic of effective teaching. Feedback about students' accurate responding increases the likelihood of future accurate responding and decreases the likelihood of incorrect responding (Fredrick & Hummel, 2004). However, feedback during the learning trial can take many forms—teachers can reinforce students' effort (e.g., persistence in the presence of challenging work), supporting one another, asking questions, and displaying behavior necessary for learning to occur (e.g., on-task).

The feedback itself serves as a consequential event to students' academic responding. With positive feedback, students know their response was correct. In addition, feedback can reinforce accurate academic responses (i.e., behavior) resulting in increases in the likelihood of correct responding in the future. Reinforcement can take the form of delivering something good to the student (e.g., praise, free time, tokens) or removing something aversive (e.g., taking away additional problems) contingent on accurate responding. Finally, feedback can serve as a discriminative stimulus for students by promoting certain behaviors that may help increase accurate responding in the future (Skinner, 1998). For example, corrective feedback delivered by a teacher might prompt a student to ask the teacher for help in the future (MacDuff, Krantz, & McClannahan, 2001).

The practice of delivering feedback for students' accurate academic responses is akin to when students are learning behavioral skills. Consideration of the positive to negative ratio, the density of the schedule, and timing are important. Borrowing from the research on teaching behavioral skills, the ratio should be at least 4:1 in favor of positive feedback, the schedule should be dense, almost continuous, when skills are first being acquired or the frequency of incorrect responses is high, and the feedback should be delivered in a way as to not disrupt students (e.g., verbal praise might serve as an antecedent for off-task behavior). According to Fredrick and Hummel (2004), corrective feedback should simply involve informing the student the response was incorrect and then providing or modeling for the student the correct response followed by a repeated trial. They noted that too much verbiage (e.g., long explanations) might interfere with the students' comprehension of what is required of them to correctly respond, or be distracting or punishing, which might result in problem behaviors.

Much has also been written about the immediacy of feedback (e.g., Alberto & Troutman, 2013; Fredrick & Hummel, 2004). Skinner (1998) observed that immediate feedback is crucial, especially when students are just beginning to acquire a skill. Incorrect responses that go uncorrected are likely to be repeated, so efforts should be made to provide feedback, especially corrective feedback, as immediately as possible. While the most economical way of delivering immediate corrective feedback is for instruction to be one-on-one, this might not be possible in a group setting like a classroom. Below are several examples that allow for the delivery of immediate feedback efficiently during learning trials with less teacher involvement:

- **Classwide peer tutoring (see Greenwood, 1997)**: Students are assigned to tutor–student pairs. The tutor presents an academic prompt, the student responds, and the tutor provides positive or corrective feedback. Pairs can earn reinforcers for correctly implementing the procedures and improvements in performance.
- **Computers**: Computer-aided practice models have been designed to specifically target different academic skills by providing a prompt, requiring the student to respond overtly, and delivering immediate feedback on performance.
- **Self-managed interventions**: Skinner (1998) suggested that self-administered interventions, such as Copy, Cover, and Compare (see Joseph et al., 2012) or using audio recordings involving response prompts, adequate time for student responding, and feedback (see Windingstad, Skinner, Rowland, Cardin, & Fearrington, 2009), can provide students with immediate feedback without direct teacher involvement.

Direct Measurement

Fredrick and Hummel (2004) noted that "every time a student responds, teachers have an opportunity to measure learning" (p.13). Learning trials, in themselves, allow for the direct measurement of student performance, as determining the accuracy of student responding is part of the feedback process. Knowing that the student was correct or incorrect is, in many ways, a direct measure of student performance. A more common measurement approach in schools involves a temporal dimension where students are formally evaluated following several days or weeks of instruction. Unfortunately, this practice fails to provide useful information on student performance for instructional decision making or offer valuable corrective feedback to students. Regardless, direct measurement of student learning should:

1. Be related to the predetermined learning objectives;
2. Directly measure skills that are modeled and practiced;
3. Be frequent enough to closely monitor student performance;
4. Provide students with performance feedback; and
5. Provide educators with information to make instructional decisions.

The Instructional Hierarchy

Haring, Lovitt, Eaton, & Hanson (1978) observed that strategies that successfully help students acquire skills were not effective when students were trying to apply those skills. Essentially, the effectiveness of instructional approaches changed as students' proficiency with the skill changed. Accordingly, they developed a framework for understanding stages of student learning called the Instructional Hierarchy (IH). Yet, although it is often considered a stage model, Martens, Daly, Begeny, and

VanDerHeyden (2011) more appropriately described the IH as a "dynamic teaching model" (p. 386) because it requires ongoing assessment of proficiency and adjustment to instructional strategies that best promote skill development. From its inception, IH has been a useful paradigm when designing educational programs for students with and without disabilities.

Most authors writing on the IH present the following phases: (1) skill acquisition, (2) fluency, (3) generalization, and (4) maintenance (e.g., Haring et al., 1978; Martens et al., 2011; Martens & Witt, 2004). These phases are often considered outcomes of effective instruction (Fredrick & Hummel, 2004). The initial phase involves acquisition of skills not in students' repertoires. Students are likely to require a significant degree of support when first acquiring a skill but supports can be faded as students demonstrate mastery (i.e., performing the skill accurately and repeatedly). The next phase focuses on fluency. The goal is for students to continue performing skills with accuracy while increasing speed of responding. Fluency building often requires repeated practice and feedback, with the goal being increased rate (e.g., responses correct per minute). When fluency is achieved, students then learn to perform skills under different conditions. Both response generalization (e.g., completing three-digit by two-digit addition problems after demonstrating proficiency with two-digit by two-digit addition problems) and stimulus generalization (e.g., applying the skill of summarizing text to different reading passages) are objectives during this phase. Some students lose proficiency with a skill after gaps in use, requiring re-teaching and re-learning. The maintenance phase emphasizes fluency but in a wide range of contexts and despite those skills not being used as often as in other IH phases.

Proficiency with a skill can be measured by assessing accurate responding (e.g., correct or incorrect response), rate of accurate responding (e.g., correct or incorrect responses per minute), and rate of accurate responding under different conditions (e.g., correct or incorrect responses per minute when given different reading material). Measurement during early phases of learning will likely focus on the first two approaches. Assessing if and how the skill is executed is consistent with understanding student learning at the acquisition and fluency phases. Identifying when the skill is executed will aid in evaluating the generalization and maintenance of a skill. Following an assessment of the student's skill proficiency, the IH can be used to identify an instructional program based on evidence-based practices that have been demonstrated to be effective at the student's level (see Table 11.3).

Skill Acquisition

Instructional strategies at the skill acquisition phase are designed to promote or enhance skills. Accuracy of responding with the use of few or no supports (e.g., demonstrations, response prompts) is the primary objective. Students at this stage are typically just beginning to learn a skill or have not demonstrated a skill consistently or with a predetermined level of accuracy. Teaching at this stage involves either incidental learning (i.e., learning that occurs during less structured activities) or structured learning trials. Structured learning trials, sometimes termed discrete trial

Table 11.3   Instructional Hierarchy, Instructional Strategies, and Sample Interventions

Learning Stage	Objective	Instructional Strategies	Example of Matched Interventions
Acquisition	Complete the skill accurately and without assistance	• Demonstrations/ modeling • Prompts/cues • Fade prompts/cues • Immediate feedback on accuracy of response • Error correction	• Copy/Cover/ Compare • Peer Tutoring • Listening Passage Preview • Roots for Numeracy • Early Learning in Mathematics • Error Monitoring
Fluency	Complete the skill accurately while increasing rate of responding	• Brief but frequent opportunities to practice • Immediate feedback on rate of responding • Combining newly acquired and previously acquired skills to solve problems	• Repeated Reading • Partnered Reading • Incremental Rehearsal • Taped Problems • Explicit Time Drill
Generalization	Increase skill usage in conditions other than what was present during instruction	• Model, practice, and reinforce skills across contexts • Structure academic tasks to require skill in new contexts • Prompt/cue usage in new contexts • Provide practice opportunities that teach discrimination between similar skills	• Self-Correction • Peer Tutoring • Roots for Numeracy • Early Learning in Mathematics • Incremental Rehearsal
Maintenance	Is fluent with the skill despite its lack of use	• Gradually increase intervals between practice sessions • Teach student to self-monitor	• Self-Management Interventions

training, involve (1) an instruction or other stimulus, (2) prompting or modeling to increase probability of accurate responding, (3) learner responding, and (4) corrective feedback for inaccurate responding or reinforcement for accurate responding (Cooper et al., 2007; Wolery, Bailey, & Sugai, 1988). In teaching an academic skill, this might look like the following:

1. Teacher presents students with addition problem "2 + 7 = _____" on the board;
2. Teacher prompts students to count out seven blocks on one side of their desks and two blocks on the other side, then instructs students to put the two piles of blocks together and count the total number of blocks;
3. Teacher provides enough time for students to respond;
4. Teacher or peers provide corrective feedback or reinforcement.

Fading assistance or supports (e.g., models, response prompts) is conducted systematically following initial acquisition of the skill. Fading and assessing for independence might be necessary when students are responding accurately to stimuli or when their learning is under stimulus control (e.g., correct responses follow an academic prompt). Additional assistance or support, or introducing easier content might be indicated when students fail to respond accurately or stimulus control is not achieved.

Fluency

Fluency is defined as automatic responding or the combination of accurate responding with appropriate pace or speed, and is an important feature of academic competency (Alberto & Troutman, 2013). Fluency development is highlighted by attempts at increasing rates of responding while maintaining a high degree of accuracy. The emphasis is no longer on individual responses to stimuli (i.e., discrete trial training) but on providing students with sufficient opportunities to learn to respond accurately and quickly to multiple stimuli (Martens et al., 2011). The instructional approaches employed during fluency development will be different than those used during skill acquisition. For example, repeated practice with the same material is often used to build fluent responding. Rereading a paragraph several times to improve oral reading fluency or reviewing math fact flash cards for math computation fluency are both examples of practice for fluency building. According to Daly, Martens, Barnett, Witt, and Olson (2007), research has found the fundamental features of effective practice to include: (1) instructional materials that closely match students' skill level so responses are more likely to be accurate with minimal support, (2) practice opportunities that are brief and immediately followed up with reinforcement or corrective feedback, (3) ongoing progress monitoring, and (4) establishment of criteria for moving to more difficult instructional material. Moreover, beginning with instructional material that is well matched to students' current skill level and gradually increasing the material's difficulty as students demonstrate fluency with the skill is important for fluency development and recommended.

Moving from skill acquisition to fluency necessitates a shift in measurement approaches. While skill acquisition involves assessing accuracy, fluency requires the evaluation of rate of accurate responding. As most school psychologists and other educators are aware, measuring rate of accurate responding is best conducted using brief (e.g., one to three-minute) academic skill probes (e.g., oral reading, math computation) that often result in 'per minute' outcome variables (e.g., 'words correctly read per minute').

Generalization and Maintenance

Generalization, in the context of the IH, is best characterized as the demonstration of fluency with a skill under conditions other than what was present during instruction (stimulus generalization). Generalization also involves being fluent with skills not specifically taught to the student (response generalization). Regarding the former, models, prompts, teachers, instructional materials, and contexts (e.g., general and special education classrooms) are all stimuli that can be altered during instruction to promote stimulus generalization. Regarding the latter, varying the instructional material is a typical strategy that enhances response generalization. For example, reading probes that include a high degree of overlap with passages used during fluency practice (i.e., similar but not identical passages) and presenting calculation problems in story format provide students opportunities to generalize skills learned during the fluency phase.

Maintenance is the continued performance of a skill following removal of contingencies or instructional supports. Removing contingencies often involves a gradual withdraw that alters the reinforcement schedule. This occurs naturally as the IH shifts from the skill acquisition to fluency phase. Initial skill acquisition is likely to require continuous reinforcement, which is gradually thinned as students become increasingly proficient with the skill. The fluency stage naturally shifts reinforcement to a ratio schedule. Student responding during the fluency stage is reinforced following many successful trials. Skinner (1983) viewed the gradual fading of reinforcement or increasing the interval between reinforcement as important for teaching students to work for longer periods of time and encouraging independence.

Research supports using different schedules of reinforcement when differentially targeting skill acquisition and fluency (Alberto & Troutman, 2013; Martens et al., 2011). In fact, varying the schedule is advised when attempting to promote or enhance academic skills. Martens and Witt (2004) cited several studies that found intermittent schedules of reinforcement promoted the acquisition of academic skills and that thinned schedules led to students' maintenance of learned academic skills when reinforcement was withdrawn. Consideration of the type of academic skill being taught might also be necessary. Ratio schedules are best suited for academic tasks that require high rates of responding (e.g., math facts, letter naming), while variable interval schedules are appropriate for academic tasks that necessitate a low to moderate response rate (e.g., math story problems, reading comprehension; Lee & Belfiore, 1997).

Basic Notetaking

World War I Notes for: <u>11/14/2016</u>
Introduction to WWI • WWI started in <u>1914</u> after the Austrian Archduke <u>Ferdinand</u> was assassinated by a Serbian Nationalist • The United States avoided the war for as long as possible but eventually joined in <u>1917</u> • Under President Woodrow <u>Wilson</u>, the US followed an *Isolationist* perspective, which means: <u>countries should not get involved in each other's conflicts</u> Causes of WWI • Several European governments took an <u>Imperialistic</u> and <u>Militaristic</u> perspective, which contributed to Nationalism or a strong sense of national <u>identity and loyalty</u> • Imperialism means: <u>a country's desire to become powerful by acquiring more territory or land</u> • Militarism is when a country maintains a strong military • Military buildups by several closely located countries can cause <u>tension and armed conflict</u> WWI Allies • <u>Great Britain, France, Russia, Serbia and Belgium</u> WWI Central Powers • <u>Germany, Austria-Hungary, Bulgaria, and the Ottoman Empire</u>

Advanced Notetaking

World War I Notes for: <u>11/15/2016</u>
WWI and the United States • The US entered the war in <u>1917</u> • Remaining neutral was <u>difficult because of our close ties with Great Britain and trade with European countries affected by the war</u> • The US became concerned about Germany because <u>of their military buildup, and use of submarines or U-Boats</u> • <u>U-Boats sank many ships, even those not part of the navy like merchant and passenger ships</u> • In <u>1915</u>, a German <u>U-Boat</u> sank the <u>Lusitania</u>, a British <u>passenger ship</u>, killing 100 <u>Americans</u>. This resulted in <u>anger in the United States and is a reason for America entering the war</u> • The Zimmerman Telegram also angered Americans. The Zimmerman Telegram was <u>when Germany's foreign minister sent a telegram to the Mexican government asking them to attack the US if the US and Germany went to war. Germany promised Mexico part of the US when they won the war</u> The US Enters the War • The US entered WWI in <u>1917</u>. Prior to entering the war, the Allies and Central Powers were at a <u>stalemate</u>, which means <u>neither side was winning</u>

Figure 11.4 Fading Visual Prompts when Teaching Notetaking

Prompt fading involves a gradual and systematic decrease in the level of assistance required to successfully complete a task. Fading instructional supports facilitates generalization and maintenance by requiring students to become more independent in their responding (Alberto & Troutman, 2013). Many commercially available textbooks fade instructional supports by initially providing students with, and then gradually removing, visual aids. Figures 11.4 and 11.5 offer examples of prompt fading.

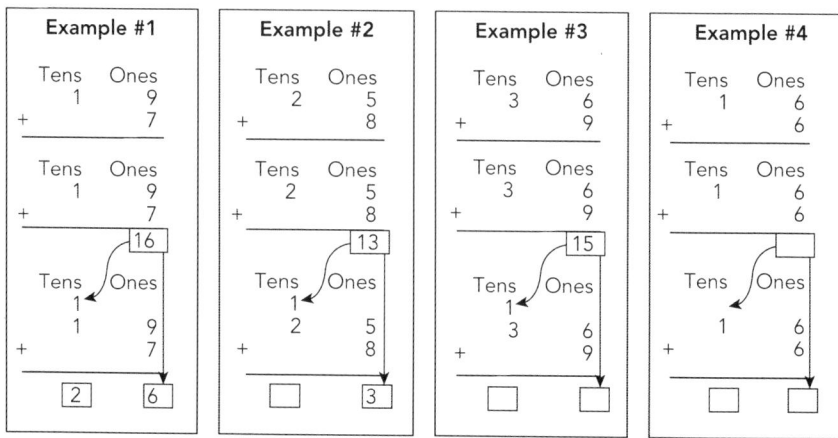

Figure 11.5   Fading Visual Prompts for Addition with Regrouping Worksheet

Finally, Martens and colleagues (2011) warned that students might demonstrate certain skill deficits that interfere with the development of more advanced or complex skills even after a fluency criterion has been achieved. For example, a student who continues to respond incorrectly to '6 × 7' might meet math fact fluency standards (e.g., digits correct per minute when practicing multiplication) but struggle when faced with long division problems that require the student to know that '6 × 7 = 42.' In these cases, Martens and colleagues recommended providing additional instruction at the skill acquisition phase by teaching the skill in isolation and concurrently with the more advanced or complex skill. This process illustrates the dynamic nature of teaching and emphasizes the importance of ongoing assessment at the individual skill and fluency stages.

Instructional Programs Derived from Behavioral Principles of Learning

Broadly speaking, academic programs based on principles of learning utilize the learning trial as its primary instructional method. Modeling and systematic prompting, providing frequent opportunities for students to respond, and delivering immediate performance feedback are all hallmarks of evidence-based instructional practices derived from ABA (Martens et al., 2011). In addition, matching instructional material to students' current level, establishing clear and objective outcomes goals, conducting ongoing direct measurement, and appropriately pacing instruction differentiate instructional models built from behavioral learning principles from constructivist or inquiry-based approaches (Kozioff, LaNunziata, Cowardin, & Bessellieu, 2001). The remainder of this chapter briefly describes Direct Instruction and Precision Teacher, two examples of comprehensive programs designed from a behavior analytic framework.

Direct Instruction

The assumptions that underlie Direct Instruction (DI) include all students can learn, learning is a function of instruction, teachers have a great degree of control over instruction, the goal of instruction is mastery of skills, students should be strategically placed within the curriculum (i.e., at their instructional level), instructional sessions should be brief (i.e., under 45 minutes) and include multiple opportunities for students to respond, and instruction is based on research-supported practices (Kozioff et al., 2001). In DI, basic skills are highly sequenced, as mastery of one skill provides students with prerequisites for the next skill, generalization and maintenance of skills are emphasized, pacing is fast, and students typically respond orally (Swanson, Hoskyn, & Lee, 1999). Moreover, instruction is explicit and follows the three-step sequence of the learning trial. Using a script, teachers describe and demonstrate the skill, elicit or prompt student responses, and provide immediate feedback including error correction for incorrect responses (Martens et al., 2011; Vargas, 2013). Error correction simply involves the teacher providing the correct response or re-modeling the skill. DI also calls on teachers to use a delayed probe to assess students' skill acquisition following several learning trials targeting the next skill (Kozioff et al., 2001). The delayed probe allows teachers to assess performance of a previously learned skill following the introduction of new skills. For students, the delayed probe provides an opportunity to demonstrate proficiency with a previously learned skill.

DI outlines procedures for encouraging the maintenance and generalization of skills. Maintenance is programmed by moving gradually from teacher- to student-guided practice sessions (Kozioff et al., 2001). For example, teachers might require students to independently use mastered skills during seatwork or homework tasks. When students initially begin independently practicing newly acquired skills, teacher-less feedback mechanisms like those described earlier could be considered (e.g., classwide peer tutoring). Critical to learning, students need to display skills outside the context of the learning trial. Consequently, planning for generalization becomes an instructional objective. Strategies include varying the teacher (e.g., peers, paraprofessionals, co-teachers) and instructional materials, using prompts and reminders (i.e., pre-teaching) when skills might be needed, and inviting students to share different ways in which skills might be used.

Several ABA texts describing DI include a description of Project Follow Through, a large-scale program designed to compare models of teaching (see Martens et al., 2011; Vargas, 2013). Parents from each school district participating in the project selected a model and teachers were trained to implement that model. The project lasted over 20 years and targeted over 75,000 students from low-income households in 170 communities. Despite some limitations with the study's methodology, students taught using the DI model outperformed all other students on measures of academic skills, comprehension and problem-solving, and affective variables (e.g., self-esteem). Moreover, long-term follow-up studies found that students in the DI group had significantly higher graduation rates than peers with similar socioeconomic backgrounds. Research since Project Follow Through continues to demonstrate the effectiveness of DI. For example, a meta-analysis of educational reform models implemented in urban and low-performing schools found DI to be in the top three of the 29 models examined (Borman, Hewes, Overman, & Brown, 2003) and DI has been used successfully with students of all ages, in various educational contexts (e.g., general education, special education), and for different academic skills (Kozioff et al., 2001; Shippen, Houchins, Stevenson, & Sartor, 2005).

Precision Teaching

Precision Teaching (PT) is more a measurement and decision-making model than an instructional program. The primary purpose of PT is to directly measure student academic behavior related to response rate, chart progress, and determine instructional program effectiveness (Vargas, 2013). Within PT, learning is measured as a change in response rate or fluency with a skill (e.g., words read correctly per minute, digits computed correctly per minute; Fredrick & Hummel, 2004). Teachers take repeated measurements of observable academic skills, record performance on a semi logarithmic or Standard Celeration Chart, and review student performance over time to make judgments about progress. Often students themselves are taught to record performance using their own data and charts provided by the teacher.

The literature investigating the effectiveness of PT is not as voluminous as that of DI, although research has shown PT's usefulness in general and special education classrooms (see Binder & Watkins, 1990). This should not be surprising, as PT includes elements of effective instruction including frequent student practice and ongoing measurement of specific academic skills. Furthermore, PT as a measurement paradigm is similar to curriculum-based measurement (CBM), which has been found to be a valid method for assessing student performance in response to instruction (Martens et al., 2011).

Conclusion

According to the National Center for Educational Statistics (2016), only 37% of twelfth graders are at or above the proficient level in reading and only one in four are at or above the proficient level in math. Moreover, the achievement gap between students with and without disabilities continues to grow. Bijou, back in 1970, suggested that the science of ABA had a lot to offer education including research-supported instructional principles, yet there is evidence that teachers do not always engage in evidence-based instructional practices (e.g., Burns & Ysseldyke, 2009; Doabler et al., 2014). This chapter presents features of effective instruction, including modeling, practice, and feedback, that are easily accessible to general and special education teachers. This chapter also describes the IH, which offers a conceptual model for matching instructional approaches to stages of learning. Together, effective instructional practices and the IH have the potential to significantly improve student learning outcomes and school psychologists should consider equipping themselves with this knowledge as they consult on referral questions involving the promotion and enhancement of students' academic skills.

References

Albers, A. E., & Greer, R. D. (1991). Is the three-term contingency trial a predictor of effective instruction? *Journal of Behavioral Education, 1,* 337–354.

Alberto, P. A., & Troutman, A. C. (2013). *Applied behavior analysis for teachers* (9th ed.). Upper Saddle River, NJ: Pearson.

Allington, R. L., & Cunningham, P. M. (2007). *Classrooms that work: They can all read and write.* Boston: Pearson/Allyn and Bacon.

Archer, A. L., & Hughes, C. A. (2011). *Explicit instruction: Effective and efficient teaching.* New York: Guilford.

Bijou, S. W. (1970). What psychology has to offer education—now. *Journal of Applied Behavior Analysis, 3,* 65–71.

Binder, C., & Watkins, C. L. (1990). Precision teaching and direct instruction: Measurably superior instructional technology in school. *Performance Improvement Quarterly, 3,* 74–96.

Borman, G. D., Hewes, G. M., Overman, L. T., & Brown, S. (2003). Comprehensive school reform and achievement: A meta-analysis. *Review of Educational Research, 73,* 125–230.

Burns, M. K. (2005). Using incremental rehearsal to increase fluency of single-digit multiplication facts with children identified as learning disabled in mathematics computation. *Education and Treatment of Children, 28,* 237–249.

Burns, M. K., & Ysseldyke, J. E. (2009). Reported prevalence of evidence-based instructional practices in special education. *The Journal of Special Education, 43,* 3–11.

Cooper, J., Heron, T., & Heward, W. (2007). *Applied behavior analysis* (2nd ed.). Upper Saddle River, NJ: Merrill/Pearson Education.

Daly, E. J., Martens, B. K., Barnett, D., Witt, J. C., & Olson, S. C. (2007). Varying intervention delivery in response to intervention: Confronting and resolving challenges with measurement, instruction, and intensity. *School Psychology Review, 36,* 562–581.

Doabler, C. T., Nelson, N., Kosty, D., Fien, H., Baker, S. K., Smolkowski, K., & Clarke, B. (2014). Examining teachers' use of evidence-based practices during core mathematics instruction. *Assessment for Effective Intervention, 39,* 99–111.

Fredrick, L. D., & Hummel, J. H. (2004). Reviewing the outcomes and principles of effective instruction. In D. J. Moran & R. W. Malott (Eds.), *Evidence-based educational methods* (pp. 9–22). New York: Elsevier, Academic Press.

Greenwood, C. R. (1997). Classwide peer tutoring. *Behavior and Social Issues, 7,* 11–18.

Greer, R. D. (2002). *Designing teaching strategies: An applied behavior analysis systems approach.* San Diego, CA: Academic Press.

Haring, N. G., Lovitt, T. C., Eaton, M. D., & Hansen, C. L. (1978). *The fourth R: Research in the classroom.* Columbus, OH: Merrill.

Hendrickson, J. M., & Gable, R. A. (1981). The use of modeling tactics to promote academic skills development of exceptional learners. *Journal of Special Education Technology, 4,* 20–29.

Joseph, L. M., Konrad, M., Cates, G., Vajcner, T., Eveleigh, E., & Fishley, K. M. (2012). A meta-analytic review of the copy-cover-compare and variations of this self-management procedure. *Psychology in the Schools, 49,* 122–136.

Kirschner, P. A., Sweller, J., & Clark, R. E. (2006). Why minimal guidance during instruction does not work: An analysis of the failure of constructivist, discovery, problem-based, experiential, and inquiry-based teaching. *Educational Psychologist, 41,* 75–86.

Kozioff, M. A., LaNunziata, L., Cowardin, J., & Bessellieu, F. B. (2001). Direct instruction: Its contributions to high school achievement. *The High School Journal, 84*, 54–71.

Lee, D. L., & Belfiore, P. J. (1997). Enhancing classroom performance: A review of reinforcement schedules. *Journal of Behavioral Education, 7*, 205–217.

Maccini, P., & Hughes, C. A. (1997). Mathematics interventions for adolescents with learning disabilities. *Learning Disabilities Research and Practice, 12*, 168–176.

MacDuff, G. S., Krantz, P. J., & McClannahan, L. E. (2001). Prompts and prompt-fading strategies for people with autism. In C. Maurice, G. Green, & R. M. Foxx (Eds.), *Making a difference: Behavioral intervention for autism* (pp. 37–50). Austin, TX: Pro-ed.

Martens, B. K., Daly, E. J., Begeny, J. C., & VanDerHeyden, A. (2011). Behavioral approaches to education. In W. W. Fisher, C. C. Piazza, & H. S. Roane (Eds.), *Handbook of applied behavior analysis* (pp. 385–401). New York: Guilford.

Martens, B. K., & Witt, J. C. (2004). Competence, persistence, and success: The positive psychology of behavioral skill instruction. *Psychology in the Schools, 41*, 19–30.

National Center for Educational Statistics (2016). *The nation's report card.* Washington, D.C.: U.S. Department of Education.

Polk, J. A. (2006). Traits of effective teachers. *Arts Education Policy Review, 107*, 23–29.

Rosenshine, B. (1995). Advances in research on instruction. *The Journal of Educational Research, 88*, 262–268.

Rosenshine, B., & Stevens, R. (1986). Teaching functions. In M. C. Wittrock (Ed.), *Handbook of research on teaching* (3rd ed.). New York: Macmillan.

Shippen, M. E., Houchins, D. E., Stevenson, C., & Sartor, D. (2005). A comparison of two direct instruction reading programs for urban middle school students. *Remedial and Special Education, 26*, 175–182.

Skinner, B. F. (1953). *Science and human behavior.* New York: Free Press.

Skinner, B. F. (1983). *A matter of consequences.* New York: Knopf.

Skinner, C. H. (1998). Preventing academic skill deficits. In T. S. Watson & F. M. Gresham (Eds.), *Handbook of child behavior therapy* (pp. 61–82). New York: Plenum.

Swanson, H. L., Hoskyn, M., & Lee, C. (1999). *Interventions for students with learning disabilities: A meta-analysis of treatment outcomes.* New York: Guilford.

Vargas, J. S. (2013). *Behavior analysis for effective teaching.* New York: Routledge.

Windingstad, S., Skinner, C. H., Rowland, E., Cardin, E., & Fearrington, J. Y. (2009). Extending research on a math fluency building intervention: Applying taped problems in a second-grade classroom. *Journal of Applied School Psychology, 25*, 364–381.

Wolery, M., Bailey, D. B., & Sugai, G. M. (1988). *Effective teaching: Principles and procedures of applied behavior analysis with exceptional students.* Boston: Allyn & Bacon.

Behavior Analysis and Mental Health Issues

12

Adolescent lifetime prevalence rates of mental health disorders are estimated to be as high as 50%, with anxiety and depression being most common (Merikangas, et al., 2010). What is more alarming is that research has found psychotherapeutic treatments for anxiety and depression in youth, including cognitive behavior therapy (CBT), are only moderately effective, with long-term positive outcomes being generally rare in the literature (Southam-Gerow et al., 2010; Weisz, McCarty, & Valeri, 2006; Weisz, Ugueto, Cheron, & Herren, 2013). Yet, ABA, a scientific field with an emphasis on targeting socially important behavior, has largely ignored mental health issues such as anxiety and depression (Friman, Hayes, & Wilson, 1998). Definitional problems involving vague topographies and attitudes about studying private events have hindered ABA research and clinical treatment efforts related to mental health (Dymond & Roche, 2009). However, basic and applied research in behavior analysis has provided evidence-based conceptualizations, and treatment efforts involving principles derived from ABA have been empirically validated. So, while ABA has historically disregarded anxiety and depression, it has provided important contributions to psychology's understanding and treatment of these disorders.

School psychologists are well positioned to support students with mental health issues through the delivery of direct intervention services and consultation with school staff and parents. Understanding anxiety and depression from an ABA perspective offers the school psychologist research-supported conceptualizations and evidence-based strategies that are practical, address environmental variables that are easily manipulated, and have the potential to be implemented in school settings.

This chapter addresses anxiety and depression, the two most common internalizing mental health problems presented to school psychologists, from an ABA perspective. The structure of each section follows a similar outline: (1) behavior analytic conceptualization, and (2) evidence-based strategies derived from ABA. Readers should note that the strategies covered in this chapter fit well within a CBT framework. In fact, the specific interventions discussed, exposure and behavioral activation, are common components of CBT (Huberty, 2012).

Anxiety

Conceptualization

Psychology has offered numerous conceptualizations and etiological formulations for anxiety. Freud's psychodynamic theory suggested anxiety was a manifestation of psychosocial conflicts occurring during development (Kalat, 2013). Beck's (1995) cognitive therapy emphasized an individual's thoughts or cognitions as the cause of most people's anxiety. These and other theories identify inner mechanisms that are ambiguous and difficult to operationally define. Furthermore, missing from each theory is supporting evidence from the basic or applied research literatures. Scholars have suggested a developmental framework for conceptualizing anxiety that includes genetic, biological and temperamental, cultural, social, familial, and school contexts (see Huberty, 2012). While offering a helpful etiological formulation for anxiety, this model fails to explain specific causal variables or inform treatment.

Current behavior analytic conceptualizations of anxiety suggest a conditioned avoidance paradigm. That is, an individual engages in behavior to avoid or escape aversive or fearful stimuli. For example, a person afraid of dogs will engage in behavior resulting in the avoidance or escape of dogs (i.e., consequential event). However, the person's behavior is resulting in more than the avoidance or escape of the physical stimulus. The behavior also allows for the avoidance or escape of a negative private, internal stimulus (e.g., fearful emotion). The person runs from the dog to escape it (i.e., physical stimulus) but also to escape the associated unpleasant internal experience. This paradigm is consistent for all anxiety disorders, as well as obsessive-compulsive (e.g., Obsessive-Compulsive Disorder [OCD]) and trauma/stressor-related disorders (Post-Traumatic Stress Disorder [PTSD]). For example, consider an individual engaging in compulsions (e.g., checking the oven pilot light 45 times). The compulsive behavior lessens the unpleasant internal experience. That is, not engaging in the behavior (e.g., checking the pilot light 45 times) leads to unpleasant internal experiences for the person such as fear or upset.

Research with animal and human models has demonstrated that avoidance is learned and maintained through classical and operant conditioning. Classical conditioning occurs when a neutral stimulus is paired with a fearful experience. The dog, by itself, might not be initially fearful but it becomes fearful when paired with a fearful experience, like the dog barking loudly. Operant conditioning occurs when the person engages in a behavior that lessens the fear-producing qualities of the stimulus. The avoidance paradigm is completed when the behavior is negatively reinforced via the removal of the fear-producing stimulus lessening any negative internal experiences that accompany the stimulus. This process is referred to as the two-factor theory. It has empirical support in the basic research literature and was important in the development of behavioral therapy (Dymond & Roche, 2009; Thorpe & Olson, 1997).

However, the two-factor theory does not explain all examples of avoidant responding. Rachman (1977) noted that the behavior analytic description of the avoidant paradigm fails to account for "fears which emerge in the absence of any identifiable learning experience" (p. 377). How can dogs become a fear-producing stimulus when the individual has never had a negative experience with a dog? Such a question likely made room for cognitive conceptualizations that posit the idea that inner processes are responsible for anxiety, and might have contributed to cognitive psychology's dominance of the anxiety literature (Marks, 1981). However, more recent behavior analytic conceptualizations have filled gaps in the two-factor theory. Research on derived stimulus equivalence has been particularly helpful in understanding how anxiety or avoidant responding might develop without direct experiences (Friman et al., 1998). Stimulus equivalence characterizes accurate responding to an untrained or nonreinforced stimulus by demonstrating reflexivity (A=A; individual matches a stimulus to itself), symmetry (if A=B, then B=A; an individual is taught to identify a written word by its picture, then without instruction the individual will identify the picture by the written word), and transitivity (if A=B and B=C, then A=C; the individual is taught that the written word represents the picture and the picture represents the spoken word, then without instruction the individual will identify the written word with the spoken word; Cooper, Heron & Heward, 2007). In addition, research has confirmed more distantly derived stimulus equivalence by showing that if A=B and A=C are taught, then B=C and C=B are derived (Friman et al., 1998). Related to anxiety, stimulus equivalence demonstrates how a neutral stimulus, such as a dog, can indirectly and without reinforcement acquire discriminative properties (Dymond & Roche, 2009). For example, observation (e.g., seeing a threatening dog on video) and verbal transmission (e.g., hearing a story of a dog-biting incident) can serve to establish a stimulus-response relationship that involves a once neutral stimulus and an avoidant response.

The three-term contingency is useful when understanding how experiences influence emotional reactions (i.e., private events), which, in turn, influence behavioral responses (see Figure 12.1 for examples). First, imagine upset as the emotional reaction. The person has an experience (e.g., cut off in traffic while driving a car), which triggers an emotional reaction (e.g., upset), which triggers a behavioral response (e.g., yelling at the other driver, honking horn repeatedly). Now apply that model to anxiety, where a person fears public spaces. The person has an experience of being in a public space, which triggers fear (i.e., the emotional reaction), which triggers a behavioral response involving screaming and running away. Practically, we can change the experience and the behavioral response to remove, reduce, or lessen the emotional reaction. However, it might be near impossible to change the emotional reaction. A person might be desensitized, over time, to the fear-producing stimulus (similar to desensitizing our skin, over time, through the development of a callous) but it is difficult to stop the person from becoming fearful. If you are skeptical of this point, run an experiment. The next time your favorite sports team loses, just don't be angry. The next time a beloved pet passes away, just don't be sad. However, while we might not be able to 'turn off' emotions, we are certainly able to engage in adaptive behavior despite our emotions. This is, perhaps, the most important point. Teaching people that they can 'sit,' metaphorically speaking, with their emotions, and still be okay, empowers people.

Although we might not be able to change emotion, we are able to change the experience and the behavioral response. In the case of anxiety, the person is typically trying to change the experience. For example, people with specific phobias tend to avoid experiences that involve the phobia (e.g., a child afraid of school will do whatever he can to avoid school). Moreover, parents and other adults often enable children by allowing them to avoid fear-producing experiences. Not only does this negatively reinforce the child's maladaptive behavior but allowing avoidance reduces, removes, or lessens the negative experience the adult is having, so both behaviors are reinforced. The alternative is to change the behavioral response. Staying with anxiety, the individual experiences a fear-producing stimulus, fear ensues, and the person now engages in some behavior that does not result in the reduction, removal, or lessening of the stimulus or internal experience. Instead, the individual engages in some adaptive behavior, such as completing a task that distracts him from the stimulus and internal experience, or a skill that is incompatible with the emotional response (e.g., relaxation via regulated breathing).

Experience ⟶	Possible Emotional Reaction ⟶	Possible Behavioral Response
Student given unfavorable response (told 'no' by teacher)	• Anger • Disappointment • Upset • Frustration	• Says 'okay' • Physical aggression
Pet runs away	• Sadness • Upset • Worry	• Cries • Isolates • Screams • Looks for pet • Calls friend for support
Public speaking assignment	• Worry • Fear • Concern	• Avoids assignment • Fails to go to school • Prepares, practices
Student teased at school	• Embarrassment • Anger • Sadness • Upset	• Asks peers for support, help • Ignores teasing • Cries • Isolates • Physical aggression

Figure 12.1 Emotional Regulation Model

Avoidant behavior characterizes all the Anxiety Disorders described in the *Diagnostic and Statistical Manual of Mental Disorders—Fifth Edition* (*DSM5*; American Psychiatric Association, 2013). Furthermore, avoidance of stimuli consistent with a traumatic event is featured prominently in PTSD's diagnostic criteria. Regarding OCD, the *DSM5* notes that compulsive behaviors or obsessive thoughts reduce upset or prevent aversive events implicating avoidance as an important clinical feature of the disorder. Students' avoidant behavior can significantly impair functioning and lead to problems in multiple domains including academic achievement and social relationships (Huberty, 2012). Moreover, avoidance might involve physical aggression, elopement, or other dangerous or difficult to manage behavior, as the student attempts any behavior that results in the avoidance or escape of the fear-producing stimulus. This might be especially true when avoidant behavior has a long history of negative reinforcement.

Treatment

Conceptually, the treatment of anxiety involves the extinction of previously reinforced behavior. Consider the three-term contingency—fear-producing physical or unpleasant internal experiences serve as stimuli that elicit responses leading to the reduction, removal, or lessening of the stimuli. Said differently, an aversive stimulus elicits a behavior that is negatively reinforced via avoidance or escape. Logically, the aim of treatment is to extinguish the behavior by not allowing it to be negatively reinforced. Specifically, "expose the anxious person to the feared phenomenon repeatedly and allow other behavioral processes (e.g., habituation, positive re-inforcement) to extinguish the maladaptive avoidance response class" (Friman et al., 1998; p. 150). Extinguishing the behavioral response to the feared stimulus is believed to concurrently extinguish the internal experience of fear (i.e., private event; Skinner, 1969). The literature cites several exposure-based treatment approaches including systematic desensitization, flooding, and response prevention. Each will be described briefly below followed by a discussion regarding implementation practices.

SYSTEMATIC DESENSITIZATION

Systematic desensitization (SD) involves gradually exposing the student to fear-producing stimuli. In most cases, SD begins with exposure to minimally intensive or low fear-producing stimuli and/or a stimulus class that is remotely like the fear-producing stimuli. For example, a student avoiding riding in cars because of fear of an accident might be initially exposed to innocuous pictures of dented fenders or asked to imagine a minor accident. With SD, exposure then proceeds systematically from moderate to high fear-producing stimuli with the stimulus class gradually resembling the exact stimuli that evokes the avoidant or escape behavior. This gradual exposure might move from pictures or imagined situations to in vivo conditions. According to Huberty (2012), the process can be slowed, stopped, or reversed in cases

Table 12.1   Examples of Using Exposure for Fear-Producing Stimuli

Fear-Producing Stimulus	Exposure Examples (from low- to high-intensity stimuli)
Food Garbage, Eating in School Cafeteria	Pictures of food garbage, eat lunch in classroom but seated on cafeteria chair, pick up food garbage while wearing gloves, eat in cafeteria before or after peers, clear peers' food garbage, eat in cafeteria with peers
Riding in Cars, Being in Car Accident	Pictures and video clips of car accidents (varying degrees from small fender benders to a 30-car highway wreck), sit in nonmoving car—gradually increase time intervals, drive in moving car—gradually increase time intervals and change locations (neighborhood or rarely used roads to busy highways)
Separation from Parent	Parent in classroom but seated away from student, parent in hallway but student can still see parent, parent checks in with student during school day (in person or via technology), student separates from parent—gradually increase time intervals
Social Interactions	Interaction with familiar adult, unfamiliar adult, familiar peer, unfamiliar peer, several familiar adults at once, several familiar peers at once, several unfamiliar adults at once, several unfamiliar peers at once—shift locations and activities from familiar to unfamiliar, increase time intervals
Crowded Places	Drive to shopping mall during nonpeak then peak times—park far from entrance—walk several car spaces (gradually increase distance walked from car to entrance), spend time in other potentially crowded locations during nonpeak then peak times (e.g., library, restaurants, movie theaters)

where the student is unable to engage in adaptive behavior because of the intensity of the exposure. Most SD protocols include mechanisms for obtaining feedback from the student and adults, and making changes to the treatment.

Not all stimuli evoke the same behavioral response or result in equal response intensities. Consequently, collaborating with students and their parents and teachers to establish a fear hierarchy is an important first step (Huberty, 2012). SD depends upon gradual and systematic exposure to fear-producing stimuli. Working to develop a list of fear-producing stimuli becomes important. Practitioners might then use a Likert-type scale (e.g., high-medium-low, zero to ten scale) to have students rank order the identified fear-producing stimuli. School psychologists might also conduct direct observations of the student or enlist the support of teachers and parents to confirm the items on the list and their rankings.

Empirical research investigating the effects of SD on anxiety-based disorders of childhood and adolescence is positive. For example, exposure therapy using SD has been found to effectively reduce behaviors associated with specific phobias, compulsions, hyperarousal, and avoidance related to trauma (e.g., Ritter & Hazlett-Stevens, 2006; Ruf et al., 2010; Shabani & Fisher, 2006). In addition, a large-scale review of the literature identified exposure therapies, such as SD within a CBT framework, as being probably efficacious based on common psychosocial treatment classification criteria (Silverman, Pina, & Viswesvaran, 2008). A similar review found SD to be the most effective intervention for child and adolescent OCD (Barrett, Farrell, Pina, Peris, & Piacentini, 2008). Finally, SD and other exposure-based approaches are featured prominently in CBT. For example, Huberty (2012) described direct exposure via SD in his comprehensive model of CBT for child and adolescent anxiety.

FLOODING

Flooding is prolonged exposure, either imagined or in vivo, to highly intense, fear-producing stimuli without a gradual introduction. It is said that flooding creates a new association between the stimuli and something positive (e.g., a different internal experience), while preventing negative reinforcement via avoidance or escape (Thorpe & Olson, 1997). With children, flooding most often involves therapist directed cues to imagine fear-producing stimuli and their responses (Saigh, 1987). However, little empirical support exists in the literature on the use of flooding with school-age youth possibly because of potential resistance from students and poor social acceptability among teachers and parents.

RESPONSE PREVENTION

Response prevention (RP) involves blocking an escape response (Thorpe & Olson, 1997). Individuals remain in contact with the fear-producing stimulus without being able to escape. For example, a student fearful of social situations would be required to remain in contact with a social situation, or an older student engaging in compulsive behavior would encounter the stimulus producing the compulsive behavior without being able to engage in the compulsive behavior. Consistent prevention of a negatively reinforced behavior in this manner helps extinguish the behavior quickly as reinforcement is withdrawn. Thus, RP is an important treatment component for certain anxiety-related problems including OCD and specific phobias.

Treatment Considerations

Using exposure for anxiety can be complicated. Students being exposed to fear-producing stimuli are likely to resist and extinction bursts are common when avoidant or escape behavior is no longer negatively reinforced. The psychological change associated with being 'okay' when in the presence of the fear-producing stimulus and associated internal experience is difficult to accomplish, and might contribute to the resistance many people have when exposed to fear-producing stimuli (see McCarthy & Foa, 1990). Thus, education about the intervention process is of upmost importance. Teaching students, teachers, and parents to conceptualize anxiety in behavior analytic terms should help support recommendations for exposure-based interventions. Other considerations include:

- **Support**: Because extinguishing the avoidant or escape behavior by eliminating negative reinforcement is likely to lead to an extinction burst, students should be provided with adult and peer support throughout the process (e.g., Foa, Chrestman, & Gilboa-Schechtman, 2009). Verbal interactions should emphasize acknowledgement (e.g., praise of approach behavior), empathy, and problem-solving.
- **Positive reinforcement**: Students' appropriate behavior should be positively reinforced. Certainly, any behavior representative of 'facing fears,' or not avoiding or escaping fear-producing stimuli, and compliance with treatment procedures should be acknowledged. However, increasing the frequency of positive reinforcement for any prosocial behavior is likely to increase the frequency of prosocial behavior and decrease the frequency of undesirable behavior including resistance to exposure, and avoidant and escape behavior.
- **Incompatible responses**: Students should be taught to engage in behaviors that are incompatible with avoidance or escape. For example, students might be taught distraction strategies involving tasks, such as working on a crossword puzzle, that can be completed when in the presence of the fear-producing stimulus or negative internal experience. Students can also be taught relaxation strategies (e.g., regulated breathing, visual imagery, tensing and relaxing the body) that might aid in reducing the physiological effects of the fear-producing stimulus (e.g., increase heart rate, rapid breathing). As with all skills instruction, modeling, practice, and feedback are necessary. In addition, adults might be instructed to prompt the student to engage in the distraction tasks or relaxation strategies when in the presence of fear-producing stimuli. It is unlikely, especially early in treatment, that students will engage in incompatible responses without prompting.
- **Behavioral Skills Training (BST)**: Students with anxiety are likely to require some degree of skills training especially when fear-producing stimuli involve social behavior, being in a social environment (e.g., interactions with peers), or performance (e.g., public speaking). Furthermore, students with anxiety might have difficulty engaging in appropriate or desirable behavior when experiencing a negative internal experience (e.g., fear, upset, frustration). For these students, BST is likely necessary for successful treatment of anxiety. The following describe BST components used to treat anxiety: identifying skill deficits, providing explicit instruction and modeling, allowing for multiple practice opportunities in non-fear-producing situations, and positive and corrective feedback.

Depression

Conceptualization

Behavior analytic conceptualizations of depression are much less developed and not as frequently studied as anxiety. This might explain why other theories of psychology have dominated the depression literature. Yet like anxiety, cognitive and psychodynamic conceptualizations of depression offer ambiguous, unobservable, and untested constructs as causes. For example, cognitive theories highlight negative cognitive structures or schema when describing the source of an individual's depression (see Huberty, 2012). Moreover, many of the symptoms of depression involve internal experiences that are difficult to define and nearly impossible to observe or measure.

Behavioral analytic models emphasize environmental rather than within-individual variables when explaining depression. For example, Lewinsohn and colleagues noted that changes in the environment elicit depressive behaviors resulting in fewer positive experiences and fewer opportunities to encounter positively reinforcing stimuli (Grosscup & Lewinsohn, 1980; Lewinsohn & Arconad, 1981). Decreases in the availability of reinforcement because of loss, skill deficits discouraging reinforcing interactions with others, and previous reinforcers losing their reinforcing qualities have been used to explain changes in reinforcement patterns. Similarly, a functional analytic perspective suggests that depressed responses are maintained by reinforcement for depressed behavior and lack of reinforcement for nondepressed behavior (see Ferster, 1973). Rehm (1977) remarked that depression occurs when self-control deficits develop following stressful experiences (e.g., loss). These deficits focus one's attention on negative events and immediate (versus delayed) reinforcement, lead to high standards of self-evaluation, and result in decreases in self-reinforcement and increases in self-punishment.

Yet while these theories offer a behavior analytic conceptualization for depression, empirical research is limited. Rehm (1989), in his review of the literature, noted that individuals report having fewer pleasurable and more negative experiences. Conversely, he stated that people report more pleasurable and fewer negative experiences as the frequency and intensity of depressive symptoms lessens. More recently, Hopko, Lejuez, Ruggiero, and Eifert (2003) suggested the matching law, which has support in the basic and applied literatures, as an explanation for depressed behavior. The matching law states that relative rates of responding (i.e., depressed and nondepressed or healthy behavior) are directly proportional to the relative rates of reinforcement in the environment. According to Hopko and colleagues, "when the value of reinforcers for healthy behavior is decreased through environmental changes (e.g., decreased availability of peers), the relative value of reinforcers for depressed behavior is simultaneously increased" (p. 705). The matching law also implies that should the relative value of reinforcers for healthy behavior increase because of environmental changes (e.g., increased access to preferred activities or peers), the relative value of reinforcers for depressed behavior is concurrently diminished.

Treatment

Behavioral Activation (BA) is an extension of the behavior analytic conceptualization described above. Jacobson, Martell, and Dimidjian (2001) noted that BA assumes depression is a response to life events and not within-individual deficits, and addresses events in the environment, the individual's response to those events, and the consequences of those responses. Specifically, BA's goal is to modify the environment so that reinforcement of healthy behavior increases, punishment of healthy behavior decreases, and reinforcement of depressed behavior decreases. This is accomplished by identifying antecedent events responsible for eliciting depressed behavior, conducting a functional assessment of consequences responsible for reinforcing and punishing depressed and healthy behavior, goal setting, teaching skills that can be used to effect change in the environment, and scheduling activities that increase the probability of reinforcement (Hopko et al., 2003; Huberty, 2012; Thorpe & Olson, 1997). The remainder of this section discusses these strategies within the context of a school-based intervention. Readers are also referred to Table 12.2 (p. 204) for BA treatment components, their purpose, and examples.

IDENTIFYING ANTECEDENTS AND CONSEQUENCES VIA FUNCTIONAL ASSESSMENT

Collaboratively identifying antecedents and consequences using functional assessment strategies is the first step in BA. The primary aim is to recognize environmental variables that are likely maintaining depressive behavior. For example, understanding that poor grades are antecedents to withdrawn behavior might assist the school psychologist in addressing environmental variables via consultation. Moreover, the school psychologist can teach the student skills involving asking for teacher assistance, which can be reinforced. Setting events, such as lack of sleep or parent-child conflicts, can also impact depressive behavior. For example, McCauley, Schloredt, Gudmendsen, Martell, and Dimidjian (2011) described a case study involving a 17-year-old boy with depression treated with BA. Parent-child conflict concerning homework and grades contributed to the boy's depressed behavior. Recognizing motivating operations, such as the reinforcement history of healthy and depressed behavior, further allows the school psychologist to consult with teachers and parents on modifying the environment to increase the frequency of reinforcement for healthy behavior, while decreasing the frequency of reinforcement for depressed behavior.

Functional assessment, a central feature of BA, is likely to identify antecedent and consequent variables that maintain depressed behavior. Moreover, functional assessment data might assist in understanding contextual variables that either act as stimuli or reinforcement for healthy behavior. Finally, a thorough assessment of a student's environment could identify potential reinforcers used in treatment. Several researchers have used semistructured functional assessment protocols that include interviews, forms, and direct observation (e.g., Ruggiero, Morris, Hopko, & Lejuez,

2007), while others have been less formal in their collection of functional assessment data (e.g., asking students questions about when the depressed behavior occurs and what typically happens after the depressed behavior; e.g., Ritschel, Ramirez, Jones, & Craighead, 2011). Interestingly, many published studies on the application of BA do not include functional assessment procedures within the discussion of methods. Regardless, some assessment of function is necessary within BA and school psychologists are encouraged to use their functional assessment expertise and knowledge of ABA when moving forward.

GOAL SETTING

Setting academic, behavioral, and social goals is the next step. Students with depression often have difficulty setting attainable goals (Huberty, 2012). In addition, their behavior tends to be mood-directed (i.e., an internal experience acts as an antecedent for depressed behavior) rather than goal-directed (i.e., the goal acts as an antecedent for healthy behavior; McCauley et al., 2011). Consequently, goals should also be attainable and short-term to increase the probability of successful outcomes. Moreover, goals should be operationally defined (i.e., clear, specific, measurable) so that everyone involved in treatment (e.g., student, teacher, parent) clearly understands the identified objectives.

TEACHING SKILLS

Problem-solving is generally taught first. This process involves teaching the student how to separate goals into obtainable steps, identifying activities the student finds reinforcing, and identifying healthy behaviors that lead to reinforcement (Chu, Colognori, Weissman, & Bannon, 2009; Ruggiero et al., 2007). Next, the student can be taught skills that recruit reinforcement (e.g., initiating social interactions), resolve conflict, and relax the body's physiology. Finally, assertiveness, compliance, and social skills are examples of skill deficits that might contribute to depressed behavior. BST can be used to teach deficient skills to students.

ACTIVITY SCHEDULING

Systematically activating responses that increase the frequency and reinforcement of healthy behavior is central to BA. This is done by developing a hierarchy that rates activities from easiest to most difficult (see Hopko et al., 2003). Students self-monitor their activities and work with the school psychologist to problem-solve barriers. There are many resources available that aid in developing BA forms and procedures (see Martell, Dimidjian, & Herman-Dunn, 2013; McCauley, Schloredt, Gudmundsen, Martell, & Dimidjian, 2016). Teachers, parents, and peers are enlisted to support the student, clear barriers, and provide reinforcement for healthy behavior and extinguish depressed behavior. In cases where the student does not engage in the identified activities, he or she can be asked to engage in healthy behavior that is not necessarily

Table 12.2 Behavioral Activation Treatment Components

Treatment Component	Purpose	Example
Antecedent Assessment	Identify antecedent events that might act as stimuli for depressed behavior	Social isolation follows arguments with parent
Functional Assessment	Identify consequential events that reinforce depressed behavior or punish healthy behavior	Student's social isolation is negatively reinforced via avoidance of embarrassment of a poor choir concert performance
Goal Setting	Orient student to become more goal-directed (vs. mood-directed)	Student sets the goal of attending more school-sponsored activities during the coming week
Teaching Skills	Develop student competencies to become more successful	Student learns skills to become more assertive in class by asking for peer and teacher assistance
Activity Scheduling	Increase contact with reinforcement for healthy behavior	Student schedules to attend a club meeting and basketball game with a friend

defined as an activity. The school psychologist then recruits teachers, parents, and peers to positively reinforce (e.g., praise, acknowledge) the healthy behaviors. For example, the student and school psychologist might select smiling or saying 'hi' to a peer as the target behavior. The school psychologist then works with others in the students' environment to positively reinforce those target behaviors.

Treatment Considerations

SELECTING TARGET BEHAVIORS

Typically, mental health professionals target negative cognitions and other private events (e.g., feelings, mood states) when treating depression. While these behaviors are important, they are not easily observable or measureable nor are they easily controllable via environmental manipulations (Hopko et al., 2003). Furthermore, there are data to suggest that increasing an individual's engagement in pleasurable activities positively affects self-reported internal states (e.g., exercise improves mood; Cuijpers, van Straten, & Warmerdam, 2007). Consequently, and consistent with a behavior analytic framework, practitioners should identify overt behaviors associated with healthy and depressed behavior when implementing BA procedures. Social engagement, exercise, and smiling are examples of healthy behavior. Social withdrawal, substance abuse, and crying are examples of depressed behavior.

PROCEDURES

Extinction, fading, and shaping are procedures featured in BA (Hopko et al., 2003). Extinction involves removing reinforcement for behavior that maintains the depression. However, the process also involves encouraging the individual to avoid antecedents that serve as discriminative stimuli for depressed behavior and seek environments that reinforce healthy behavior. Conceptually, differential reinforcement of incompatible behavior describes the process whereby healthy behavior inconsistent with depressed behavior is reinforced. For example, attending a school concert (i.e., healthy behavior) is incompatible with social isolation (i.e., depressed behavior). Conceptually, this involves reinforcing a student's approach behavior while ignoring any avoidant behavior. Furthermore, the extinction process calls for the withdrawal of reinforcement for depressed behavior. This might be difficult for adults who regularly positively reinforce depressed behavior with attention in the form of sympathy. Consequently, teachers, parents, and peers should be educated about the subtle but important differences between sympathy and empathy (i.e., expressing an understanding of someone else's experience).

Fading is also used in BA. Hopko and colleagues (2003) noted that individuals being treated using BA are "likely to benefit from the support of structure," (p. 710) including verbal prompts from adults or peers, and self-monitoring of healthy and depressed behavior. These supports can be gradually faded, however. In addition, planned reinforcement (e.g., reinforcement from parents, teachers, or selected peers) of healthy behavior can be gradually faded to include more naturally occurring reinforcement. Fading is planned when the student has demonstrated independence with a skill, or generalization of a skill is the target, healthy behavior has come under stimulus control, or depressed behavior has been extinguished.

Although shaping describes successive approximations of a skill not currently in a student's repertoire, the concept is appropriate when describing the reinforcement of skills that are in a student's repertoire but not consistently applied (Hopko et al., 2003). In the case of BA for depression, shaping small approximations of healthy behavior might be important when depressed behavior is significantly interfering with the students' functioning, or the student is resistant to or noncompliant with treatment. In practice, shaping is likely to take one of two forms. First, shaping might involve reinforcing an initial or small step of a scheduled activity (e.g., reinforcing a phone call to a friend as the first step to seeing a movie). Second, shaping might reinforce a similar but less effortful behavior (e.g., reinforcing watching a football game on television when the scheduled activity is watching a football game in person). One advantage of using shaping is that the small step, itself, might act as an antecedent for other healthy behaviors. For example, attending a club meeting might lead a student to participate by interacting socially at the meeting.

RESEARCH SUPPORTING BA WITH CHILDREN AND ADOLESCENTS

The literature on BA's effect on adults with depression is very positive. Meta-analyses have found BA to be equally effective as cognitive and medication therapies at decreasing depressive symptoms, with treatment gains maintained at six month and one year follow-ups (see Cuijpers et al., 2007), and a recent study with adults demonstrated BA was more effective than cognitive therapy for reducing symptoms of depression (Soleimani et al., 2015). With children and adolescents, the literature on BA is much less developed. Recent research has found BA to be highly effective at eliminating symptoms of depression in adolescent subjects with follow-up assessments indicating sustained effects (Ritschel, Ramirez, Cooley, & Craighead, 2016). Moreover, several recent pilot and case studies have shown BA to be effective with adolescents with depression and anxiety in both clinical and school settings (e.g., Chu et al., 2009; McCauley et al., 2011; Ritschel et al., 2011). Taken altogether, BA is a promising intervention for adolescents exhibiting depressed behavior. In addition to having support in the empirical literature, BA is easy to implement, does not demand specialized training, can generate positive results quickly, and fits well within a school-based intervention delivery model.

Conclusion

Mental health problems, especially anxiety and depression, are a great source of stress for students, impacting their academic, behavioral, psychological, and social functioning. Although research is emerging supporting CBT-based interventions in school settings, predictors of outcomes and barriers to implementation require more exploration (Mychailyszyn, Brodman, Read, & Kendall, 2012). School psychologists, often with limited time, resources, or mental health training, are frequently called upon to support students with anxiety and depression. This chapter offers school psychologists practical, conceptually sound, evidence-based approaches to treating anxiety and depression. Both exposure for anxiety and BA for depression hold promise for school psychologists looking for mental health interventions that are appropriate for the school setting.

References

American Psychiatric Association. (2013). *Diagnostic and statistical manual of mental disorders—fifth edition*. Arlington, VA: Author.

Barrett, P. M., Farrell, L., Pina, A. A., Peris, T. S., & Piacentini, J. (2008). Evidence-based psychosocial treatments for child and adolescent obsessive-compulsive disorder. *Journal of Clinical Child and Adolescent Psychology, 37*, 131–155.

Beck, A. T. (1995). Cognitive therapy: A 30-year retrospective. In S. O. Lilienfeld (Ed.), *Seeing both sides: Classic controversies in abnormal psychology* (pp. 303–311). Pacific Grove, CA: Brooks/Cole (Original work published in 1991).

Chu, B. C., Colognori, D., Weissman, A. S., & Bannon, K. (2009). An initial description and pilot of group behavioral activation therapy for anxious and depressed youth. *Cognitive and Behavioral Practice, 16*, 408–419.

Cooper, J., Heron, T., & Heward, W. (2007). *Applied behavior analysis* (2nd ed.). Upper Saddle River, NJ: Merrill/Pearson Education.

Cuijpers, P., van Straten, A., & Warmerdam, L. (2007). Behavioral activation treatment of depression: A meta-analysis. *Clinical Psychology Review, 27*, 318–326.

Dymond, S., & Roche, B. (2009). A contemporary behavior analysis of anxiety and avoidance. *The Behavior Analyst, 32*, 7–27.

Ferster, C. B. (1973). A functional analysis of depression. *American Psychologist, 28*, 857–870.

Foa, E. B., Chrestman, K. R., & Gilboa-Schechtman, E. (2009). *Prolonged exposure therapy for adolescents with PTSD emotional processing of traumatic experiences: Therapist guide.* Oxford: Oxford University Press.

Friman, P. C., Hayes, S. C., & Wilson, K. G. (1998). Why behavior analysts should study emotion: The example of anxiety. *Journal of Applied Behavior Analysis, 31*, 137–156.

Grosscup, S. J., & Lewinsohn, P. M. (1980). Unpleasant and pleasant events, and mood. *Journal of Clinical Psychology, 36*, 252–259.

Hopko, D. R., Lejuez, C. W., Ruggiero, K. J., & Eifert, G. H. (2003). Contemporary behavioral activation treatments for depression: Procedures, principles, and progress. *Clinical Psychology Review, 23*, 699–717.

Huberty, T. J. (2012). *Anxiety and depression in children and adolescents: Assessment, intervention, and prevention.* New York: Springer.

Jacobson, N. S., Martell, C. R., & Dimidjian, S. (2001). Behavioral activation treatments for depression: Returning to contextual roots. *Clinical Psychology: Science and Practice, 8*, 255–270.

Kalat, J. W. (2013). *Introduction to psychology* (10th ed.). Belmont, CA: Wadsworth.

Lewinsohn, P. M., & Arconad, M. (1981). Behavioral treatment of depression: A social learning approach. In J. F. Clarkin & H. I. Glazer (Eds.), *Depression: Behavioral and directive intervention strategies* (pp. 33–67). New York: Garland.

Marks, I. M. (1981). Behavioral concepts and treatment of neuroses. *Behavioral Psychotherapy, 9*, 137–154.

Martell, C. R., Dimidjian, S., & Herman-Dunn, R. (2013). *Behavioral activation for depression: A clinician's guide.* New York: Guilford.

McCarthy, P. R., & Foa, E. B. (1990). Obsessive-compulsive disorder. In M. E. Thase, B. A. Edelstein, & M. Hersen (Eds.), *Handbook of outpatient treatment of adults: Nonpsychotic mental disorders* (pp. 209–234). New York: Plenum.

McCauley, E., Schloredt, K. A., Gudmundsen, G. R., Martell, C. R., & Dimidjian, S. (2011). Expanding behavioral activation to depressed adolescents: Lessons learned in treatment development. *Cognitive and Behavioral Practice, 18*, 371–383.

McCauley, E., Schloredt, K. A., Gudmundsen, G. R., Martell, C. R., & Dimidjian, S. (2016). *Behavioral activation with adolescents: A clinician's guide.* New York: Guilford.

Merikangas, K. R., He, J., Burstein, M., Swanson, S. A., Avenevoli, S., Cui, L., . . . Swendsen, J. (2010). Lifetime prevalence of mental health disorders in US adolescents: Results from the national comorbidity study—adolescent supplement (NCS-A). *Journal of the American Academy of Child and Adolescent Psychiatry, 49*, 980–989.

Mychailyszyn, M. P., Brodman, D. M., Read, K. L., & Kendall, P. C. (2012). Cognitive-behavioral school-based interventions for anxious and depressed youth: A meta-analysis of outcomes. *Clinical Psychology: Science and Practice, 19*, 129–153.

Rachman, S. J. (1977). The conditioning theory of fear acquisition: A critical examination. *Behaviour Research & Therapy, 15*, 375–387.

Rehm, L. P. (1977). A self-control model of depression. *Behavior Therapy, 8,* 787–804.

Rehm, L. P. (1989). Behavioral models of anxiety and depression. In P. C. Kendall & D. Watson (Eds.), *Anxiety and depression: Distinctive and overlapping features* (pp. 55–78). San Diego, CA: Academic Press.

Ritschel, L. A., Ramirez, C. L., Cooley, J. L., & Craighead, W. E. (2016). Behavioral activation for major depression in adolescents: Results from a pilot study. *Clinical Psychology: Science and Practice, 23,* 39–57.

Ritschel, L. A., Ramirez, C. L., Jones, M., & Craighead, W. E. (2011). Behavioral activation for depressed teens: A pilot study. *Cognitive and Behavioral Practice, 18,* 281–299.

Ritter, M. R., & Hazlett-Stevens, H. (2006). The use of exposure and ritual prevention in the treatment of harm obsessions with covert compulsions. *Clinical Case Studies, 5,* 455–476.

Ruf, M., Schauer, M., Neuner, F., Carani, C., Schauer, E., & Elbert, T. (2010). Narrative exposure therapy for 7- to 16-year-olds: A randomized controlled trial with traumatized refugee children. *Journal of Traumatic Stress, 23,* 437–445.

Ruggiero, K. J., Morris, T. L., Hopko, D. R., & Lejuez, C. W. (2007). Applications of behavioral activation treatment for depression to an adolescent with a history of child maltreatment. *Clinical Case Studies, 6,* 64–78.

Saigh, P. A. (1987). In vitro flooding of childhood posttraumatic stress disorder: A systematic replication. *Professional School Psychology, 2,* 135–146.

Shabani, D. B., & Fisher, W. W. (2006). Stimulus fading and differential reinforcement for the treatment of needle phobia in a youth with autism. *Journal of Applied Behavior Analysis, 39,* 449–452.

Silverman, W. K., Pina, A. A., & Viswesvaran, C. (2008). Evidence-based psychosocial treatments for phobic and anxiety disorders in children and adolescents. *Journal of Clinical Child and Adolescent Psychology, 37,* 105–130.

Skinner, B. F. (1969). *Contingencies of reinforcement: A theoretical analysis.* New York: Appleton-Century-Crofts.

Soleimani, M., Mohammadkhani, P., Dolatshahi, B., Alizadeh, H., Overmann, K. A., & Coolidge, F. L. (2015). A comparative study of group behavioral activation and cognitive therapy in reducing subsyndromal anxiety and depression symptoms. *Iranian Journal of Psychiatry, 10,* 71–78.

Southam-Gerow, M. A., Weisz, J. R., Chu, B. C., McLeod, B. D., Gordis, E. B., & Connor-Smith, J. K. (2010). Does CBT for youth anxiety outperform usual care in community clinics? An intial effectiveness test. *Journal of the American Academy of Child and Adolescent Psychiatry, 49,* 1043–1052.

Thorpe, G. L., & Olson, S. L. (1997). *Behavior therapy: Concepts, procedures, and applications.* Boston: Allyn & Bacon.

Weisz, J. R., McCarty, C. A., & Valeri, S. M. (2006). Effects of psychotherapy for depression in children and adolescents: A meta-analysis. *Psychology Bulletin, 132,* 132–149.

Weisz, J. R., Ugueto, A. M., Cheron, D. M., & Herren, J. (2013). Evidence-based youth psychotherapy in the mental health ecosystem. *Journal of Clinical Child and Adolescent Psychology, 42,* 274–286.

Index

Italic numbers indicate figures; bold numbers indicate tables.